DATE DUE

Cambridge studies in sociology 3

THE AFFLUENT WORKER
IN THE CLASS STRUCTURE

Cambridge Studies in Sociology

The affluent worker
in the class structure

JOHN H. GOLDTHORPE
Official Fellow, Nuffield College, Oxford

DAVID LOCKWOOD
Professor of Sociology, University of Essex

FRANK BECHHOFER
Lecturer in Sociology, University of Edinburgh

JENNIFER PLATT
Lecturer in Sociology, University of Sussex

CAMBRIDGE
at the University Press, 1969

Published by the Syndics of the Cambridge University Press
Bentley House, 200 Euston Road, London N.W.1
American Branch: 32 East 57th Street, New York, N.Y. 10022

Standard Book Numbers: 521 07231 x cloth edition
521 09533 6 paperback edition

Printed in Great Britain by
William Clowes and Sons, Limited, London and Beccles

Contents

Contents

Preface

In 1962 the two senior authors initiated a research project into the sociology of the affluent worker. Late in that year field work was started with the financial support of the Department of Applied Economics of the University of Cambridge. Additional support was later provided by a grant from the Human Sciences Committee of the Department of Scientific and Industrial Research—the forerunner of the present Social Science Research Council. Throughout the period in which field work was being undertaken and its results analysed, the two junior authors were members of the research staff of the D.A.E. The following were also at various times engaged on the project: as research officer, Mr Michael Rose; as research assistants, Mrs D. Dutkiewicz, Miss P. Ralph and Mrs R. Crompton; and as interviewers, Messrs P. Batten, J. Dichmont, D. Goddard, P. Jenkins and R. Payne. We acknowledge their valuable collaboration and, in particular, that of Mr Rose during the period of the main interviewing programme. Our appreciation must also be expressed to the many members of the D.A.E. computing and typing staff who have given assistance to the project at all stages.

From 1963 onwards we have published papers arising out of our work in various professional journals. More recently, two longer reports have appeared—*The Affluent Worker: Industrial Attitudes and Behaviour* and *The Affluent Worker: Political Attitudes and Behaviour*.[1] As their titles imply, both of these books were concerned with somewhat specialised aspects of our research. The first was in fact a by-product of our work, prompted by findings of a kind we did not altogether anticipate: the second deals with a particular topic which had aroused some considerable interest and which we thought worthy of separate treatment. The present report is the final one of book-length that we shall produce and, while a number of other journal articles are still to come, it is to be regarded as marking the effective conclusion of our project. The position of the affluent worker in the class structure has from the outset been the central concern of our research, and we here set out our findings and conclusions on those issues which our research was specifically designed to investigate.

[1] Both published in 1968 by Cambridge University Press as numbers 1 and 2 of Cambridge Studies in Sociology. For convenience, these items will be subsequently cited as *IAB* and *PAB*.

In so doing, we have frequently had need to draw on material which we have already presented and discussed at length elsewhere. In some such cases we have simply alluded to our earlier publications; but on all matters of major importance we have recapitulated the relevant data and arguments in order that our final report should be a reasonably self-contained one. The amount of repetition thus occasioned is less than might at first sight appear, since often the 'old' material is introduced into quite new contexts.

This book appears some five years after the collection of data came to an end. This is a considerable time-lag—although, unfortunately, one which is in no way exceptional in the sociological field. However, the delay has afforded us one definite advantage. In recent years a number of other research projects have been started which are in some way related to ours, and in writing the present volume we have been able to make use of at least the preliminary findings of several of these enquiries. We would wish to thank in particular those colleagues who have sent us communications on their work in progress, and also the many others who have commented helpfully on our own previous contributions.

1. Introduction: the debate on the working class

Any study which is concerned with the evolution of the working class within western industrial society must, in one sense at least, be controversial: inevitably, it will be read and evaluated within the context of the great debate on this theme which has been in progress now for more than a century. This being so, it seems to us advisable that at the outset of this book we should say something, if only briefly, about the way in which we ourselves see the progress of this debate, and about the origins of our study in relation to its most recent phases. Such an introduction may also have the advantage of providing some wider perspective in which can be viewed the variety of more specific arguments that will subsequently be raised and discussed.

It need scarcely, perhaps, be added that we do not regard problems of the kind we consider in this initial chapter as ones that will ever be definitively resolved purely on the basis of sociological enquiry and analysis. And we are, moreover, well aware that the conclusions from any single study, restricted in time and space, are likely to be of only limited application. Thus, while we do in fact believe that the results of our research should enable *some* particular issues to be settled, our ultimate aim is certainly not the vain one of bringing controversy to an end. It might more accurately be defined as that of providing controversy with more and better material on which to feed.

The debate on the working class to which we have referred has its origins in the work of Marx and Engels. Marx was not the first to recognise that the growing numbers of wage workers in the towns and cities of early nineteenth-century Europe represented a new social phenomenon. He was not the first to distinguish this emerging urban proletariat from the 'lower orders' or 'labouring poor' of previous times. Nor indeed was he the first to see in this proletariat a social force with the potential ultimately to dominate and transform the society within which it had been created. Such insights and speculations were ones which Marx was able to take over from a wide variety of sources during the period in which his own ideas were forming. However, what *is* distinctive, and of major importance, in Marx is the part that is given to a *theory* of the evolution of the working class within his finished 'system'. Such a theory is not only presented in some detail but is moreover closely interrelated with a number of other theories—economic, philosophical, political—so that it becomes in fact the crucial element in the entire construction: the lynch-pin, one could say, in Marx's total theory of man, history and society.[1]

For example, in Marx's system the growth of working-class conscious-ness and organised power, culminating in the revolutionary overthrow of capitalism, is basically to be accounted for in terms of successive crises of the capitalist economy; it is in this sense an inevitable outcome of capital-ism. At the same time, though, this process is also the means whereby the breakdown of capitalism is followed by the creation of the post-capitalist order and of the new, communist society. In other words, the revolutionary action of the proletariat typifies the process that is at the core of 'historical materialism': that through which men 'make their own history'—even if not out of whole cloth. Again, working-class action is of central signifi-cance in Marx's philosophical anthropology. In this perspective, the in-surgent proletariat represents 'in the midst of degradation, the revolt against degradation'; and it is, moreover, through this revolt that man-kind will be at last liberated from the alienated condition in which it has existed since private property and the division of labour in production were first established. It is through the victory of the proletariat, in the last great struggle between the classes, that these sources of man's alien-ation will be ultimately destroyed and the conditions created for a society in which man can for the first time become fully human. Finally, it may be noted that Marx's theory of the working class is also fundamental to the claim that within his system theory and practice are completely unified, and thus that Marxian socialism is 'scientific' as opposed to merely 'utopian'. In Marx's work, the ideals of the society of the future are not simply proclaimed: they are related to a particular agency—the working class—which, it is held, is destined to achieve their realisation: 'the proletariat finds its intellectual weapons in philosophy' but 'philosophy finds its material weapons in the proletariat'.

Thus, it is not difficult to appreciate why successive critiques of Marx have almost invariably raised important questions concerning the working class; and conversely, given the intellectual and political impact of Marx-ism, why successive examinations of the position of the working class within western society have, with equal regularity, taken Marx as an

[1] Cf. C. Wright Mills, *The Marxists* (New York, 1962), ch. 4.

important point of reference. From either angle, the basic issues have been ones such as the following: How far have Marx's expectations concerning the evolution and the political mission of the working class been borne out by the course of events? To the extent that Marx's predictions in this respect have not been supported, is this to be seen as the result largely of the intrusion of factors 'external' to the situation that was the subject of his analysis? Or, rather, is it the case that these predictive failures imply, and reveal, serious flaws within the analysis itself?

Such issues have in fact been under continuous and usually intense discussion virtually from the time when Marx's work first appeared. To take one matter of particular interest here, it was among the early Marxists themselves that the problem of the so-called *embourgeoisement* of the worker and its political implications was initially raised. Engels especially, in course of the 1870s and 1880s concerned himself with the question of why the working class in Britain—the most developed in existence—failed to exploit the new franchise of 1867 and to secure working-class dominance in Parliament. He recognised as a factor of immediate significance the British worker's craving for 'respectability' and enhanced social status which thus led to a willingness, indeed eagerness, to accept bourgeois social values, life-styles and political ideas. But he then argued further that this situation had to be seen as an exceptional and temporary one—as one in fact *deriving from* Britain's current position as the world's leading industrial nation. It was only because of British economic supremacy and the colonial exploitation that accompanied this, that it became possible for a sizable section of the labour force to enjoy a standard of living sufficient to encourage bourgeois aspirations, and for the development of true working-class consciousness to be in this way retarded. Such a check was not therefore seen as in any way affecting the *ultimate* validity of Marx's theory. The British situation was not a stable one, the contradictions inherent in capitalism would continue to work themselves out and, at some point, the revolutionary proletariat would of necessity make its appearance and assume its historic role.[1]

[1] See in particular 'The English Elections', 1874 and 'Trades Unions', 1881; also Engels' letters to Marx, 7 October 1858; to Marx, 18 November 1868; to Kautsky, 12 September 1882; to Kelly-Wischnewetzky, 10 February 1885; and to Sorge, 7 December 1889. All the above are reprinted in Karl Marx and Frederick Engels, *On Britain* (Moscow, 1953). The problem of *embourgeoisement* was, of course, taken up again later by Lenin in his discussion of working-class 'aristocracies', occasioned chiefly by the collapse of the Second International. See, for example, V.I. Lenin, 'Imperialism, the Highest Stage of Capitalism', ch. 8, and 'The Collapse of the Second International' in J. Fineberg (ed.), *Lenin: Selected Works*, vol. 5 (London, n.d.).

This position, it may be observed, is essentially the same as that subsequently adopted by most orthodox Marxists when compelled to face the fact that quite generally in advanced capitalist societies the working class has failed to develop into a highly organised political force, ready for the overthrow of the *status quo*. Characteristically, the explanations provided for this fact have been in terms of the ability of capitalism simply to protract its death agony—through taking advantage of the various possibilities offered for survival by nationalism, imperialism, militarism, the 'artificial stimulation of demand' and so on. That is to say, it has not been allowed that what has actually happened in the world since Marx laid down his pen demonstrates any basic inadequacy in his exposé of the internal dynamics of the capitalist order.[1]

However, outside the circle of 'fundamentalist' believers, the continuing lack of historical validation for Marx's theory of the working class encouraged numerous more critical appraisals. Sympathisers as much as adversaries attempted to identify the particular deficiencies in Marx's analysis of capitalism which could be related to developments within modern western society that he had manifestly failed to anticipate. In this respect, three arguments may be distinguished in which the majority of commentators have shared. These can be summarised as follows.[2]

(i) Marx's economics were at fault in leading him to expect the 'polarisation' of classes under capitalism, with the wage workers being forced down into ever greater poverty. Rather, the economic development of capitalist societies, despite periodic crises, has brought general and substantial increases in living standards and, furthermore, has led to a considerable expansion of the 'intermediate' strata of nonmanual, salaried employees. Thus, in effect, the reverse of polarisation has occurred.

(ii) Marx seriously misjudged the role of the State within capitalist society in seeing this as merely the coercive instrument of the bourgeoisie and in regarding political power as invariably subordinate to economic power. Rather, as a result of party political action, the State has played an important and relatively independent role in limiting the powers attaching to property and in giving common civil, political and social rights to all members of the national community regardless of their economic position.

(iii) Marx in general exaggerated the importance of property ownership as a source of social cleavage and of disruptive conflict. Income, occupation

[1] As a typical example of such argument, see Eugene Varga, *20th Century Capitalism* (Moscow and London, n.d.).
[2] A more detailed review can be found in Ralf Dahrendorf, *Class and Class Conflict in Industrial Society* (London, 1959), ch. 2.

4

and education have all proved to be further important bases of stratification within capitalist society, and widely accepted *status* differences have
reduced the saliency of purely *class* divisions. Moreover, conflict between
employers and employees, as between rival political groupings, has in
various ways become accommodated and institutionalised.

Thus, following arguments of this kind, not only a systematic critique
of Marx but also an alternative theory of the evolution of the working class
became possible. That is, a theory asserting not the inevitable transformation of a 'class in itself' into a 'class for itself'—which would then,
until the day of reckoning, encamp within capitalist society like a hostile
army—but rather a theory of the progressive *integration* of the working
class into the institutional structure of capitalism; this being brought
about on the one hand by the purposive modification of this structure
and on the other by the 'natural' development of the capitalist economy. A
theory on these lines, although never fully worked out by any one writer,
could in fact be regarded as at least the implicit basis of the case against
Marx as this stood around the mid-point of the twentieth century.[1] What
essentially was called into question was the *revolutionary potential* of the
working class—its mission to act as the gravedigger of capitalism:
what was emphasised was the apparent readiness of the mass of wage
workers under capitalism to accept the responsibilities along with the
rights of national citizenship and to pursue their objectives through
organisations which recognised 'the rules of the game' within both the
industrial and political sectors.

This, then, was the stage which the debate on the working class had
reached by the time that the advanced societies of the West began to
recover from the effects of the second world war. From this period onwards, however, it is important to recognise that a further distinctive
phase in the debate commences. Against a background of sharply acceler-
ating social change, new issues were opened up and old ones appeared in
different forms.

In the years in question, economic growth, in North America and
western Europe in particular, went rapidly ahead. The era of 'high mass
consumption' was generally achieved and the coming of the 'affluent

---

[1] As among the most important of the works in which this case is embodied, although in differing contexts and with differing emphases, one could cite the following: Theodor Geiger, *Die
Klassengesellschaft im Schmelztiegel* (Cologne and Hagan, 1949); T. H. Marshall, *Citizenship
and Social Class* (Cambridge, 1950); Dahrendorf, *Class and Class Conflict in Industrial
Society*; and Reinhard Bendix, *Work and Authority in Industry* (New York, 1956). See also
the important essay by Bendix, 'Transformations of Western European Societies since the
Eighteenth Century', in his *Nation Building and Citizenship* (New York, 1964).

society' was, at all events, frequently proclaimed. At the same time further important, if less widespread, changes were occurring on the side of production. The second industrial revolution was sweeping aside the satanic mills of the first and creating new types of factory. Managements were becoming increasingly concerned with 'human relations', while automated or process production systems gave rise to conditions of work which, from both a physical and a social point of view, differed markedly from those characteristic of an earlier age of industry. Further still, extensive changes were also in progress in patterns of residence and community life. On the one hand, the movement of population from rural to urban areas continued, and at an increasing rate in many regions; on the other, the great towns and cities in all the advanced societies of the West spilled out the inhabitants of their older, more central districts into the suburbs or rapidly expanding fringe areas and commuter belts. Thus, many long-established communities were disrupted and many new ones created, together with their distinctive opportunities and problems.

Under the impact of changes of these kinds, new lines of thought emerged concerning the destiny of the working class, and ones which went clearly beyond the former, negative argument that this class could no longer be realistically considered, even in potential, as a revolutionary force. Rather, a major and recurrent theme—and most notably in liberal quarters—was that of the incipient *decline* and *decomposition* of the working class. As the development of industrial societies continued, it was suggested, the working class, understood as a social stratum with its own distinctive ways of life, values and goals, would become increasingly eroded by the main currents of change. The very idea of a working class had been formed in, and in fact belonged to, the infancy of industrial society: in the era to come it would steadily lose its empirical referent. Social inequalities would no doubt persist; but these would be modified and structured in such a way that the society of the future would be an overwhelmingly 'middle-class' society, within which the divisions of the past would no longer be recognisable.

In other words, the developmental—even, perhaps, the historicist—perspectives of Marx and the Marxists were revived. But in place of a theory of working-class revolution as the inevitable culmination and conclusion of capitalism, there was proposed a theory of the progressive disappearance of the working class as part of the inherent logic of industrialism. The Marxist claim that the development of the forces of production is the ultimate determinant of the pattern of stratification and of the balance of cohesive and disruptive forces within society was generally accepted: but a radically different view was taken of the consequences of this relationship in the past and for the future. In brief, the contention was that, as expressed by one prominent author, 'history has validated a basic premise of Marxist sociology, at the expense of Marxist politics'.[1]

What, then, in more detail are the arguments that have been advanced in support of this theory of the working-class in decline? Three main types of change which stimulated new thinking have been alluded to: economic, technological and managerial, and ecological. The ways in which each of these have been seen as shaping and defining the future of the working class may be usefully considered in turn.

So far as the consequences of economic changes are concerned, the particular development to which most importance has been attached is that usually referred to as the 'homogenisation' of incomes and living standards. In the course of the 1950s, statistics became available in most of the advanced societies of the West which suggested that, concomitantly with the general increase in prosperity, a significant expansion was taking place in the numbers of individuals or families in receipt of middle-sized incomes. Quite apart from the degree to which the overall range of economic inequality was being reduced, an increasing proportion of the population appeared to be falling into the intermediate brackets of the income scale—to the extent, in fact, that several writers referred to the need to discard the old idea of an income pyramid and to think rather of a 'diamond-shaped' distribution.[2] Moreover, the major source of this expansion it could be claimed, lay in the marked increase in incomes that had been achieved, from around the end of the 1940s, among many sections of the working class: that is to say, the new middle-income group was to be seen as largely the result of the relatively rapid economic advance of substantial numbers of manual workers and their families who had been able to

[1] S. M. Lipset, 'The Changing Class Structure of Contemporary European Politics', *Daedalus*, vol. 63, no. 1 (1964). Probably the most comprehensive statement of the theory in question is to be found in Clark Kerr, John T. Dunlop, Frederick H. Harbison and Charles A. Myers, *Industrialism and Industrial Man* (London, 1962). Also influential, though containing few direct references to changes in class structure, has been W. W. Rostow, *The Stages of Economic Growth: a Non-Communist Manifesto* (Cambridge, 1960). For a critique of the views of Kerr and his associates as a form of 'evolutionary para-Marxism', see John H. Goldthorpe, 'Social Stratification in Industrial Society' in P. Halmos (ed.), *The Development of Industrial Societies*, Sociological Review Monograph no. 8 (Keele, 1964).

[2] See, for example, Kurt Mayer, 'Recent Changes in the Class Structure of the United States', *Transactions of the Third World Congress of Sociology*, vol. 3 (London, 1956); 'Diminishing Class Differentials in the United States', *Kyklos*, vol. 12 (October 1959); and 'The Changing Shape of the American Class Structure', *Social Research*, vol. 30 (Winter 1963). Cf. also Robert Millar, *The New Classes* (London, 1966), pp. 27–8.

secure incomes comparable to those of many white-collar employees and smaller independents.

Consistently with this, statistics on consumption patterns could also be adduced as evidence of the blurring of class differences, in economic terms at least. For example, the possession of various kinds of consumer durables—television sets, record players, vacuum cleaners, washing machines—was evidently becoming fairly general, while increasingly too manual workers were invading the hitherto almost exclusively middle-class preserves of car- and house-ownership. Surveys carried out by consumer research agencies led to enthusiastic reports on the immense possibilities offered by the newly emergent 'middle market'.[1]

On this basis, it became possible to argue that one defining characteristic of the working class, as traditionally conceived, was fast being obliterated: that is, its clearly inferior position in terms of economic resources and consumer power. The existence of a large class of 'have-nots', it could be held, was a necessary feature of industrial society in its early phases; but at the stage of development now being attained, the nature of the economy ensures—and indeed requires—that the bulk of the population enjoy middle-class living standards. Severe economic deprivation may still exist in the case of certain special groups, but this can no longer be the lot of the mass of the manual labour force. In the words of one exponent of this point of view: 'A mass-oriented economy depends on a mass-market ... The very existence of families able to afford Cadillacs depends on the existence of millions of families able to buy Chevrolets.'[2]

Furthermore, arguments concerning the homogenisation of living standards have typically led on to claims concerning homogenisation at a cultural level also. The achievement by increasing numbers of manual workers of middle-sized incomes has been widely regarded as providing them with their *entrée* into middle-class worlds from which they were

[1] See, for example, for Great Britain, Lintas Research, *The Changing Consumer* (London, 1961); and for the United States, The Editors of *Fortune*, *The Changing American Market* (New York, 1955). As well as giving consumption statistics, these publications also present survey data showing the extent of the 'overlap' between manual and nonmanual incomes. See in the Lintas report, ch. 2, 'The Middle Market—or Social Class Outmoded', and in the *Fortune* report the discussion of 'the new bourgeoisie' in ch. 3, 'The Rich Middle-Income Class'. Also for the United States, see 'Worker Loses his Class Identity', *Business Week*, 11 July 1959, being a summary of a report by the U.S. Department of Labor, 'How American Buying Habits Change' (Washington, 1959).
[2] Jessie Bernard, 'Class Organisation in an Era of Abundance', *Transactions of the Third World Congress of Sociology*, vol. 3 (London, 1956), p. 27. Cf. also the discussion of the process of *embourgeoisement* in Raymond Aron, *La Lutte de Ceasses* (Paris, 1964), pp. 205-13.

previously excluded; as enabling them to participate in middle-class life-styles which were previously beyond their means and to share in values that were hitherto inappropriate to their material conditions and expect-ations. In regard to modes of speech and dress, eating habits and styles of décor, entertainment, leisure activities, child-rearing practices and parental aspirations—to mention only some topics—it has been argued that the more affluent sections of the working class at least are taking over middle-class models, norms and attitudes. As the working class ceases to be distinctive in terms of its economic position, so its distinctiveness as a cultural entity is also steadily diminished.[1]

In this way, then, the Marxian notion of the *embourgeoisement* of the manual worker re-appears: this process being now understood, however, not as some temporary irregularity, occasioned by the uneven develop-ment of capitalism, but rather as an integral part of the evolution of industrial society in its post-capitalist phase. Indeed, what is being claimed is another complete reversal of a Marxian prediction: instead of salaried employees becoming homogeneous in all important respects with the proletariat and joining the latter in its political struggle, 'the "proletarian" workers are becoming homogenous with the white-collar workers and are joining the middle class'.[2]

Turning next to changes in technology and industrial management, the implications of these have been seen as reinforcing the process of *embourgeoisement* in two major ways. In the first place, a connection is made between technological progress in industry and the sharp increase in incomes experienced by certain groups within the labour force; that is, by those workers who are employed in the most advanced sectors and plants and who benefit from the fact that in the enterprises in which they work productivity is exceptionally high and labour costs represent only a relatively low proportion of total costs. Furthermore, with some forms

[1] This, for example, was the view taken in all the publications referred to in n.1 p. 8 above. See further for Great Britain, F. Zweig, *The Worker in an Affluent Society* (London, 1961); for the United States, Mayer, 'The Changing Shape of the American Class Structure' and other papers already cited; for France, Albert Détraz, 'L'Ouvrier Consommateur', in Leo Hamon (ed.), *Les Nouveaux Comportements Politiques de la Classe Ouvrière* (Paris, 1962) and Edgar Morin, 'La Mue d'Occident' in *Introduction à une Politique de l'Homme* (Paris, 1965); for Germany, H. P. Bahrdt, 'Die Angestellten' and 'Die Industriearbeiter' in Marianne Feuersenger (ed.), *Gibt Es noch ein Proletariat?* (Frankfurt, 1962).

[2] Mayer, 'Recent Changes in the Class Structure of the United States', p. 78. Cf. Bernard: 'The "proletariat" has not absorbed the middle class but rather the other way round . . . In the sense that the class structure here described reflects modern technology, it vindicates the Marxist thesis that social organisation is "determined" by technological forces. The precise manner in which these forces operate and the result they bring about, however, belie the Marxist dialectic.' 'Class Organisation in an Era of Abundance', pp. 30–1.

9

of advanced technology, the work-tasks employees perform do not require great physical exertion and the level of output is not primarily determined by the degree of effort they expend. This is so, for example, where their work is mainly concerned with the monitoring or regulating of largely automatic or 'continuous flow' production systems. Consequently, it has been also argued that men performing such tasks are differentiated from the traditional type of industrial worker in more than economic terms alone. While the latter earns his livelihood through selling his labour power—through engaging in a direct 'money for effort' bargain—these new workers are employed chiefly to exercise their knowledge and experience and, above all, to act responsibly in regard to the requirements of the production process. They perform therefore the functions of technicians rather than of hands or operatives; and increasingly too, it is claimed, this is being recognised by management in that these workers are often accorded virtually white-collar status within the plant including conditions of service of a 'staff' character.

In sum, then, the contention here is that in the most progressive branches of industry—those which may be expected to set the pattern for the future—the division between manual and nonmanual grades, between 'works' and 'staff', is breaking down. The work situation of the majority of employees is such that these categories no longer apply: it was through the development of the 'forces of production' that such categories were initially created and it is through this development too that they are now being outmoded.[1]

Secondly, technological change has also been seen as having an important influence within the enterprise in altering attitudes to work and in restructuring social relationships at shop-floor level. As industrial technology goes beyond conventional mass production methods, it is held, not only do work-tasks become in general less stressful and more inherently rewarding but, in addition, advanced production systems and the progressive management policies associated with them are such as to further encourage the 'integration' of rank-and-file workers into their employing organisations.

For instance, while mass production typically involves individuals working at fragmented and repetitive work-tasks under restrictive conditions, automated or process production often brings men together in

---

[1] For argument on these lines, see in particular M. M. Postan, *An Economic History of Western Europe, 1945–1964* (London, 1967), pp. 320–6, 335–6; and for less considered statements, Millar, *The New Classes*, pp. 81–5; and J. K. Galbraith, *The New Industrial State* (London, 1967), chs. 23 and 24 esp.

relatively small and tightly-knit teams within which they can perform a variety of tasks. At the same time, such workers usually enjoy greater autonomy in planning and organising their work and greater freedom of movement about the plant. Then again, most advanced production systems make it likely that both specialist staff and operating managers will be brought into direct and frequent contact with members of the rank-and-file, and on an essentially consultative and collaborative basis. The primary function of works management is no longer that of maintaining discipline or extracting effort but that of collecting and disseminating information and of giving expert advice and assistance: consequently, the possibility of relatively harmonious and co-operative management–worker relations is significantly enhanced. Finally, it is suggested that the social integration of the enterprise is further aided by the fact that the operation of a highly complex technology imposes a *common* discipline upon superiors and subordinates alike. In, say, a fully automatic factory or a chemical plant or refinery, the system of control which bears upon employees is recognised by them as being inherent in the production process itself and as applying to the enterprise as a whole. It is not interpreted as an exercise of managerial authority in pursuit of specifically managerial interests. Once more, then, the likelihood of harmony rather than of conflict is favoured; workers are helped to *identify* with their enterprise instead of viewing the employment relationship in the old oppositional terms of 'us' and 'them'.

In these several ways, therefore, it is claimed that the alienation of the industrial worker is being progressively overcome. As one author, Robert Blauner, has expressed it, alienation in industry is to be seen as following 'a course that could be charted on a graph by means of an inverted U-curve'. That is to say, alienation was at its most extreme in the period which followed the disruption of craft industry and which saw the introduction of large-scale mass production based on the assembly-line principle. But, with the still further technological advances of recent years, conditions have again been created under which men can perform 'meaningful work in a more cohesive, integrated industrial climate'. As a result, the 'social personality' of workers in the most evolved types of enterprise now 'tends toward that of the new middle class, the white-collar worker in bureaucratic industry ... Generally lukewarm to unions and loyal to his employer, the blue-collar employee in the continuous process industries may be a worker "organisation man" in the making'.[1]

---

[1] Robert Blauner, *Alienation and Freedom: the Factory Worker and his Industry* (Chicago and London, 1964), pp. 181–2. Cf. Galbraith, *The New Industrial State*, pp. 226–7, 276. Blauner

Lastly, then, in regard to what we have termed ecological changes, we can again distinguish two main lines of argument that have been advanced in support of the thesis of 'the worker turning middle class'. As was noted earlier, the changes in question involve the continuing expansion of the urban population as a result of the 'drift' from the countryside and at the same time the spread of urban areas as central districts are redeveloped and new suburbs, estates and satellite communities are created. A variety of writers have sought to show that through both of these processes the distinctiveness of the working class as a cultural and social entity is being reduced and further that the merging of working class and middle class is thereby facilitated.

The effect in this direction of rural emigration has been most emphasised in countries such as France, where the trend is quantitatively most important, but has also been commented on in most other of the more economically advanced western societies. In general, the argument is that under present conditions, workers of rural origin do not aim, as they did mostly in the past, simply at becoming part of the urban proletariat. Rather, they see their membership of the industrial labour force as being only a transitional phase in a movement of social ascent which will ultimately bring them to at least *petit bourgeois* status. Thus, while greatly concerned with the economic returns from their work, they tend not to adopt the solidaristic, class-conscious orientation of the established working class. They retain the more individualistic and basically conservative values of their original culture, and are reluctant to define their social position by reference to their present work situation. They are, in other words, in the working class but not of it. Consequently, it is claimed, in communities or sectors of industry in which new workers of this kind are numerous, the working class becomes 'diluted' and old ways of life, old modes of thought and belief tend to disappear. Furthermore, in such situations, and particularly in regions where modern industry has only recently been introduced, the emergence of 'integrated' industrial relations and of new patterns of industrial life in general is encouraged —patterns, it is suggested, in regard to which the class divisions of the

is the most notable exponent of the view that the evolution of industrial technology will lead workers to adopt distinctively middle-class attitudes towards their work and their employing organisations, but a number of other industrial sociologists have argued that the more advanced types of production system tend to be associated with more harmonious work relations and with the greater normative integration of the industrial enterprise. See, for example, for Great Britain, Joan Woodward, *Management and Technology* (London, H.M.S.O., 1958); 'Industrial Behaviour—Is there a Science?', *New Society*, 8 October 1964; and *Industrial Organisation: Theory and Practice* (Oxford, 1965), pp. 160–8, 198–205.

past have no relevance but which are indicative of the model for the future.[1]

In this way, then, rural emigration has been regarded as a factor reducing the cohesiveness of the working class from without: in contrast, the changes attendant upon urban growth and renewal have been seen as operating—and far more generally—to decompose the working class *from within*. The particular type of development on which interest has focused has differed somewhat from country to country: for example, in Great Britain it has been the extensive building of new estates and new towns mainly through the agency of public authorities; in the United States, the creation of vast new suburban 'tracts' largely through private enterprise. But in all cases one common outcome has been stressed: the decline of the traditional type of working-class community, the decline of the 'urban village', founded upon the residential stability and social homogeneity of its inhabitants.

As communities of this kind have been disrupted or deserted, so, it has been argued, has the matrix of the traditional working-class way of life been destroyed. It was through the network of kinship, the pattern of neighbouring, the collective activities and rituals of communal solidarity which characterised such districts that working-class culture was transmitted and preserved. Once this basis is gone, therefore, the local and particularistic nature of working-class life is immediately threatened. In the new communities that have been formed, manual workers and their families are often physically separated from their extra-familial kin and live in far less intimacy with their neighbours than previously. Thus, they become more fully exposed than before to the varied and powerful pressures of the wider society—to the impact of mass media and to the influences exerted through their greater contact with other social groups and strata than their own. And in this way, it is then claimed, they are made more receptive to the appeals of higher standards and new styles of living; their expectations and aspirations cease to be defined by traditional norms and values. In contrast with the class-based solidarity and equalitarian emphases of the old community, a concern with *status* and with status distinctions emerges. In other words, these families aim to share, and indeed come to share, along with those of the bulk of white-collar

[1] An influential French study which stresses the weak integration of workers of rural origin into the urban working class, in consequence of their projects of mobility and *a-socialisation préventive*, is Alain Touraine and Orietta Ragazzi, *Ouvriers d'Origine Agricole* (Paris, 1961). See also William E. Powles, 'The Southern Appalachian Migrant: Country Boy turned Blue-Collarite' in Arthur B. Shostak and William Gomberg (eds.), *Blue-Collar World: Studies of the American Worker* (Englewood Cliffs, 1964).

workers, in the way of life of what one writer has referred to as the 'middle mass'—a vast, amorphous collectivity within which no clear-cut lines of economic or socio-cultural division can be drawn.[1]

Here, therefore, the argument obviously links with those concerning 'homogenisation' which were outlined earlier. The shifts in residence and the social relocation following on urban development have in fact been widely regarded as offering the crucial *opportunity* for affluent working-class families to translate their economic advance into status terms. The new American suburbs, for example, have been referred to as a 'second melting pot', in which class rather than ethnic differences are dissolved and where *arriviste* workers learn the folkways of the new social *milieux* to which they aspire.[2] Similarly, it has been suggested that for manual workers in Great Britain 'A move to a new neighbourhood provides the opportunity to break with old habits and adopt new ones, particularly when the shift is from an East End street by the railway to a semi-detached home in a new town.'[3]

The theory of the break-up and progressive *embourgeoisement* of the working class in the context of advanced industrialism is, then, one which rests impressively on a number of more limited yet often interrelated and mutually supportive analyses of current trends of social change. Although it has many variant forms, in which the arguments set out above appear with sometimes widely differing emphases, and although often, as will be seen later, there is some serious lack of clarity as to exactly what is being claimed, the appeal and persuasiveness of the theory cannot be denied. They are amply demonstrated by the extent to which, from country to country, it has won approval among social scientists as well as among journalists, publicists and politicians.[4] The main attraction, one would suggest, lies precisely in the evolutionary perspective which is offered: to advocates of the theory, it must surely appear that it is they, and not the

---

[1] See Harold Wilensky, 'Work, Careers and Social Integration', *International Social Science Journal*, vol. 12, no. 4 (1960); 'Orderly Careers and Social Participation: the Impact of Work History on Social Integration in the Middle Mass', *American Sociological Review*, vol. 26, no. 4 (August 1961); and 'Mass Society and Mass Culture', *American Sociological Review*, vol. 29, no. 2, (April 1964). In using the term 'middle mass', Wilensky explicitly recognises this as 'the vanguard population' identified by the *Fortune* surveys (see n., 1 p. 8 above).

[2] W. H. Whyte, Jnr, 'The Outgoing Life', *Fortune*, vol. 49 (July 1953). Cf. Mayer, 'Diminishing Class Differentials in the United States'.

[3] D. E. Butler and Richard Rose, *The British General Election of 1959* (London, 1960), p. 11.

[4] Some indication of the widespread support for the theory in Great Britain is given below pp. 22–3 and footnotes. It would not be difficult to compile similar evidence for other advanced western societies.

Marxists they oppose, who have interpreted the past correctly and who now have history on their side. However, in order to complete our account of how the debate on the working class has recently progressed, we must next go on to consider the way in which those who are in some sense or other adherents of Marxism have responded: both to the actual developments within western society that have not accorded with Marx's expectations and also to the rival interpretations of capitalism and industrialism which these developments have inspired.

Among entirely orthodox Marxists, as we have already implied, the tendency has been simply to fall back on explanations of events designed to show that Marx's analysis of the dynamics of capitalism remains fundamentally valid; and that, for reasons he set out, the contradictions inherent in the system must sooner or later bring about a revolutionary situation. On the other hand, though, reactions of a far more interesting kind have come from thinkers who have accepted to some extent the failure of Marx's historicism yet who have sought to account for this failure in essentially Marxian terms. For example, the relative economic stability and the decline in class conflict that have characterised capitalist societies in recent decades have led to some radical rethinking on the part of Marxian economists as a prior undertaking, it would appear, to a reassessment of the evolution of working-class movements.[1] At the same time, and of more immediate relevance here, the evident durability of capitalism has also stimulated a new critical interpretation of the nature of capitalist society and culture which draws primarily on the more philosophical writings of the young Marx. Most notably, this finds in the theme of alienation a key to the understanding both of working-class passivity and compliance in the past and also of possible new sources of social and political radicalism in the future. Studies inspired in this way have varied a good deal in their particular focus and in their emphases; none the less, there are certain features which would appear common to all.

In regard to the decline, rather than development, of the working class as a revolutionary force, two closely related arguments have been generally advanced. In the first place, it has been denied that the seeming acceptance by the working class of the existing form of western industrial society—'neo-capitalism'—in any way implies the end of alienation: on the contrary, it is the persistence, indeed the intensification, of alienation that goes far to explain the absence of a revolutionary class consciousness. That the increasing impoverishment of the working class has not occurred

---

[1] See, most notably, Paul A. Baran and Paul M. Sweezy, *Monopoly Capital* (New York and London, 1966).

and that living standards have, in fact, substantially improved has to be recognised. But, it is claimed, although the immediate 'survival' needs of the worker may thus have been largely provided for, his fundamental needs as a human being—those essential to the free development of his human potentialities—remain unfulfilled and indeed deliberately frustrated, and at the same time the worker's awareness of this fact is systematically inhibited. For example, while affluence gives the worker increased possibilities as a consumer, his greater income is taken up merely in the satisfaction of the 'false' needs that are imposed upon him by prevailing institutions and interests—the need to live in the manner prescribed by advertisements and the mass media, the need to 'have fun', to 'relax', to 'escape' and so on. No matter how strongly these needs are actually felt, they are false in that they do not derive from real freedom in self-expression but are rather the result of indoctrination and manipulation. Through such needs, the worker's alienated condition is made manifest.[1]

Furthermore, it is also stressed that, in the last analysis, the alienated consumer has to be understood in terms of the continuing alienation of labour in the organisation of production. Advanced technology may change the nature of industrial work, even the pattern of management–worker relations; domination may be transfigured into administration. But this does not alter the case that under capitalism of any kind the industrial worker is in a subordinate position, a mere instrument without control over the processes of production or over that which is produced. And it is, then, ultimately on account of *this* fact that it is possible for the worker to be made into the kind of consumer that the capitalist system requires. As one author puts it:

It is precisely because the worker is not 'at home' in 'his' work; because, denied him as creative, active function, this work is a calamity, a *means* solely of satisfying needs, that the individual is stripped of his creative, active needs and can find his own power only in the sphere of non-work—the satisfaction of the passive needs of personal consumption and domestic life . . . Capitalism sells the means of a *make believe* human existence—since there is no question of actually *making* such an existence—through the possession of pre-packaged symbols of humanity. The further it goes in this direction, the more it numbs a stunted, mass-produced humanity with satisfactions that leave the basic dissatisfaction untouched, but still distract the mind from it: the more it hopes that these men, preoccupied with various means of escape and oblivion, will forget to question the basis of the whole system: the alienation of labour. Capitalism civilises consumption and leisure to avoid having to civilise social

[1] This position is taken up most clearly by Herbert Marcuse, *One-Dimensional Man* (London, 1964). See, in particular, part 1, 'One-Dimensional Society'.

relationships, productive and work relationships. Alienating men in their work, it is better equipped to alienate them as consumers; and conversely, it alienates them as consumers the better to alienate them in work[1].

This, then, is the alleged strategy of capitalism in its advanced phase: to create the 'happy robot', to establish a soft, euphoric totalitarianism. But this argument is in itself incomplete. Why, it may be asked, is this strategy so successful? Why is the vicious circle of alienation, once exposed by critical intellectuals, not more widely recognised and rejected? Why cannot social criticism and related political agitation produce mass support for movements that are directly aimed at liberating man through the destruction of the capitalist system?

In order to deal with such questions as these, a second argument, and one that is of yet wider compass, has been developed. This refers to the 'hegemony' which, in most advanced societies, the dominant class is able to exercise over subordinate strata: that is, a form of dominance 'not simply by means of force or wealth, but by a *social authority* whose ultimate sanction and expression is a profound cultural supremacy'.[2] In other words, it is held that in the case of neo-capitalism, the dominant class characteristically retains its power not only, or even primarily, through its control over the means of violence or of production but, more fundamentally, through its control over cultural institutions and agencies: schools and universities, literature and the arts, mass *and* minority media —in fact over the entire set of means of creating social consciousness. In this way, the handful of dissident intellectuals can be isolated and their influence minimised; and the bulk of the population can be largely prevented from comprehending the possibility of any alternative form of society to that which the ideology of the dominant class prescribes and supports. Social life and social thought become, in Marcuse's phrase, 'one-dimensional'.

Thus, it may be observed, a curious paradox arises. While, as we have seen, anti-Marxist adherents of the thesis of *embourgeoisement* stress the importance of changes in the 'material basis' of modern society, the

---

[1] André Gorz, 'Work and Consumption' in Perry Anderson and Robin Blackburn (eds.), *Towards Socialism* (London, 1965), p. 349. See also by Gorz, *Stratégie Ouvrière et Néocapitalisme* (Paris, 1964); and *Le Socialisme Difficile* (Paris, 1967).
[2] See Perry Anderson, 'Origins of the Present Crisis', in Anderson and Blackburn (eds.), *Towards Socialism*, p. 30. The idea of 'hegemony' in this sense derives directly from Gramsci but has obvious affinities with Marx's thesis that the ruling class tends to control the means of intellectual as well as of economic production. Cf. Marcuse, *One-Dimensional Man*, part 2 especially, where an extreme 'pessimistic' view is advanced; also Peter Worsley, 'The Distribution of Power in Industrial Society', in Halmos (ed.), *The Development of Industrial Societies*.

defenders of a Marxian standpoint are led in the end to underline the importance of 'superstructural' factors in rejecting the idea that the political potential of the working class is no longer of major significance. In the latter view, what now appears as necessary for the emergence of radical political action on a mass scale is that the *subjective* conditions for this should be brought about; and this in turn means the left-wing vanguard gaining victory in the crucial struggle for hegemonic power. In the context of neo-capitalism: 'La bataille culturelle pour une conception de l'homme, de la vie, de l'enseignement, du travail, de la civilisation, est la condition de la réussite de toutes les autres batailles pour la socialisme, puisqu'elle fonde leur signification.'[1]

At the same time, though, it should further be noted that in considering ways in which false, or at any rate unduly restricted needs might come to be seen as such and false consciousness be pierced, writers who share in the views in question *have* also referred to the possible consequences of ongoing social change. And what is of particular interest here is that they have fixed their attention on essentially the *same* processes as those that are emphasised by their opponents.

Not surprisingly, perhaps, given the insistence that alienation stems fundamentally from the work situation, major interest has tended to centre on the radical possibilities seen as implicit in the new industrial technology and its functional exigencies. It has been pointed out that in enterprises where advanced technology is in operation, the potential, if not the actual power of the rank-and-file is in various ways enhanced. Such concerns are particularly vulnerable to strike action, which would seriously disrupt production and keep expensive plant idle, and in general their managements must seek to ensure a stable and responsible work force. Thus, in return for helping to meet these requirements of the production system, workers are in a strong position to extract from management the right to an effective voice in the decision-making process within the enterprise. 'Integration', in other words, can be double-edged. Moreover, it has also been suggested—most notably by Serge Mallet—that the solidarity between workers, technicians and operating managers which advanced technology encourages could become the basis for a recognition of common interests and for unified action on the part of all employees, manual and nonmanual, against the directors and executives of the concern: the basis, in fact, of a new form of plant unionism of a syndicalist character with 'worker control' as its major objective. Thus, from this point of view, the progress of industrial technology may be envisaged as leading to the

[1] Gorz, *Stratégie Ouvrière et Néocapitalisme*, p. 123.

democratisation of industry and to the ending of alienation in a sense clearly different from that intended by writers such as Blauner. At all events, Mallet would argue, the fact that the social situation within the modern enterprise does not readily give rise to violent, expressive demonstration of worker opposition cannot be taken to mean that such opposition no longer exists. Rather, as industrial relations become less emotionally charged and as working-class consciousness 's'épure de ses aspects sentimentaux', it becomes possible for this opposition to assume a more calculative and rational nature—and thus more probable that it will be carried through to its logical, socialist conclusion.[1]

Although less widely discussed, an argument in very similar vein has in fact also been advanced in regard to the disruption of long-established working-class communities and the dilution of their traditional culture. This process, it has been held, cannot be simply equated with the decomposition of the working class and with a decline in working-class consciousness—except on the assumption that such consciousness is the particular product of deeply felt ties of neighbourhood and kinship. However, such an assumption is a highly questionable one: 'For it implies that the solidarity of class—which is societal in its sweep, and draws no nice distinction between men of this place and that, this name and that, this dialect and that—is rooted in the kind of parochial solidarity which is its very antithesis.'[2] Rather, it has been suggested, the ending of working-class particularism, the forcing of workers and their families out into the mass society, may be seen as a prerequisite for the development of class consciousness at its highest level: one which transcends parochial or sectional loyalties and which is based upon a rational appreciation of class interests and class enemies. In this way, the best possibility may exist of the working class at last shedding its 'corporate' character—its acceptance both of its own distinctiveness and of the social order within which it is contained—and committing itself to the transformation of capitalist society more decisively than ever before. In the words of one commentator on recent changes in working-class life in England:

[1] See Serge Mallet, *La Nouvelle Classe Ouvrière* (Paris, 1963) (quotation from p. 171); also Pierre Belleville, *Une Nouvelle Classe Ouvrière* (Paris, 1963), ch. 5. Cf. Gorz, *Stratégie Ouvrière et Néocapitalisme*, pp. 105–24 esp. Although Mallet would regard himself as a Marxist of sorts, the developments within the industrial sphere which he anticipates seem often closer to those expected, or at least hoped for, by Veblen than by Marx himself. See Thorstein Veblen, *The Engineers and the Price System* (New York, 1933), and especially ch. 6, 'A Memorandum on a Practicable Soviet of Technicians'.

[2] John Westergaard, 'The Withering Away of Class' in Anderson and Blackburn (eds.), *Towards Socialism*, p. 107. See also Alain Touraine, 'La Vie Ouvrière', in Touraine (ed.), *Histoire Générale du Travail*, vol. 4, *La Civilisation Industrielle* (Paris, 1961).

The incursion of rationalism into the hermetic world of the . . . working class is a necessary stage in its emancipation—however limited or confusing its initial manifestations. It is the precondition of a genuinely ideological collectivism—founded on *ideas*, and not merely on instinct. Above all, this rationalism is likely to be directly destructive of the mystical values of deference, the paralysing complex which imprisons so many working class Conservatives today. Capitalist hegemony in Britain is founded on an ideology of stupefied traditionalism and empiricism, an anti-ideology which is the enemy of all ideas and all calculation . . . The battle for the working class can, as we have seen, only be won on the plane of ideology. The new rationalism may be preparing the conditions for real victory[1]

Finally, one may note, the possibility has been raised that growing working-class prosperity itself, although so far a seemingly anodyne influence, could eventually give rise to a significant increase in discontent and social protest. Under the stimulus of a period of steadily rising living standards, expectations and aspirations could in fact race ahead, far beyond the rate at which material advance could conceivably continue. In such circumstances, therefore, a far more acute sense of deprivation and social injustice might be created than was ever possible while the restricted horizons of the traditional working class were maintained. Furthermore, as affluence makes possible the satisfaction of the more obvious personal and domestic wants, urgent new wants may be expected to develop of a kind less readily met through increasing private incomes—for improved environmental conditions, especially in towns; for more *public* amenities for leisure and cultural activities; for better and more equal educational and work opportunities, and so on. And since within the capitalist system there exist serious barriers to making such provision, a greater awareness of the oppressive nature of this form of society and of its inherent irrationality will thus be provoked, and the possibility and desirability of radical change become more widely realised. In sum, it is envisaged that affluence could in the long term become a dynamic, liberating force; a solvent of crystallised attitudes of acceptance and passivity.[2]

From the foregoing paragraphs it is, then, apparent that neo-Marxist

---

[1] Perry Anderson, 'Problems of Socialist Strategy', in Anderson and Blackburn (eds.), *Towards Socialism*, p. 265.

[2] For arguments on these lines see, for example, Anderson, 'Problems of Socialist Strategy', and also Westergaard, 'The Withering Away of Class'. It may be remarked that while Anderson and Westergaard are both exponents of the idea of alienation, they differ notably from many others in recognising that social changes of basic political significance may occur elsewhere than in relationships of production. Cf. our own assessment of future possibilities below, pp. 188–95, which has certain obvious affinities with theirs although not couched in the language of alienation.

writers share with proponents of the *embourgeoisement* thesis a surprising amount of common ground as to the basic processes of change within advanced societies that are of greatest importance for the destiny of the working class. The argument between the two camps in some part concerns the rate and extent of such changes;[1] but, essentially, it is about the ways in which the changes in question are being experienced and given meaning by the individuals and groups upon whom they impinge and, consequently, about the nature of the latter's response. The debate is one that *centres* not on questions of income, standards of living, conditions of work or patterns of residence but on questions of social values, social relationships and social consciousness.

The research on which this volume reports arose out of the debate on the working class in the particular form in which this was being carried on in one industrial country, Great Britain, at one period of time, the late 1950s and early 1960s.

In 1959 the British Labour Party was defeated at the polls on the third successive occasion and the Conservatives increased their parliamentary majority as in fact they had done at the previous general election in 1955. At the election of 1951, although they were then removed from office, the Labour Party had received a record number of almost 14 million votes, equal to 49% of the total poll; but in 1955 their share had fallen to 46% and in 1959 the figure fell again to 44%. The psephological evidence suggested that this decline in support for Labour was most marked in those areas of the country that were most prosperous and economically progressive, and also in the New Towns and in constituencies in which extensive rehousing programmes had been carried through.[2]

At the same time, information was becoming available of the general improvements in living standards experienced by the British population, and most notably by wage earners, in the course of the previous decade.

---

[1] For example, as regards the extent of the overlap between manual and nonmanual incomes. The idea of declining differentials has been questioned or qualified by a number of writers. For Great Britain, see Blackburn, 'The Unequal Society' in Blackburn and Alexander Cockburn (eds.), *The Incompatibles: Trade Union Militancy and the Consensus* (London, 1967); for France, Gilbert Mathieu, 'La Réponse des Chiffres', *Les Temps Modernes*, nos. 196–7 (September–October 1962); and for West Germany and the United States, Richard F. Hamilton, 'Affluence and the Worker: the West German Case', *American Journal of Sociology*, vol. 71 (September 1965) and 'The Income Differential between Skilled and White Collar Workers', *British Journal of Sociology*, vol. 14 (December 1963). A critique of the latter paper has been made by Gavin Mackenzie, 'The Economic Dimension of *Embourgeoisement*', *British Journal of Sociology*, vol. 18 (March 1967).

[2] Butler and Rose, *The British General Election of 1959*, pp. 2, 200.

For example, it was estimated that the average real earnings of industrial workers had risen by more than 20% between 1951 and 1958; and that by the spring of 1959 the average working-class household income was about £850 per year (gross), with nearly half of all employed working-class families having an annual income of over £1,000. It was revealed further, as a result of national surveys, that by 1959 among this more prosperous half of the working class 85% of all households had a television set, 44% a washing machine, 44% a lawnmower, 32% a car and 16% a refrigerator. In addition 35% of the families in question owned, or were buying, their own house. Finally, official statistics showed that between 1948 and 1958 one family in every six in Great Britain—and certainly a higher proportion among the working class—had moved into a newly built house or flat, whether rented or owner occupied.[1]

Given such circumstances, it was then obviously a tempting idea to place the outstanding economic and political trends of the period in a relationship of cause and effect, and to see as the crucial mediating process a shift among certain sections at least of the British working class towards middle-class life-styles and social attitudes. Increasing affluence and other changes in the material basis of working-class life could be regarded as prompting this re-orientation, which in turn could be related to the secular decline in Labour voting among manual workers that electoral statistics appeared to indicate. In this way, it appeared, some general understanding could be gained of the rapidly evolving pattern of British social and political life.

At all events, the thesis of the incipient *embourgeoisement* of the working class—whether explicitly related to political events or not—gained considerable popularity in Great Britain in the years in question. It was accepted in Conservative circles as largely accounting for the party's unprecedented run of electoral success and as a guarantee that this would continue (indeed, the future of the two-party system was held to be in doubt). It was widely regarded by Labour politicians and supporters as the basic factor underlying the failures of the 1960s and as one making imperative a radical reshaping of Labour policies and of the party's 'cloth-cap' image.[2] And, in testimony to the non-controversial nature of

[1] Data on incomes and rehousing are taken from Butler and Rose, *The British General Election of 1959*, p. 12; those on the ownership of consumer durables and house purchase are given by Mark Abrams, 'New Roots of Working Class Conservatism', *Encounter* (May 1960). Cf. also Robert Millar, *The Affluent Sheep* (London, 1963), chs. 1 and 2.

[2] See in particular, Anthony Crosland, *Can Labour Win?*, Fabian Tract 324, 1960; and Rita Hinden, 'The Lessons for Labour', in Mark Abrams and Richard Rose, *Must Labour Lose?* (London, 1960).

the thesis, it was eventually incorporated in a semi-official broadsheet of the Central Office of Information, aimed at presenting the new Britain to the world. This document stressed the shift that had occurred during the 1950s from low-level to middle-level incomes, chiefly among wage-earning manual workers, and went on to claim that British society was now characterised by 'a swelling middle class'. There could be no return to the working-class conditions of the thirties for 'The average man now has much more to lose, and has made too great an investment in his own future as a middle class citizen and householder.'[1]

Moreover, among the ranks of academic social scientists there were not a few who were ready to share in this consensus. For example, in the inquest on the 1959 election the majority of academic commentators—including writers such as David Butler and Richard Rose, Mark Abrams and S. M. Lipset—saw a connection of some kind between working-class affluence, the spread of a middle-class outlook and the drift of support away from the Labour Party.[2] In addition, several studies made at this time of the social life of manual workers and their families claimed to offer direct evidence of the fact that large sections of the working class were, as one author put it, 'on the move towards new middle class values and middle class existence'.[3] At the end of a comprehensive review of research into family and community living in modern Britain, Josephine Klein was prepared to advance the conclusion that:

The white collar is ceasing to be the easily identified distinguishing mark of the middle-class man. Not only have many clerks of middle class origin suffered a relative reduction in their standard of living, not only have many clerks come from manual working-class families and made changes in their manner of life accordingly, but manual workers themselves are also adopting a middle-class way of life.[4]

However, there were also those who regarded the thesis of the worker turning middle-class with some marked degree of scepticism or who, at any rate, could see a number of serious difficulties in the thesis as it was

[1] Central Office of Information, *Social Changes in Britain*, December 1962. The report was reprinted in *New Society*, 27 December 1962.
[2] See Butler and Rose, *The British General Election of 1959*, chs. 2 and 13 esp.; Abrams, 'New Roots of Working Class Conservatism'; and S. M. Lipset, 'The British Voter', *The New Leader*, 7 and 21 November 1960.
[3] Zweig, *The Worker in an Affluent Society*, p. ix; cf. also Zweig, 'The New Factory Worker', *The Twentieth Century* (May 1960).
[4] Josephine Klein, *Samples from English Cultures* (London, 1965), vol. 1, p. 420. For other, more journalistic, accounts which also advance the idea of *embourgeoisement*, see Millar, *The New Classes*, and also George Steiner, 'The Decline of the Labour Party', *The Reporter*, 29 September 1960, and Graham Turner, *The Car Makers* (London, 1963).

being currently presented. We ourselves were of this number, and in papers published in 1960, 1962 and 1963[1] we noted a series of objections and reservations relating to both conceptual and factual matters. The more important of the critical points contained in these publications can be briefly restated as follows.

(i) Proponents of the *embourgeoisement* thesis, as applied to the British case, have been generally imprecise as to exactly what changes in the existing pattern of social stratification they are claiming. In particular, there has been a failure to distinguish clearly between what might be termed the *economic*, the *normative* and the *relational* aspects of the problem. It is scarcely ever made explicit whether *embourgeoisement* is being taken to refer simply to the acquisition by manual workers of incomes and living standards that are comparable to those of many white-collar groups; or, further, to their adoption of a new social outlook and social norms that are of a distinctively middle-class kind; or, further still, to their general acceptance by white-collar persons on a basis of equality and their assimilation into middle-class 'society'. Typically, it would appear, the first of these processes has been taken, more or less unthinkingly, as implying the second, and then these two together as implying the third. But the assumptions that are being made in this case have no very sound empirical foundation.

(ii) The emphasis placed on the increasing comparability of standards of income and consumption of those in manual and white-collar occupations has led to neglect of the fact that the two categories remain much more clearly differentiated when their members are considered *as producers*. Despite the possibly levelling effects of some forms of advanced technology and of modern employment policies,[2] the work situation of white-collar employees is still generally superior to that of manual wage earners in terms of working conditions and amenities, continuity of employment, fringe benefits, long-term income prospects and promotion chances. Class position is not merely a matter of consumer power: the function and status of a group within the social division of labour must still be regarded as being of basic importance.

(iii) Many of the newly observed features of the social life of manual

---

[1] David Lockwood, 'The "New Working Class"', *European Journal of Sociology*, vol. 1, no. 2 (1960); John H. Goldthorpe and David Lockwood, 'Not so Bourgeois After All', *New Society*, 18 October 1962, and 'Affluence and the British Class Structure', *Sociological Review*, vol. 11, no. 2 (July 1963).

[2] It may be noted that in specifically British versions of the *embourgeoisement* thesis the significance of developments in industrial technology and management have in fact been far less emphasised than in, say, the French or American cases.

workers and their families—most notably, their home- and family-centredness—have been too readily interpreted as implying a shift in values and norms in a specifically middle-class direction. To a large extent, ongoing changes in working-class life-styles are open to an alternative explanation in terms of the *adaptation of traditional patterns*, either to the problems posed by new conditions (e.g. physical separation from kin) or to new opportunities (e.g. those provided by better accommodation, greater security and higher wages). Indeed, the assumption that middle-class life-styles are being emulated is not only unnecessary but is also suspect: for there appear to be certain quite distinctive features of middle-class social life that members of the new working class characteristically do *not* display (e.g. regular mutual entertaining between couples and a relatively high level of participation in clubs, societies, etc.).

(iv) In arguing their case, supporters of the *embourgeoisement* thesis have, in fact, referred primarily to changes in the standard and style of living of manual workers and their families. But social class is also importantly manifested in the nature of actual *relationships* between individuals and groups; and little or no evidence has been provided to show that manual workers are now being increasingly regarded and treated by white-collar persons as social equals and thus incorporated into distinctively middle-class status groups. Rather, such information as is available points to the continuance of the manual–nonmanual division as one of the sharpest lines of status demarcation—in work, in local communities, in voluntary associations.

(v) Finally, there is again an absence of evidence to indicate that middle-class social acceptance is indeed something to which manual workers, whether affluent or not, *actually aspire*. There is no evidence, in other words, that to any significant degree manual workers are now rejecting working-class social norms and are identifying rather with the norms of white-collar reference groups to which they would like to belong. Data which show that some proportion of manual workers choose to think of themselves as 'middle-class' are of little value in this respect: for it can be demonstrated that such self-ratings can, and often do, carry some other meaning than either a claim or a desire to be middle-class in the sense of participating in a largely white-collar social world. Powerful economic aspirations—for continually improving standards of living—can be readily found, especially among workers who have become isolated from traditional working-class *milieux*: but specifically status aspirations have rarely been documented. If anything, studies of the new working class, as of the old, suggest that attitudes towards middle-class persons are often critical (e.g. in regard to their anxiety over 'keeping up appearances' and 'class distinctions', and their 'pretensions' to gentility).

On such grounds, therefore, we held to the view that the thesis of the progressive *embourgeoisement* of the British working class was, to say the very least, not proven; and that, as usually presented, it involved a variety of confused and dubious assertions. Several other authors, we may add, subsequently arrived at a similar verdict, even if via different routes from our own; and comparable critiques of the thesis as applied to the working classes of other advanced industrial societies also appeared.[1]

However, while this rejection of rather superficial analysis and over-hasty conclusions was clearly necessary, it was at the same time quite obvious, at all events in the British case, that relatively rapid and possibly far-reaching changes *were* occurring in the pattern of working-class life—changes that certainly called for investigation and appraisal of a more detailed kind than they had so far received. Consequently, as a first step towards such a re-evaluation, we were led to suggest in our 1963 paper—'Affluence and the British Class Structure'—an alternative interpretation of these changes which, while a good deal less sweeping in character than that of *embourgeoisement*, appeared somewhat more closely related to the available research findings.

In brief, this interpretation was the following: that what the changes in question predominantly entailed was not the ultimate *assimilation* of manual workers and their families into the social world of the middle class, but rather a much less dramatic process of *convergence*, in certain particular respects, in the normative orientations of some sections of the working class and of some white-collar groups. In other words, we suggested that the major ongoing modifications in manual–nonmanual differences were occurring at the level of values and aspirations, rather than through any radical reshaping of status hierarchies and relationships in either work or community life; and further, that these modifications resulted from shifting orientations among white-collar as well as among manual strata.

[1] For other discussions of the British case, see Peter Willmott, *The Evolution of a Community* (London, 1963), chs. 9, 10 especially; W. G. Runciman, '*Embourgeoisement*, Self-Rated Class and Party Preference', *Sociological Review*, vol. 12, no. 2 (July 1964); and Westergaard, 'The Withering Away of Class'. For criticism of the *embourgeoisement* thesis as applied to the United States, see S. M. Miller and Frank Reissman, 'Are Workers Middle Class?', *Dissent*, vol. 8 (Autumn 1961); also Richard F. Hamilton, 'The Behaviour and Values of Skilled Workers' and Gerald Handel and Lee Rainwater, 'Persistence and Change in Working Class Life-Style', both in Shostak and Gomberg (eds.), *Blue-Collar World*; for France, see Touraine, 'La Vie Ouvrière'; and P. Chombart de Lauwe, 'Y-a-t-il encore une Classe Ouvrière?', *Revue de l'Action Populaire*, no. 134 (January 1960); and for Germany, Hamilton, 'Affluence and the Worker: the West German Case'.

Spelled out in somewhat more detail, our argument was that the most significant effect of the economic, industrial and ecological changes of the recent past had been to weaken simultaneously *both* the traditional 'collectivism' of manual wage earners *and* the traditional 'individualism' of nonmanual employees. To quote from 'Affluence and the British Class Structure':

On the side of the working class, twenty years of near full employment, the gradual erosion of the traditional, work-based community, the progressive bureaucratisation of trade unionism and the institutionalisation of industrial conflict have all operated in the same direction to reduce the solidary nature of communal attachments and collective action. At the same time, there has been greater scope and encouragement for a more individualistic outlook so far as expenditure, use of leisure time and general levels of aspiration are concerned. Within the white-collar group, on the other hand, a trend in the opposite direction has been going on. Under conditions of rising prices, increasingly large-scale units of bureaucratic administration and reduced chances of upward 'career' mobility, lower level white-collar workers, at any rate, have now become manifestly less attached to an unqualified belief in the virtues of 'individualism' and more prone to collective, trade union action of a deliberately apolitical and instrumental type—especially as the nature of many manual workers' philosophy of unionism is steadily coming nearer to that which they themselves find acceptable.[1]

The convergence implied here had then a twin focus: first, on the acceptance of collective trade union action as a means of economic protection and advancement; and second, on the acceptance of the individual conjugal family and its fortunes as a central life interest. 'Instrumental collectivism' and 'family-centredness' were thus proposed as the major points of increasing similarity in the socio-political perspectives and lifestyles of manual and nonmanual strata. But, we emphasised, convergence should not be assumed to imply identity. In particular, working-class adoption of new ends and aspirations for the family would appear to be occurring less rapidly than the conversion of white-collar employees to collective means, and in any case differences might still be thought likely in the *nature* of the goals pursued by new working- and middle-class families; the former being overwhelmingly economic, the latter still probably reflecting some concern with status differentiation.

In advancing this alternative to the idea of *embourgeoisement*, and in arguing that, in the light of the existing evidence, it appeared the more plausible, we reached in effect the point at which further research became a clear prerequisite for further discussion of a profitable kind. The major

[1] P. 152.

question which arose, therefore, was that of the direction that such research might most usefully take.

After considering the various lines of approach open to us, we arrived at the conclusion that the most logical procedure to follow in this respect would be to devise a study with the primary aim of testing the *embourgeoisement* thesis in as complete and rigorous a fashion as possible. This was the thesis which, as it were, claimed most and which, if valid, would carry the most significant implications. We had shown that it could by no means be taken as generally established, but the possibility none the less remained that it might prove to be confirmed at least in certain respects and under certain conditions. Thus, it seemed to us appropriate to take this as our main point of reference. At the same time, though, we also regarded it as desirable and possible that our research should be so designed that, in the event of the *embourgeoisement* thesis not being supported, it would still be possible for us to check on the applicability of our own more conservative view of the changes taking place on the manual–nonmanual frontier—or, at all events, of those occurring among working-class groups. This, then, became an important secondary objective in the planning of our enquiry.

The details of the strategy and conduct of the research, as related to these concerns, are discussed at length in chapter 2. But, before going on to this, we should finally note here that while our project was actually under way, ideas and possibilities other than those with which we had been initially preoccupied emerged into greater prominence and were clearly relevant to the general question of the future of the working class. First, growing disaffection with Conservative rule, the Labour Party's ultimate return to electoral success in 1964 and 1966, and accentuated conflict between governments and trade unions, both before and after Labour's accession to power, all served to draw attention to arguments of the kind outlined earlier in this chapter in which affluence and its concomitants appear less as harmonising influences than as likely sources of working-class discontent and unrest. Subsequently, the record of the Wilson administrations has served to confirm long-standing doubts on the Left as to the viability of democratic socialism, and has led to the thesis of working-class alienation being given increased emphasis as a means of interpreting the existing situation and, in some cases, as the basis of continued hope in revolutionary possibilities.[1] Thus, since those who see the working class as decomposing and those who still regard it as at least a potential agency of radical change appear to appeal largely to the

[1] See, for example, Blackburn and Cockburn (eds.), *The Incompatibles*.

same emergent social conditions, we have thought it worth while in writing the present volume to try to say something about the implications of our findings for the latter point of view as well as for the former. However, given of the fact that our research was designed to focus specifically on the *embourgeoisement* issue, we have not attempted to go much beyond this in the main body of the book: our attention is there concentrated on examining versions of the *embourgeoisement* thesis in the several contexts of work, sociability, social aspirations and imagery, and so on. We have widened our frame of reference only in our final chapter in which, by way of a conclusion to our project as a whole, we take up again the broad issues of class and politics out of which our interest in the affluent worker initially stemmed.

2. The design of the research

In seeking to test the thesis of working-class *embourgeoisement*, the first problem we faced was that of how, with limited resources, we could most effectively investigate the occurrence of a social process which was not clearly defined, even by those who asserted its importance, and which in our view was decidedly problematic. In particular, the question arose of how, if the thesis were in fact a mistaken or much exaggerated one, this could be indicated in a reasonably convincing manner. Simply to show that there were some, or indeed many, manual workers in Great Britain who were still far from being middle-class on any definition would not in itself be of any great relevance. For virtually all of those who had put forward the idea of *embourgeoisement* had obviously regarded this as an incipient process, as yet fully revealed only among certain more 'advanced' sections of the working class, whose chief significance lay not in their present numerical strength but rather in the pattern they set for the future.[1] Thus, what was required was a research design that would enable conclusions to be drawn not simply as to the current extent of *embourgeoisement* but also, and more importantly, as to the reality or otherwise of the specific mechanisms and sequences of change which this reshaping of the class structure was held to involve or would appear to entail. On such a basis it would then be possible, according to the nature of the evidence produced, either to accept *embourgeoisement* as probably an integral feature of the dynamics of modern British society or, alternatively, to establish a strong argument in support of the negative position.

In order to approximate as near as we could to a design which would afford possibilities of this kind, we decided that we should concentrate our resources on a single case-study; that is to say, on the study of one 'population' of manual workers in one particular context at one particular time. This would allow us to carry out a relatively intensive enquiry and to collect information about the social lives of the workers we selected of a range and degree of detail not generally found in the studies on which current discussion of the new working class chiefly rested. For example,

---

[1] This point is particularly stressed in Postan, *An Economic History of Western Europe, 1945–1964*, pp. 328–31.

nationally based poll-type surveys had traced seemingly important differences among the working class in social and political attitudes—but without showing how, if at all, the groups thus differentiated were distinctively located within the social structure and experienced distinctive social pressures and opportunities.[1] Again, accounts of new patterns of working-class family and community life had rarely given serious attention to the influence of different types of employment and work relationships, while investigations using work-based samples had generally failed to produce detailed information on respondents' out-plant activities and associations. Our objective, then, was to bring together data which pertained both to attitudes and to social behaviour and relationships, and to cover work and non-work *milieux* alike; the ultimate aim being that of forming some idea of the *total* life-situations and life-styles of the individuals and groups we studied.

At the same time, of course, this decision in favour of a single, intensive enquiry gave rise to certain fairly evident problems: most notably, that of how we should choose our case and of how this could be made an adequate basis for some degree of generalisation. The way in which these problems were to be handled was obviously a matter of crucial importance for the success of the entire project. On consideration, however, it seemed to us that there was one solution which could be attempted which was clearly preferable to all others. This was, quite simply, to select our case so that, in the light of all previous discussion, this would be *as favourable as possible* for the confirmation of the *embourgeoisement* thesis: in other words, to focus our enquiry on a population of manual workers whose social characteristics and social setting appeared highly conducive to the whole series of shifts in values and norms, in reference groups and in patterns of association that *embourgeoisement* could be taken as implying. In this way we would, on the one hand, gain the best chance of being able to study workers who were actually in course of changing their class situation; while, on the other hand, if in the case in question this process was *not* in evidence, we would then be in a position to claim that *a fortiori* it was unlikely to be occurring to any significant extent within British society at large. Furthermore, in this latter eventuality we would also be well placed to show where the various arguments involved in the thesis of *embourgeoisement* actually broke down, despite conditions being systematically biased towards their validation; and also to explore, in part at least, our own alternative idea of 'normative convergence'.

[1] For a critique of one such study, see David Lockwood and John H. Goldthorpe, 'Dr Abrams on Class and Politics: a Second Opinion', 1962 (available from the Department of Applied Economics, University of Cambridge).

In sum, the strategy we elected to follow was that of finding and examining a *critical* case: one which would either provide us with an opportunity to study the phenomenon of the worker turning middle-class at first hand; or which would enable us to confirm in as decisive a manner as possible the doubts about *embourgeoisement* that we had previously expressed.

To put such a strategy into effect entailed preparatory work which fell into two main stages. First, we had to specify, on a theoretical basis, the set of attributes that a critical case of the kind we sought should ideally possess; and then secondly, we had to discover some real-life situation which could be shown to approximate to this theoretical model sufficiently closely to make our strategy a practicable one. Both these tasks posed difficulties; but carrying them through was not only a necessary exercise but also one that proved to be of interest and value in itself.

As regards the specification of the critical case, we were chiefly guided in this by the literature in which the thesis of *embourgeoisement* was presented. From the review of this literature contained in the previous chapter, it can be seen that the conditions that have been regarded as necessary to, or as predisposing for, *embourgeoisement* are multiple, and that not only economic conditions are involved but also ones associated with particular developments in industrial technology and management and with changing patterns of residence. Moreover, and again as was earlier indicated, the arguments in question include many implicit elements and require some elaboration if they are to be made entirely clear. Thus, on close examination the complete catalogue of features which, it appeared, should be present in the critical case turned out to be a quite lengthy and complex one. The following represents an attempt at a systematic exposition.

A. *Required social characteristics of the population of workers*

(i) *Affluence*: personal and family incomes comparable to those of many white-collar employees, minor professionals and smaller independents.

(ii) *Economic security*: good prospects for continuity of high-paying employment; also no widespread experience of insecurity—as, for example, through unemployment—in the past.

(iii) *Physical mobility*: a high incidence of migration away from community of origin, associated with changes in job or residence and resulting in physical separation from kin.

(iv) *Consumption-mindedness*: a high motivation to attain standards and styles of domestic living in advance of traditional working-class norms, resulting in extensive ownership of consumer durables and house purchase.

B. *Required characteristics of the industrial setting*

(i) *Advanced technology*: high productivity and high wage plants; work-tasks demanding a relatively low level of physical effort but a high level of skill or responsibility, and conducive to the formation of rewarding work relationships.

(ii) *'Progressive' employment policies*: management policies aimed at increasing worker integration into the enterprise through security guarantees, profit-sharing, fringe benefits, welfare programmes, 'promotion from within', consultative practices etc.

(iii) *Harmonious industrial relations*: a favourable industrial relations 'atmosphere' uninfluenced by traditions of class-based hostility or suspicion; efficient procedures for grievance settlement, consultation and negotiation capable of eliminating unregulated disputes and strikes.

C. *Required characteristics of the community setting*

(i) *Newness, instability and 'openness'*: an absence of tightly-knit kinship networks and of established patterns of neighbourhood life, giving maximum exposure to the influence of mass media in shaping beliefs, values, norms, tastes etc. and minimum social control over consumption behaviour and life-styles.

(ii) *Social heterogeneity*: a high degree of mixing within residential localities of individuals and families of differing status, occupation, regional origin etc., offering wide possibilities for emulation and status competition.

(iii) *Economic expansion, 'optimism' and relative isolation from older industrial regions*: a high rate of economic growth associated with general optimism about the future and positive attitudes to change; an absence of long-standing traditions of industrial working-class life—as for example, ones centering on trade unionism, Labour politics or Nonconformist religion.

Given such a specification, which appeared to be both reasonably comprehensive and logically consistent, we were then prepared to move on to the task of finding some actual population and setting which would 'match up' to the requirements in question. At this point, however, the major difficulties arose. It quickly became evident that although the set of features that should be found in our critical case might fit well together as an ideal-type, they did not always do so empirically. Rather, there were a

2*

number of instances where particular features showed, if anything, a tendency to be *negatively* associated.

For example, among those types of worker who would qualify as 'affluent' there proved to be a relatively large number who in fact received their high wages in return for work which was physically unpleasant and stressful, if not actually hazardous, and which was also in some cases irregular—thus giving rise to marked fluctuations in earnings. Considerations of this kind meant that we had to regard as generally unsuitable for our enquiry affluent groups in such industries as mining, fishing, iron and steel, sea and road transport, docking and construction.[1] Similarly, another possible type of affluent worker—the skilled craftsman —also presented problems from our point of view which arose from his characteristic industrial environment. Craft grades tend to be distinguished by their often conservative attitudes towards trade unionism, industrial relations and industrial life generally,[2] and the industries in which such grades are today most heavily represented—such as shipbuilding and heavy engineering—are ones renowned for traditionalism on the part of workers, managements and employers alike.[3] Furthermore, it may be added that both these latter industries and most of those mentioned previously are ones typically located in long-established industrial regions, some of which, together with their associated industries, are now in economic decline. In short, then, a considerable proportion of affluent workers in modern Britain are still to be found in industrial settings which, for one reason or another, seem unlikely to encourage their assimilation into middle-class society—on the basis of arguments that exponents of the *embourgeoisement* thesis have themselves advanced.

Moreover, approaching our objective of a real-life critical case from the side of the community revealed yet other complications. To begin with, there was the difficulty that the large majority of new communities in which manual workers and their families live are in fact little less homogeneous in their social composition than the kinds of community these families have traditionally inhabited. Most of the new municipal estates built on the outskirts of large towns and cities have been specifically designed in order to provide 'working-class' housing; and even where, as

[1] In addition, of course, certain of these industries are noted for their high propensity for labour disputes and strikes.
[2] For a good example of this, in the context of a process production plant, see Allan Flanders, *The Fawley Productivity Agreements* (London, 1965), pp. 92–4, 214–19 esp.; see also I. C. Cannon, *The Social Situation of the Skilled Worker* (University of London, Ph.D. thesis, 1961).
[3] See, for example, Geoffrey Roberts, *Demarcation Rules in Shipbuilding and Shiprepairing* (Cambridge, 1967); also J. E. T. Eldridge, *Industrial Disputes* (London, 1968), chs. 3 and 4.

in some of the New Towns, efforts have been made to promote social 'balance' through juxtaposing houses of differing quality, this policy seems to have failed more often than not.[1] In so far as examples of new and relatively mixed communities could be discovered, these tended to be rather small and also to be somewhat removed from major centres of industrial activity—as, say, in the case of those forming parts of 'expanded' country towns. And here the problem which occurred in turn was that of finding sufficient manual workers who could be reasonably classed as affluent; for in such localities wage levels were generally lower than in areas where the demand for industrial labour pressed harder on supply, and family incomes were kept down through the limited opportunities for female employment.[2] In other words, a further contradictory tendency within our ideal-type critical case was exposed: empirically, it appeared, the kinds of community setting in which affluent workers are most likely to be encountered are ones which, even if new, are not distinctive for their degree of heterogeneity in occupational and status terms.

The preliminary investigations which led us to appreciate these difficulties in locating our critical case were, therefore, of some substantive significance. They suggested fairly clearly that the coincidence of *all* the conditions that had been seen as favouring working-class *embourgeoisement* was still probably a rare situation in present-day British society, and that any assumption that the main 'modernising' trends of social change ran in close parallel was likely to be misleading. Put more concretely, it became evident, even at this early stage in our research, that the manual worker earning, say, a regular twenty pounds a week from physically undemanding employment in a progressive 'integrated' enterprise and living in prosperous style together with his white-collar neighbours in a new 'integrated' community was, if not a myth, then at all events a far less conspicuous figure on the contemporary scene than had often been implied.

However, despite both the practical problems encountered and the further indication these gave that the thesis of the worker turning middle-class was, to say the least, an overstated one, we maintained our intention of trying to test this thesis in as detailed and decisive a manner as could be arranged. We continued the search for a suitable *locale* for our enquiry but modified somewhat our expectations of how near we could come to

[1] See, for example, J. H. Nicholson, *New Communities in Britain: Achievements and Problems* (London, 1961), pp. 65–7, 132–3; and B. J. Heraud, 'Social Class and the New Towns', *Urban Studies*, vol. 5, no. 1 (February 1968).

[2] Cf. Nicholson, *New Communities in Britain*, pp. 86–91.

meeting the full range of criteria that we had set out. Proceeding on this rather less ambitious basis, we were in fact eventually able to identify a population of manual workers whose characteristics and social context came very close to our requirements in most respects, and which, moreover, appeared to us to be *as* appropriate to our objective as any that was likely to be found. This, we believed, could then reasonably be taken as constituting a critical case for the purposes of our study, although not fully matching our ideal specification at every point.

The population in question was one located in the town of Luton in south-west Bedfordshire and was made up of workers in a number of selected high-wage occupations who were employed at the Luton plants of three major manufacturing concerns. These were: Vauxhall Motors Ltd, a totally owned subsidiary of General Motors; the Skefko Ball Bearing Company Ltd, a member of the international SKF organisation; and Laporte Chemicals Ltd, a member of the Laporte Group of companies.[1] In order now to support our claim that a study of these men and their families may be regarded as a critical test of the *embourgeoisement* thesis, the following information is presented under headings corresponding to those that were previously established.

A. *Social characteristics of the population studied*

(i) *Affluence*: We limited our attention to workers who were married men and who in October 1962, were *regularly* earning *at least* £17 per week gross. In fact, in the sample we drew from our population just over half (53%) of those interviewed reported *net* weekly earnings (i.e. 'take-home pay') averaging over £18 per week.[2] Thus the workers we studied, as we have shown in a previous publication,[3] could certainly be regarded as affluent relative to the bulk of manual wage earners at the time in question. Moreover, their earnings also compared favourably with those of a sample of lower grade (i.e. non-managerial) white-collar workers which, for comparative purposes, we drew from the staffs of two of our firms, Skefko and Laporte.[4] Among the latter sample, only 38% reported having

---

[1] For further details of the plants, see *IAB*, pp. 3–4 *et passim*, and below pp. 39–43.

[2] Full details of the sampling procedure are given in *IAB*, pp. 4–6 and appendix B, and in *PAB*, pp. 3–6 and appendix B; see also pp. 47–8 below.

[3] See *PAB*, p. 36, n. 1 especially.

[4] For details of this sample, see below, pp. 52–3. It may be underlined here that for the purposes of testing the *embourgeoisement* thesis, as this has been typically set out, it is such a comparability with white-collar incomes that is the essential requirement. Thus, to observe that the manual workers we studied were not the *most* affluent that could have been found is rather beside the point, and in any case neglects the difficulties of finding an entirely 'ideal' case which we have discussed above. To argue that in face of these difficulties we should have

average take-home pay at above the £18 per week level. As regards family incomes, the white-collar workers were at some advantage since more white-collar than manual wives were in gainful employment (48% compared with 32%); but even so, the differences between the two samples were not marked and in both cases the median figure came into the £18–24 per week range. Finally, we may note that 40% of the manual workers we studied had Post Office Savings Bank accounts and that 64% had money in a building society or the Trustee Savings Bank; the corresponding figures for the white-collar sample being 46% and 67%.[1]

(ii) *Economic security*: The general prospects for continuity of employment varied somewhat between the three firms on which our study was based, but the prospects for all the groups of workers with whom we were particularly concerned were very good. At Skefko, no-one had been laid off since 1926, and Laporte too had a reputation for providing secure jobs. A recent closure of one unit at the plant had been carried through with only a small number of redundancies among employees with less than three years' service. In the case of Vauxhall there was, as with any car firm, a history of redundancies but, in comparison with experience elsewhere in the industry, these had been remarkably limited. Between the end of the war and the time when our study began (1962) there had been only one occasion on which men with more than one year's service had lost their jobs. In the case of the Vauxhall workers who satisfied our earnings criterion, all but a handful had been with the firm for at least two years.

Among all the groups of workers we interviewed the degree of security they enjoyed was widely appreciated. Overall, only 7% regarded their present job as being 'fairly insecure' and 1% as 'very insecure', compared

concentrated on workers with the highest incomes that could be discovered, even at cost of neglecting other *desiderata*, would be to give greater weight to affluence alone than exponents of the *embourgeoisement* thesis have generally done. Finally, we would note that commentators on our previous publications appear not always to have appreciated the significance of the fact that the men in our sample were *regularly* earning over £17 per week—whereas the men represented in the upper quartile, decile, etc., of the income distribution of an occupational group, industrial sector or other collectivity will not, of course, be entirely the *same* men from week to week or month to month. Thus, for example, our own comparison of earnings, referred to in the preceding note, actually underemphasises the relative affluence of the workers we studied.

[1] The two samples were also broadly similar in the extent to which various kinds of insurance policy were held, the only appreciable difference being that the white-collar workers were more often insured against fire and theft. Two other marked differences were that 19% of the white-collar workers as against only 4% of the manual workers held stocks or shares, and that 89% of the former as against 34% of the latter had bank accounts. This last difference was obviously related to the fact that virtually all the white-collar workers were paid by cheque.

with 71% who believed it to be 'fairly safe' and 18% 'dead safe'.[1] Furthermore, chiefly to eliminate men with earlier experience of un-employment during the inter-war years, we restricted our study to workers in the age-range 21–46. Consequently, it proved that the very large major-ity of our sample, 88% overall, had had no experience of unemployment at any time in their lives, and that only 4% had ever been out of work for a period of longer than three months.

(iii) *Physical mobility*: Between 1951 and 1961 the population of Luton grew from 110,400 to 131,600, and of this increase more than 60% was attributable to net migration. This trend was reflected in the findings that in our sample of affluent workers only 30% of those interviewed had lived chiefly in the Luton area[2] up to the time that they were first employed, and that nearly half (46%) had grown up outside of the entire London and South Eastern region. It also proved that a majority of our respondents' wives (56%) were similarly not natives of Luton.

The attractions that had been mainly responsible for bringing these migrants to the town appeared to be two: first, better housing and second, the prospect of well-paid and relatively stable employment; the former being the more important among migrants from the London area, the latter among those from other parts of the country.[3] As a result of their physical mobility, a high proportion of the couples we studied were separated from their kin and often by some considerable distance. For example, of those who still had parents alive, only 13% of the men and 18% of the wives had parents living within ten minutes' walk of their homes; and in the case of 56% of the men and 48% of the wives their parents were living entirely outside Luton. The degree of separation from siblings was slightly less marked, since sometimes they too had moved to Luton. But, even so, only 36% of the couples interviewed had a majority of their closer kin (parents, siblings and in-laws) living in the town. The remaining couples were almost equally divided between those with the majority of their kin living within a 50 mile radius of Luton and those whose kin were for the most part yet further afield.

(iv) *Consumption-mindedness*: As we have just noted, a majority of the

---

[1] These figures are all the more impressive in view of the fact that just at the time when our 'work' interviews were starting, two other Luton firms laid off numbers of men (for quite unrelated reasons) and thus gave rise to much discussion in the local press of the degree of job security in the town generally and to speculations about the situation in the three major firms with which we were concerned. In the event, none of the pessimistic forecasts were borne out.

[2] I.e. the town of Luton and all territory within ten miles of the town boundaries.

[3] See *IAB*, pp. 152–4.

workers with whom we were concerned had come to Luton primarily in quest of higher incomes and better living conditions. Moreover, our interviews also suggested that among our sample as a whole the aspirations that were most commonly held for the future were ones relating to steadily increasing consumer capacity and to yet higher material standards of life.[1] In the sphere of domestic consumption, at least, there was little evidence at all of any restricting influence being exerted by traditional working-class norms. Considering, for example, refrigerators and cars—two high-cost and characteristically 'middle-class' possessions—the extent of ownership proved to be roughly comparable between our manual and nonmanual samples: 58% of the former as against 56% of the latter had refrigerators and 45% as against 52% owned cars. Furthermore, on what might be regarded as the still more revealing matter of house purchase, it emerged that 57% of our affluent workers—compared with 69% of the white-collar sample—owned or were buying their present homes. It is of interest to contrast these figures with those reported by Abrams (and noted in the previous chapter) for the 'more prosperous half' of the British working class in 1959: the latter show only 16% of households having a refrigerator and 32% a car; and only 35% of families being house-owners or buyers. Even allowing for the fact that our data relate to 1962–3, the differences indicated may be taken as testifying further to both the high degree of affluence and the marked consumer orientation of the workers we studied.

B. *Characteristics of the industrial setting*

(i) *Advanced technology*: It was in this respect that the case we selected for study most obviously fell short of the 'critical' specifications that we had initially laid down. Two of the plants at which our affluent workers were employed—those of Vauxhall and Skefko—would in fact have to be allocated to those 'intermediate' ranges of the technology scale which, in the view of Blauner and other writers, provide the context most conducive to worker alienation and class consciousness and to conflict-ridden industrial relations.[2] Vauxhall is a car and van manufacturing plant in which the majority of production workers are engaged in the mass production of vehicle bodies or in the various stages of vehicle assembly; while the Skefko establishments[3] are geared to the machining of varying,

---

[1] See *IAB*, ch. 6 and pp. 77–9 below.

[2] See above, pp. 10–11.

[3] Skefko have in fact two physically separate plants in Luton. These are, however, in many ways interdependent and for our purposes could reasonably be treated as one.

but often large, quantities of many different types of ball and roller bearings. Only the Laporte plant would approximate to the kind of industrial environment that has been seen as favouring the breakdown of traditional antagonisms within the enterprise and the existence of a high level of normative consensus. This establishment comprised a number of process production units, turning out in bulk a range of ammonium, potassium, sodium and barium compounds and sulphuric acid. Some units were rather old and physical conditions were quite often unpleasant; none the less, most of what have been taken to be the characteristic socio-technical features of process production were readily observable: for example, the lack of any direct relationship between worker effort and the level of output, highly stable production routines, the relatively relaxed pace of work in production departments, and the freedom of operatives from close supervisory or technological constraints.

The acceptance of plants with such varying production systems as the basis of our sample of affluent workers was largely implicit in the choice of Luton as the *locale* for our study[1]—a choice which, we believed, was overall the best we could make. However, we were in fact more inclined from the first to settle for something short of the ideal in this aspect of our research design than in any other. This was so for two main reasons: first, because, as we have already noted, arguments relating to the influence of technological developments were relatively little emphasised in specifically British versions of the *embourgeoisement* thesis; and secondly, because such arguments appeared empirically to be the least convincing elements in the thesis as a whole. A steady accumulation of research findings from the mid-1950s onwards already justified considerable scepticism over the idea that the spread of advanced technology was regularly a factor conducive to greater employee satisfaction and more harmonious work relations.[2] In this respect, therefore, there seemed to be some possible virtue in the necessity of deviating from the strict requirements of

[1] Vauxhall was by far the largest firm in Luton, employing over a fifth of the town's workers, while Skefko was among the three or four next largest employers. Laporte was the only sizable process production plant. The three firms together accounted for approximately 30% of the total labour force of the Luton area.

[2] Briefly, the relevant findings could be said to show that the development of automated (including continuous flow) production systems (i) has very variable effects on skill levels and 'mixes' within industrial plants; (ii) *may* give rise to new forms of strain and monotony in work—e.g. ones associated with continuous concentrated attention; (iii) *may* increase operatives' feelings of lacking control over, and of being divorced from, the production process; (iv) *may* prevent work group formation through dispersing men widely over large areas of plant; (v) tends to increase shift-working substantially. See, for example, P. Naville, 'The Structure of Employment and Automation', *International Social Science Bulletin*, vol. 10, no. 1 (1958) and *L'Automation et le Travail Humain* (Paris, 1961); W. A. Faunce, 'Automation

our critical case and in including among the workers we studied men employed under more than one general type of technology.[1]

Moreover, this view proved to be amply justified by the actual results of our research. As we have described in some detail in an earlier report[2] our findings gave little support to the idea that any close connection necessarily exists between workers' immediate experience of, and response to, their work situation, as technologically conditioned, and the attitudinal and behavioural patterns that they more generally display as industrial employees. For example, with the men we studied, attitudes and behaviour—in regard to workmates, supervisors, management, the firm as an employer, trade unions, etc.—showed in the main a high degree of *similarity* among assemblers, machinists and process workers alike, despite the widely differing kinds of production system within which these groups worked. And while our respondents' dispositions towards management and their employers were in general relatively favourable, this tendency was, if anything, *more* marked among the assemblers and machinists than among the process workers, even though the latter appeared to experience least deprivation in the actual performance of their work-tasks and -roles.[3] Under these circumstances, then, the fact that a majority of the men in our sample were employed in fairly conventional mass production enterprises becomes far less damaging to the general design of our project than might otherwise have been the case.

(ii) '*Progressive*' *employment policies*: All three firms on which our study was based followed employment policies of a liberal character and regarded these as contributing to the effectiveness of the enterprise as a whole as well as to the well-being of employees. Each firm had standardised procedures for the induction of newly engaged workers which involved presenting information on the history, established practices and organisation of the firm in addition to technical instruction. Each firm also offered an extensive welfare programme including *inter alia* subsidised

---

and the Automobile Worker', *American Sociological Review*, vol. 28 (August 1958); B. Karsh, 'Work and Automation', in Howard Boone Jacobson and Joseph S. Roucek (eds.), *Automation and Society* (New York, 1959); Ronald Gross, 'The Future of Toil', in Shostak and Gomberg (eds.), *Blue-Collar World*; and P. Blumberg, *Industrial Democracy: the Sociology of Participation* (London, 1968), pp. 53–64.

[1] It might be added that all three firms in question were in the van of technical progress in their own fields and that all had very good business records. See *IAB*, p. 79, n. 2.

[2] *IAB*, chs. 1–4 especially.

[3] Disaffection on the part of the process workers was concentrated on wage levels, while an important consequence of the technological environment in which they worked appeared to be that of impeding communication between different groups of workers and thus inhibiting collective action. See *IAB*, pp. 73–8, 88–9.

canteen arrangements, a pensions scheme, a sickpay scheme (except at Skefko), medical facilities and provision for a wide range of 'social' and recreational activities through a 'works club'. Furthermore, there were from firm to firm various other policies in operation yet more directly aimed at bringing home to employees the extent to which their own interests and those of the firm could be allied. All the firms, for example, ran suggestions schemes through which workers could win often quite substantial cash prizes for submitting ideas which led to more efficient production. Again, it was the declared intention of all the firms both to 'promote from within' and to 'train for promotion' wherever possible; and, so far at least as supervisory and lower-level technical and managerial grades were concerned, this policy appeared to be generally adhered to. In Vauxhall, where the concern for employee 'integration' was most highly developed, there was also a profit-sharing scheme and an elaborate consultative system whereby constituencies of employees elected men to serve, on an almost full-time basis, as members of a Management Advisory Committee. Finally, it may be noted that in the brochures and house journals of all three firms there could readily be found open expressions of management's desire to 'build up worker interest in the company', 'create team spirit at all levels', 'foster attitudes of co-operation and trust' and so on; in other words, to make the enterprise, in the eyes of its employees, something more than merely an economic association founded on the labour contract.

(iii) *Harmonious industrial relations*: All three of our firms had notable records of industrial peace. The Skefko and Laporte plants had in fact been strike-free at least from the end of the war, while Vauxhall was well known for its success in avoiding all but very infrequent disputes in an industry in which labour unrest and stoppages of work are particularly common.[1] Relationships between Skefko and Laporte and the unions representing their employees were on a more or less orthodox pattern, Skefko being in principle a '100% union' firm. In the case of Vauxhall, on the other hand, arrangements were less conventional as a result of the firm not belonging to the Engineering Employers Federation and having negotiated special agreements at district level with the Amalgamated Engineering Union and the National Union of Vehicle Builders. However, these institutional differences were probably of far less consequence for industrial relations in the three firms than was the character of local union leadership. The officials chiefly concerned included few militants, at least

[1] For some observations on the disputes that occurred at Vauxhall during 1965–7, after the completion of our study, see *IAB*, appendix D.

of a class-conscious type, and prevailing attitudes tended to be those rather of 'business' unionism. Furthermore, such attitudes were largely consistent with those displayed by the members of the rank-and-file whom we interviewed in the course of our enquiry. As we have previously shown, a majority of our respondents regarded their relationship with their employer as being, within limits, one of collaboration and inter-dependence, and saw their firm's avoidance of strikes as a positive achievement attributable to sound industrial relations practice.[1]

One other aspect of the 'favourable' labour situation in Luton which has been commented on is the high proportion of workers in the major firms who have not before been employed in large-scale manufacturing industry; that is, who have worked hitherto mostly in agriculture, services or small concerns, where union organisation is often weak and overt conflict between employers and labour exceptional. Among the workers in the several occupational groups we studied, from a third to two-thirds had not been unionists before coming to their present firms; and among those in semi-skilled jobs, less than a fifth had any previous experience of their present type of factory work.

C. *Characteristics of the community setting*

(i) *Newness, instability and 'openness'*: As we have already noted, the population of Luton has grown rapidly in the post-war period, with net migration contributing more to this growth than natural increase. Concomitantly with this, extensive house building programmes have been carried through. According to Moser and Scott, the new housing rate for Luton over the years 1945–58 was tenth highest among the 157 British towns with 1951 populations of over 50,000;[2] and a recent writer on the ecology of Luton has calculated that in 1960, 12,000 or about a third of all houses in the town had been erected in the previous fifteen years.[3] In consequence, then, of the amount of both immigration and new housing development, it is evident that a relatively high proportion of individuals and families in Luton must be living in residential areas which are at least new to them if not new altogether. Among the couples who figure in our enquiry, only 30% had not changed their place of residence since marriage or since coming to Luton as a couple; and of the remainder, 30% (21% of

---

[1] See *IAB*, ch. 4, and also, for details of our affluent workers as trade unionists, ch. 5.

[2] C. A. Moser and Wolf Scott, *British Towns* (Edinburgh and London, 1961), appendix B, p. 112.

[3] D. W. G. Timms, 'Distribution of Social Defectiveness in Two British Cities: a Study in Human Ecology' (University of Cambridge Ph.D. thesis, 1963), p. 90.

the total sample) had been in their present accommodation for not more than two years and 64% (44% of the total) for not more than five years.

Some indication has earlier been given of the extent to which our affluent workers and their wives were physically separated from their kin, and it may also be noted that our research findings point to the absence of familiar relationships between immediate neighbours as another fairly typical situation: 49% of the couples we interviewed reported no more than casual contacts (i.e. no visiting or 'dropping in') with the families living next door, while only 21% were on 'regular' visiting terms. Indeed, there was little evidence that our respondents were involved in any specifically 'neighbourhood' life at all, in the sense of subcultural patterns shaped and sustained through the close interpersonal ties of the locality.[1]

(ii) *Social heterogeneity*: In addition to having a notably high rate of new housing, Luton is yet more distinctive in the extent to which this housing has been in the form of *private* developments. Of the 12,000 houses built since 1945, less than half—5,500—were the result of local authority schemes.[2] The bulk of the private development consists, moreover, of large estates of moderately priced houses which have been built specifically to attract the town's affluent industrial workers as well as the lower middle class. Thus, on these estates the residential mixing of manual and nonmanual families, which has proved so difficult to achieve in public housing, is clearly in evidence. Among the couples we studied, we have already noted that a majority (57%) were house owners or buyers, and this is closely related to our further finding that 55% lived outside distinctively working-class localities such as those in the centre of the town or the corporation estates. In the case of these couples it then proved that as many as 44%, compared with 17% in the rest of the sample, had at least one next-door neighbour who was not himself a manual worker.

It is, of course, true that the existence of private estates of the kind in question may well mean that on the corporation estates in Luton white-collar workers are in an even smaller minority than elsewhere. However, in these localities the significance of occupational homogeneity would appear to be typically over-shadowed by the marked heterogeneity of

---

[1] This view is supported by Zweig's remarks on Luton as compared with the other towns on which his study of industrial workers was based—Sheffield, Workington, Erdington (Birmingham) and Mitcham. See *The Worker in an Affluent Society*, pp. 234–6.

[2] Timms, 'Distribution of Social Defectiveness in Two British Cities', p. 90. In the Moser and Scott analysis of British towns, Luton, as noted, ranks tenth in terms of its new housing rate for 1945–58: over the same period, however, it ranks only forty-sixth on the basis of its 'local authority' rate and one hundred and thirtieth (out of 157) in terms of new local authority housing as a percentage of all new housing.

residents in terms of their regional origins. Native Lutonians live along-side, and are often out-numbered by, the families of newcomers. And from our interviews and from a reading of the local press it was evident that consciousness of such differences was a quite definite influence on individuals' attitudes and behaviour towards each other. Stereotypes of Londoners, Irish, Scots and 'northerners' were all fairly well developed and formed a ready basis for invidious comparisons of psychological and moral attributes. In other words, no matter how 'working-class' they might be in occupational composition, the corporation estates were evidently not the repositories of any widely shared traditions of working-class community life.

(iii) *Economic expansion, 'optimism' and relative isolation from older industrial regions*: The best available indicator of the rate of economic expansion in Luton in post-war years is the extent and nature of the increase in the town's population that we have referred to. The growth of Luton's industry has produced a situation of chronic labour shortage to which the continuous influx of migrants has been the response. Even so, several Luton firms, including Vauxhall and Skefko, have at various times had to organise national recruiting campaigns. Among its inhabitants themselves, awareness of Luton's prosperity and progressiveness appears to be highly developed. In interviews, we were frequently told: 'This is a boom town.' The majority of the workers we studied reported that their living standards had risen substantially in recent years, and the majority, too, were hopeful about the future—chiefly, it seemed, because of a belief in the virtual inevitability of economic progress either in general or in the particular industries and firms in which they were employed.[1] There was little sign of the 'fatalism' characteristic of the more traditional industrial worker, or of the suspicion and fear of the future that could readily be found among, for example, even the most affluent of miners, shipyard workers or dockers.

A further factor directly conducive to such relatively confident and forward-looking attitudes could well be the extent to which Luton is set apart from the major industrial areas of the North and Midlands. Certainly Luton has had far less experience than most factory towns of economic hardship in the past[2] and conspicuously lacks the collective memory of 'the bad old days' which remains strong elsewhere. Moreover, largely because of its location and the pattern of its economic history, Luton has no long-established working-class institutions through which industrial

[1] See *IAB*, pp. 138–42.
[2] See Timms, 'Distribution of Social Defectiveness in Two British Cities', pp. 88–90.

attitudes formed in the struggles of previous generations might be preserved. Trade unionism, for instance, has been a force in local industry only in the last three decades; and in the political sphere it is still doubtful if the Labour Party has established its supremacy in Luton despite the very high proportion of factory workers among the electorate.[1]

Finally, it may be added that this absence of strong Labour traditions in the town and the fact that it is situated beyond the range of activities of militants in either North London or Birmingham have often been advanced as additional reasons for Luton's avoidance of industrial unrest.[2] Left-wing comment in particular has often represented Luton as a 'turnip-patch': a place where workers' awareness of the hard facts of industrial life and of the basic conflicts this involves has never been aroused, and where class consciousness is thus feeble and unformed.

It is, then, on the content of the foregoing paragraphs that we chiefly rest our claim that the population of workers we selected for study was, in all probability, as well-fitted as any available to our objective of testing the *embourgeoisement* thesis in a critical way. However, there is one further piece of supporting evidence which might also be noted: namely, that in the British context Luton has been frequently singled out by sociologists, journalists and others as the *locus classicus* of the affluent, aspiring, status-conscious type of worker. For example, Zweig, in the study referred to in chapter 1, describes Luton as '... rapidly expanding, prosperous, its people running after jobs and money more or less in American fashion'. Luton is 'a slice of America in Britain, self-assured, beaming with vitality and go-aheadness, a cosmopolitan community ...'.[3] Moreover, the Vauxhall men included in Zweig's study, and particularly the younger ones, are reported as having a much weaker sense of working-class identification than affluent workers in the other towns that were covered.[4] In a very similar manner, Graham Turner characterises Luton as 'Gadgetville, U.K.', a town with 'a perpetual gold rush mentality'; and he discerns, at least among Vauxhall employees, 'a new status conscious drive for posi-

---

[1] *Ibid.*, pp. 79–80. Luton ranks ninth in Moser and Scott's analysis in terms of the percentage of its gainfully occupied population engaged in manufacturing. However, from 1950 to the 1963 bye-election, Luton was a Conservative seat, the majority having steadily risen to 5,019 in 1959. At the bye-election, Labour won the seat with a majority of 3,749. This was reduced to 723 in 1964 but rose again to 2,464 in 1966.

[2] See for example, George Cyriax and Robert Oakeshott, *The Bargainers* (London, 1960), p. 133; Graham Turner, *The Car Makers*, pp. 116–17; and Ken Weller, *Truth about Vauxhall*, Solidarity Pamphlet No. 12 (Dunstable, n.d.), p. 10.

[3] See *The Worker in an Affluent Society*, pp. 234–5.

[4] *Ibid.*, pp. 136–8.

tion' and indeed 'all the signs of a nascent middle class'.[1] Even in a highly academic study, Timms has advanced the idea that although Luton has an exceptionally high proportion of factory workers, to call the town 'working-class' would be a misnomer; for such a description is belied by its prosperity, by the character of its housing and also by its voting patterns.[2] And this same interpretation would no doubt have been accepted by the Conservative Party spokesman who stated in 1963 that 'Luton is a microcosm of the kind of society we [Conservatives] are trying to create'.[3]

Our choice of Luton was not in fact greatly influenced by this attention the town received as the prototype of the new 'middle-class' Britain: a good deal of the comment in question came after our enquiry had begun. Nonetheless, the outcome is a fortunate one in that it means we are able, in a more or less literal sense, to meet supporters of the *embourgeoisement* thesis on their own ground. Quite apart from the theoretical justification we have given for our selected *locale*, we cannot be accused of seeking for workers turning middle-class where no-one had ever claimed or supposed that such a pattern of change was likely.

It remains in this chapter for us to raise and discuss certain problems relating to the actual conduct of our enquiry—that is, to the implementation of our research design—and to possible limitations of the design itself. To some extent, the problems in question are ones that we have already dealt with in previous publications; where this is so, the fact is noted and the present discussion is kept relatively brief.

In the first place, we must refer to difficulties associated with the way in which, for interviewing purposes, we sampled the affluent workers who made up the—highly specialised—population of our critical case. As we have already indicated,[4] this population was basically one of workers in a number of high-wage occupational categories, employed at three industrial establishments with broadly contrasting production technologies. The occupational categories were selected so that in the case of each plant they would cover men performing types of work that were central to the main production systems in operation. Thus, in Vauxhall we concentrated on assembly-line workers; in Skefko, on machine operators involved in batch production, together with machine setters and craftsmen who were concerned in some way with the servicing of machines; and in Laporte, on

---

[1] *The Car Makers*, pp. 99, 101.
[2] 'Distribution of Social Defectiveness in Two British Cities', pp. 79–80.
[3] Mr John Hare (later Lord Blakenham) speaking on the eve of the Luton bye-election.
[4] P. 36, above.

process workers and on craftsmen engaged in process maintenance. In addition, for reasons that have mostly been elaborated above, we further restricted our interest to men who were: (i) between the ages of 21 and 46; (ii) married and living with their wives; (iii) *regularly* earning *at least* £17 per week gross (October 1962); and (iv) resident in Luton itself or in immediately adjacent housing areas.

The sample we took of this population was not a simple random one. On a number of grounds, mostly of a practical kind, it seemed to us advisable to confine the sample within each firm to certain major departments;[1] and although within each occupational group these covered an estimated 60–70% of our population, the question of 'representativeness' was in this way inevitably raised. Furthermore, while in most of the departments selected, we included in our sample *all* those men who were eligible, this 100% sampling could not be maintained in the case of the two largest of the Vauxhall assembly divisions—thus leading to the under-representation both of men in these divisions among the assemblers and of the assemblers within the sample as a whole.

Such imperfections would obviously threaten to make generalisations about our critical case a hazardous, or at best a complicated matter. However, as a result of the checks which we were able to make, and which we have previously described,[2] we are satisfied that interview data from our sample are in fact unlikely to be misleading—*provided that* due attention is always given to any significant differences in response occurring among the occupational groups on which the sample is based.[3] In the course of the chapters that follow, such variation is from time to time noted; and it may be assumed that wherever *un*qualified reference is made to the pattern of response of the sample as a whole, differences between occupational groups are, so far as we can ascertain, of no great importance to the argument. In table 1, details are presented of the distribution of our sample by firm and occupational category, and also of the response rates that were obtained in our interviewing programme.

[1] In Vauxhall, six of the major assembly divisions; in Skefko, most of the larger machine shops, two millwrights' shops and the toolroom; and in Laporte all process departments other than those on pilot schemes. For further details see *IAB*, appendix B or *PAB*, appendix B.

[2] *Ibid*. Briefly, no grounds could be found for supposing that those men in our population in the excluded departments differed in their basic social characteristics from those in the departments studied; and, as regards the assemblers, the interview data showed no systematic differences in patterns of response between the men from the under-represented divisions and the rest.

[3] To the extent that such differences do exist, the 'overall' pattern of response of the sample will obviously be in part a function of the number of respondents in each group—which, quite apart from different sampling ratios, is a somewhat arbitrary feature of our population.

TABLE I. *Distribution of sample and response rates by firm and occupational category*

Firm	Occupational category	Number in original sample	Number in final sample	Overall response rate (percentage)*
Vauxhall	assemblers	127	86	68
Skefko	machinists	65	41	63
	setters	31	23	74
	craftsmen	58	45	78
Laporte	process workers	31	23	74
	craftsmen	14	11	79
TOTALS		326	229†	70

* *Two* interviews were involved (see text below). The figure given in this column refers to men who agreed to *both*. Of the total of 326 men in the original sample, 12 (3.7%) could not be contacted and 46 (19.6%) declined to be interviewed. A further 21 (6.4%) agreed to the first interview but not to the second.

† In all subsequent tables relating to this sample, N = 229 unless otherwise indicated.

A second issue that should be raised concerns the methods used in collecting information about the social attitudes, behaviour and relationships of the workers we selected for study. As we have implied, the interview was our main research instrument. Those men in our sample who agreed to co-operate were interviewed first of all at their place of work and then again, some weeks later, in their own homes and together with their wives. The average duration of the first interview was approximately one hour, and of the second—sometimes divided in two sessions—approximately three hours.[1] So far as our respondents' working lives were concerned, interviewing was supplemented by observational studies, made in all the departments from which our sample was taken. But as regards out-plant life, no comparable observational work was carried out—and this might well be regarded as a serious shortcoming. It means, for example, that our information about respondents' relationships with their kin, neighbours or friends, or about their leisure activities or participation in various clubs and societies is all based upon the accounts that they themselves gave to us in interviews and not upon our own 'direct' study. The possibility thus exists of bias and distortion occurring in the data as a result of respondents' attempts, conscious or otherwise, to present themselves in a certain manner; as the social anthropologists have traditionally

[1] For the first interview, respondents, 'lost time' was made good by their firms; for the second, we offered a compensatory payment of £1 which some couples refused.

49

insisted, it is wise to distinguish between what people say they do and what they do in fact.

The problem here is not, however, an unfamiliar one to sociologists, and it needs to be said at once that neither is it so intractable as is sometimes suggested. Interview data, when obtained by well-qualified personnel and carefully interpreted, *can* provide valid information on social behaviour and relationships as well as attitudes.[1] Respondents are rarely able to maintain a 'front' throughout an entire interview and, more importantly, few appear even to attempt this. In our own interviews, we were strongly impressed by the open manner in which questions were generally answered and issues discussed, and by respondents' preparedness to show themselves in what, to them at least, appeared as an unfavourable light. Where it was possible to check on the response to interrelated questions, no serious degree of inconsistency was found in the answers that individuals gave.

Moreover, there is one other very powerful justification for relying heavily upon interviewing in the case of the men and women with whom we were concerned: namely, that outside the work-place observational methods would have been difficult to apply, and would have yielded only very limited results, because of the actual style of social life that the couples in question most typically displayed. As we describe in detail later on, this style was a highly *privatised* one, decisively centred upon the home and the conjugal family. Consequently, little opportunity existed for 'field work' of the conventional anthropological kind or for any more refined techniques of observation. Typically, there was no local community of a 'public' kind in the midst of which the investigator could, as it were, sit down and take notes; nor many important forms of communal sociability which he could participate in or analyse. To a surprising degree, the social lives of our affluent workers and their families were carried on behind closed doors or were built around such essentially private occasions as the family walk or car-ride, the visit to relatives, or the couple's 'evening out' at a cinema or restaurant.

Thus, while the limitations and possible dangers of our heavy dependence upon interview material must always be borne in mind, we do not believe that there are grounds here for doubting the validity of our findings

[1] See, for example, the discussion in Johan Galtung, *Theory and Methods of Social Research* (London, 1967), part 1, ch. 5; also Herbert H. Hyman, *Interviewing in Social Research* (Chicago, 1954). All assistants who participated with the authors in the interviewing programme were graduates with at least some social science training, and prior to entering the field all received intensive instruction on the nature and aims of the project and carried out a series of trial interviews.

in any general sense. And we would at all events argue that the methods of enquiry we followed were by far those best-suited to the nature of the case with which we were concerned. If the social lives of individuals such as those who made up the bulk of our sample cannot be adequately investigated by means of interviews, then it is difficult to see how they are to be studied at all.[1]

Finally, there is an important question to be faced as to the appropriateness of our research design for a study that is focused on a problem of social change. Our interest centres on the *process* of *embourgeoisement*; yet, for the most part, the material we have collected about our sample of affluent workers enables us to build up only a static picture—a snapshot— of their social lives at one particular point in time. The information we have about their previous lives is largely restricted to details of work histories, changes in residence and so on; few questions were asked about the past, other than quite specific and factual ones, because of obvious doubts about the quality of 'retrospective' data. This means, therefore, that we can say relatively little about changes actually experienced by our respondents themselves. We cannot, for example, compare their present attitudes or life-styles with those they displayed say five or ten years before; and because this is not possible, it is difficult for us to discuss, other than in a highly inferential way, the likely direction or pattern of change in their lives in the future. In other words, the design of our research does not allow us, strictly speaking, to say anything decisive at all about whether or not the workers we studied were *on the move* towards 'middle-classness'. Such a judgment would clearly have to rest on the results of a longitudinal study of a kind that we were not able to attempt.

Does this lead, then, to the conclusion that we are not after all in a position to apply an effective test to the *embourgeoisement* thesis? That this is not in fact so should become clear from a re-examination of our earlier discussion of the thesis. It is quite apparent that what is claimed, or perhaps more often implied, by the majority of its proponents is not simply that the trend of change among the working class is—in some degree or other—in the direction of middle-class standards and styles of living; but further, that among certain more 'advanced' groups of manual workers and their families distinctively middle-class values and patterns of social life are *already* established; and further still, in some cases, that these groups have already become assimilated into middle-class social worlds. Such arguments have been made the basis for explanations of observed, or alleged, changes in family and community life, in economic behaviour, in

[1] Cf. Ronald Frankenberg, *Communities in Britain* (London, 1966), pp. 15–16.

political behaviour and so on. And in turn the generalisation of a middle-class way of life and of middle-class society has been specifically related to economic and social conditions brought about as part of the unfolding of the inherent logic of advanced industrialism.

In the case we selected for study nearly all of these conditions, as we have endeavoured to show, were in existence and had been for some time. Thus, if the *embourgeoisement* thesis is a sound one, it follows that we should expect to find among the workers in our sample not merely evidence of some partial acceptance of seemingly middle-class attitudes and behaviour—such as might be covered, for example, by our own much more limited thesis of 'normative convergence'—but rather some sizable proportion of men who, apart from being manual wage workers, are virtually indistinguishable in their typical life-styles and patterns of association from persons of nonmanual status who would be generally thought of as at least 'lower' middle-class. On the other hand, though, if middle-class manual workers of this kind are *not* to be found in the case in question —and if the critical nature of this case is not impugned—then serious doubt must necessarily fall upon the argument that such workers constitute a significant stratum within British society at large: that is to say, in these circumstances the *embourgeoisement* thesis would be powerfully controverted.[1]

To facilitate detailed comparisons between our affluent manual workers and men in lower level nonmanual occupations was the major reason for including in our research design the sample of white-collar employees to which we earlier referred. This sample was one of men in all main clerical grades in the Skefko and Laporte establishments.[2] Interviews, which took in respondents' wives, were based on a schedule consisting of parts of both the 'home' and the 'work' schedules used with our manual respondents. Thus, over quite a wide range of items directly matching data

[1] It could, of course, still be held that our affluent workers will *eventually* become middle-class or, say, that the decisive shift in this direction will be made by their children. But such arguments would obviously imply major qualifications and additions to the *embourgeoisement* thesis as it has thus far been presented: quite new mechanisms and sequences of change would have to be postulated—for example, to account for the 'time-lag' involved—and these in turn would then require empirical examination.

[2] It was initially planned to include the appropriate grades of employee from Vauxhall also but unfortunately this proved not to be possible because of administrative and other difficulties. In Skefko, the grades covered were those of general clerk, cost clerk and correspondent (or order clerk); and in Laporte, general clerk and commercial assistant. We restricted our attention, as in the case of the manual workers we studied, to married men between the ages of 21 and 46, and our sample included all those in the grades in question who met these specifications. In all, 75 men were approached and of this number 54 (72%) agreed to be interviewed. In all tables relating to this sample, N= 54 unless otherwise indicated.

for the two samples were obtained. However, it should be added that in view of the very restricted nature of the white-collar sample, we have not attempted to give any great weight to the findings it produced except where these are broadly in line with those from more extensive studies of members of white-collar strata. In other words, we have chiefly used this sample as a source of data, in the same form as data for our sample of manual workers, which can be taken as *illustrating* already well-documented features of white-collar social attitudes and behaviour.

In sum, then, we feel able to claim that our research design is adequate to its purpose and that a straightforward description of the social lives of our affluent workers and their families, set against the available comparative material from studies of white-collar groups, can provide an appropriate and cogent test of the *embourgeoisement* thesis in the form in which this has been generally advanced. Such a description constitutes the main content of the chapters that follow.

3. The world of work

We have previously noted that in British versions of the *embourgeoisement* thesis—as compared, say, with French or American versions—the possible effects on class attitudes and behaviour of long-term developments in industrial technology and management have been relatively little emphasised.[1] In our initial criticisms of the thesis, as applied to the British case, we were led to remark that the discussion had been concentrated on the worker as consumer almost to the exclusion of any consideration of the worker as producer—despite the obvious relevance of this latter issue to the claims that were being advanced. However, in designing our own enquiry we attempted, so far as this was consistent with other *desiderata*, to give ourselves the opportunity of studying industrial workers in Britain under conditions which writers elsewhere had associated with the decline of traditional status distinctions and class antagonisms and with the emergence of new, more 'integrated' modes of industrial life. As we have described, one of the establishments on which our research was based— that of Laporte—although not a particularly modern plant, could be placed towards the 'advanced' end of the technology scale; and while the other two plants were of a fairly conventional mass production type, management policies and practices were in all three cases alike highly progressive and employee-oriented. Furthermore, all three firms had achieved considerable success in providing relatively stable as well as highly paid employment, and in avoiding disputes and stoppages of work. All three were recognised leaders, both technically and commercially, within their particular branches of industry.

What, then, do our findings tell us about the *experience* of work and about the *expectations* and *aspirations* in work of the men we studied in these firms? And what are the implications of our findings for the *embourgeoisement* thesis?

The point that is most immediately evident about the way in which our affluent workers actually experienced their employment is the generally low level of satisfaction that they derived directly from their work-tasks

[1] Only Zweig's work contains more than passing references to this aspect of the matter.

54

and -roles. Only a minority appeared to find the work they performed inherently rewarding, while on the other hand work-related stresses of one kind or another were quite frequently reported and in some groups were obviously acute. The data on which these assertions rest have been fully discussed in an earlier publication;[1] here it will be sufficient simply to restate three specific conclusions that emerge.

(i) Judging by the findings of more extensive studies of factory workers, it would seem that at least among the assemblers and machinists in our sample—whose jobs were particularly fragmented and 'rationalised'—the numbers stating that their work is monotonous, that their job does not absorb their full attention, and that the pace of their work is too fast are, on any comparison, notably high.[2] Moreover, our interview material suggests that within our sample as a whole such experiences are a major source of job dissatisfaction: men reporting them were, in each case, significantly more likely than others to express a preference for having a different shop-floor job to their present one.[3] In addition, evidence also existed of other discontents, fairly general in one occupational group or another, centering on such matters as physical conditions, supervisory practices, methods of organising work, work-loads, the operation of piece-rate systems and the lack of opportunity for job changes. In all these respects except the first, one common factor could be identified: namely, the dislike of work rules which were felt by workers either to restrict their freedom of action unduly or to lead to unfair outcomes in terms of the allocation of work and levels of pay.

(ii) While very few of our affluent workers could have been forced into their present employment for want of alternative opportunities, a sizable proportion stated that they had liked some previous job more. This was the case with 66% of the machinists, 59% of the assemblers, 47% of the more skilled men (craftsmen and setters) and 44% of the process workers. As might be expected, the reasons given for such preferences related very

[1] See *IAB*, ch. 2, 'The Worker and his Job'.
[2] In the case of these groups, job-cycles tended to be of short duration—for the majority of assemblers being less than three minutes. We would, incidentally, regard as perverse the argument recently advanced that assembly-line work in car factories is comprehensive and meaningful, and not at all without variety, and that widespread complaints by workers of monotony and so on might be better understood as a bargaining tactic or as the 'feedback effect' of previous research findings. See H. A. Turner, Garfield Clack and Geoffrey Roberts, *Labour Relations in the Motor Industry* (London, 1967), p. 169. The body of evidence indicating that real deprivation is experienced in performing such work consists of more than simply attitudinal data, and the fact that it comes from samples 'in different countries decades apart' (*ibid.*) would seem to add to, rather than detract from, its significance and reliability.
[3] I.e. a different job in the same firm.

largely to intrinsic factors—to the greater variety, autonomy or responsibility that previous jobs had offered, or to the less severe deprivations that they had entailed. The kinds of job most frequently mentioned were either ones at a higher skill or status level than the respondent's present work,[1] or jobs in agriculture, transport, services or other forms of employment which do not usually involve the physiological or psychological rigours of large-scale factory industry. Around a quarter of the more skilled workers and three-quarters of the semi-skilled men had held jobs in one or other of these categories at some earlier time in their working lives. What is indicated here is then that many of our affluent workers were attracted into their present employment primarily by the extrinsic, economic returns that it offered *in compensation for* its inherent 'disutility'.[2] In other words, it is indicated that the current orientation of these men towards their work was a decidedly *instrumental* one.

(iii) Consistently with this interpretation, the reason that our respondents by far most frequently gave for remaining in their present jobs—and most appeared to be quite firmly attached[3]—was in fact the high level of pay that they could earn. As can be seen from table 2, this reason was given by half the process workers, by two-thirds of the more skilled men and by three-quarters of the assemblers and machinists; and with 1 in 4 of the latter, this was the *only* consideration mentioned. The reason next most frequently advanced was security of employment (referred to by 38% of our respondents overall) and taking all economic factors together—level of pay, security, extent of social welfare and other fringe benefits—one or more of these was referred to by 87% of the craftsmen and setters in the sample and by 82% of the semi-skilled men. In contrast, in no occupational group did as many as a third of our affluent workers make any mention of staying in their jobs because they liked the work they did; and among the assemblers and machinists the proportion was as low as 1 in 8. If for purposes of comparison we now turn to our sample of white-collar employees, we find a very different situation. A clear majority (70%) did *not* refer to the level of pay as a factor attaching them to their present employment, while the nature of their work was mentioned by two-fifths—this

[1] In course of their work history, 7% of our sample had held professional, managerial or other white-collar jobs; 9% had been self-employed; 18% had attained supervisory, inspectional, minor official or service positions; 26% had been craftsmen; and a further 18% had been in manual jobs classified as skilled. In other words, only a little over a fifth had been entirely confined in their working lives to semi-skilled or unskilled manual work. See *IAB*, table 16, p. 32.

[2] In this respect it is interesting to note that of the 138 men who advanced reasons for preferring some previous job, only 7 (5%) mentioned the better pay that was offered.

[3] See below p. 77 and for full details, *IAB*, pp. 25–6.

being the reason given more often than any other.[1] In much the way that would be expected from the results of more extensive research at white-collar level, the actual performance of their work-tasks and -roles appeared to provide these men with a degree of direct satisfaction significantly more often than happened in the case of our manual workers.[2]

TABLE 2. *Level of pay and nature of work as reasons for staying in present employment*

	Assemblers and machinists (N = 127)	Craftsmen and setters (N = 89)	Process workers (N = 23)	White-collar (N = 54)
	Percentage			
Level of pay given as only reason for staying	27	7	9	4
Level of pay given as one reason for staying (with at least one other)	46	58	39	26
TOTALS	73	65	48	30
Level of pay not mentioned as reason for staying	27	35	52	70
Nature of work given as a reason for staying	12	29	26	39

[1] The reason next most often given was, as with the manual sample, security of employment, being referred to by 35%. The proportion of the white-collar workers mentioning *any* economic factor was 59%.

[2] Among studies showing the importance of the nature of work performed to white-collar job satisfaction, we may cite the following: (1) Walker found that office workers in two large industrial firms rated 'interest of work' first out of ten features of their jobs in terms of attractiveness, while civil servants rated the same item third after job security and pensions rights. Pay was rated third and fifth respectively. (Nigel Walker, *Morale in the Civil Service: a Study of the Desk Worker* (Edinburgh, 1961), pp. 199–203.) (2) Dufty has shown that among a sample of Australian rail clerks and clerks in a training organisation 'type of work' was rated a close second to security as the most important of a list of eleven job satisfaction factors. Pay was a poor third. 90% of the respondents stated that they liked their jobs primarily on account of their 'interest'. (N. F. Dufty, 'White Collar Contrasts', *International Journal of Comparative Sociology*, vol. 4, 1963.) (3) Dale found that while among a sample of clerks working in five industrial firms 'monotony, worry, and low job satisfaction' were the reasons most often given for disapproving of clerical work, they were referred to by only 17% of respondents; and that on the other hand 58% reported that the work they did was 'very interesting all the time' or 'interesting most of the time', as against only 11% rating it 'mostly rather boring' or 'very dull all the time'. (J. R. Dale, *The Clerk in Industry* (Liverpool, 1962), pp. 20–4.) (4) Weir and Mercer report that in a sample of white-collar workers employed in ten large-scale organisations and consisting of clerks, local government officials, technicians and draughtsmen, between a half and two-thirds in each group referred either to the actual content of their work-tasks or to 'doing my job well' when asked: 'What about your job gives you most satisfaction?' (D. T. H. Weir and D. Mercer, 'Orientations to Work among White-Collar Workers', *Proceedings of the S.S.R.C. Conference on Social Stratification and Industrial Relations*, January 1969).

3+

From the findings we have reviewed, it is therefore fairly apparent that for many of the affluent workers we studied, affluence had been achieved only at a price: that of accepting work which affords little in the way of intrinsic rewards and which is likely to be experienced essentially as *labour*—as the expenditure of effort motivated simply by the extrinsic reward of payment. Indeed, one could say that many of these men have gained their 'middle-class' incomes and standards of living through taking and holding down jobs which offer higher pay than do most types of manual work *because of* the stresses and deprivations they impose: be- cause, that is, they imply a kind of work experience that contrasts particu- larly sharply with that characteristic of the white-collar clerk, technician or administrator. These remarks are most obviously relevant in regard to men whose work is physically demanding,[1] who are tied to the compulsive rhythms of the conveyor belt, or who are compelled to earn their high wages through 'racing the clock' on piece-work. But it would be a mistake to suppose that the seemingly more favoured groups in our sample—the craftsmen and the process workers—have not also had to 'buy' their afflu- ence in an essentially similar manner. This becomes evident if we examine the position of these two groups rather more closely.

The craftsmen clearly had opportunity in their work for the exercise of skill, judgment and initiative—far more so than the semi-skilled men; yet within this group over half claimed that their jobs did not absorb their full attention, discontent over methods of supervision and work organisation was widespread, and just under half reported having had at least one previous job that they had found more likeable. In interpreting this situ- ation, one important clue is provided by the nature of the jobs to which these latter respondents referred. With few exceptions, these were jobs which, in one way or another, were of a less restricted and routinised character than the ones they and their fellow craftsmen at present per- formed; for example, maintenance jobs in relatively small firms in which they 'had to do everything' or were given a 'roving commission', or tool- making jobs in which they had worked closely with development engineers or designers. In Skefko and Laporte, however, as in large-scale plants generally, even skilled work is subjected to the logic of specialisation and bureaucratic control,[2] and in this way the autonomy of craftsmen and

---

[1] Within our sample, the physical strain of work seemed to be most felt among the setters—not because their work was heavy but because of the pressure under which they worked and the long hours they usually put in. Of the men in this group, 65% reported that they found their jobs physically tiring, as compared with a quarter of the craftsmen and process workers and slightly under half of the machinists and assemblers. See *IAB*, pp. 21–2.

[2] Most notably, through the standardisation of toolmaking work and also through the operation of 'planned maintenance' systems.

their opportunities for applying their skills are inevitably curtailed. When this is borne in mind, then, the grievances and frustration expressed by the men we interviewed become somewhat easier to understand. At the same time, though, it proves to be the case that only 2 out of the 56 craftsmen stated that they preferred a previous job on account of the better pay it had offered, while two-thirds mentioned the high level of pay as a factor attaching them to their present jobs.[1] In other words, it would appear that in much the same way as with the assemblers and machinists, the craftsmen in our sample have been prepared to sacrifice, or to forgo, work satisfactions of an immediate kind in order to maximise their economic gain. And it may well be that because of their craft training, the *relative* deprivation that they thus experience is *greater* than that of men for whom it is easier to accommodate to the idea of work as an almost exclusively instrumental activity.[2]

As regards the process workers, the nature of their work-tasks and -roles undoubtedly gave rise to fewer and less severe stresses than those typically created by assembly-line work or piece-rate machining. Consistently with this, the process workers displayed no strong dislikes concentrated on particular features of their job. On the other hand, however, there was no indication that they experienced any great degree of positive satisfaction, either in the immediate performance of their work-tasks or from the social relationships of their work. In this last respect, in fact, our findings go directly contrary to what would be expected from the analyses of writers such as Blauner and Woodward. Far from showing the highest degree of integration into their employing organisation, the process workers in our sample were *less* likely than men in other occupational groups to have close ties with workmates or to participate in work-based clubs and societies and, in addition, were *more* likely to reveal critical or hostile attitudes towards their firm.[3] This discontent, it would seem, largely resulted from the fact that while the satisfactions they sought and derived from their employment were just as restricted as those of the assemblers and machinists to economic returns, the wage levels they enjoyed were

---

[1] And over 90% mentioned some economic factor: i.e. either pay, security or welfare and other fringe benefits.

[2] Support for this idea comes from the findings (i) that only among the craftsmen were those who said they had never thought of leaving their present employment in a minority, and (ii) that half of the craftsmen, as compared with around a quarter in each other occupational group, had at some time thought of leaving *and* had taken some action to this end, such as investigating other employment possibilities, approaching other employers, etc. See *IAB*, pp. 25–6.

[3] See *IAB*, ch. 4, 'The worker and his firm', pp. 72–8, 90–2 especially.

below those of semi-skilled grades in Vauxhall and Skefko.[1] In effect, therefore, one might say that the process workers were party to a 'money for effort' bargain struck at a somewhat lower level than in the case of the assemblers and machinists: in comparison with the latter groups, they carried out usually less taxing but still inherently unrewarding work for lower, although still quite high, economic compensation. As one Laporte man put it: 'Of course, you could make more at Vauxhall, but life here is just that much easier.' However, the process workers were not in the main appreciative of the actual 'deal' that they received—96% thought that Laporte could afford to pay them more—and the discrepancy between the level of wages aspired to and that obtained appeared certainly to be wider among the process workers than in any other group in our sample.[2]

What then proves to be distinctive about the craftsmen and the process workers is not that they enjoy relatively advantageous conditions of employment in 'money for effort' terms but that, if anything, they are more likely than the other workers in our sample to be *dis*satisfied with their position in this respect: the former group because of the extent to which they feel deprived of opportunities for intrinsic rewards in work, the latter because they do not regard their economic return as being sufficiently high. It is in these groups, in fact, that wants and expectations from employment appear to be *least* adequately fulfilled. We can thus conclude that few at all of our affluent workers, no matter what their skill level or technological environment, are likely to have found the road to affluence an easy one; and further, and more importantly, that while in the white-collar world the achievement of higher pay is usually associated with taking on a more complex, autonomous and responsible job, something like the *reverse* of this has been the typical experience of the manual workers we studied.[3]

The nature of the work they perform is not, moreover, the only cost of affluence that these men have to bear: two other factors that have also to be taken into account are the actual amount of work they do and when they do it. In previous discussion of the new industrial worker and of 'declining class differences' between manual and nonmanual strata surprisingly little

[1] While all the process workers in our sample were, of course, regularly earning more than £17 p.w. gross (our cut-off point for inclusion in the sample) the median reported take-home pay for the group was under £18. See *IAB*, table A.2.

[2] See *IAB*, pp. 86–9, 138–9.

[3] A partial exception to this statement must be noted in the case of the setters: in being promoted from machining to their present jobs they had achieved both an increase in pay and more skilled and directly satisfying work. But it would appear that in becoming machinists in the first place, they had, like the machinists we interviewed, often sacrificed intrinsic for extrinsic rewards in work.

attention has been given to the prevalence in modern industry of overtime working and of shiftwork. However, for most of the men who made up our critical case these were important aspects of their working lives, and ones which could exert a considerable influence upon the pattern of their out-of-work lives as well.

At the time when our study was carried out, the three plants on which the research was based operated standard working weeks for their production employees of from 40 to 42 hours. In each case, though, overtime working was more or less institutionalised and formed a regular feature of the employment of the mass of the manual labour force. Among the men we interviewed, the amount of overtime being currently worked varied a good deal from group to group—averaging around 8–9 hours per week with the setters and machinists, 5–6 hours with the craftsmen, 4–5 hours with the process workers and 2–3 hours with the assemblers. However, too much should not be made of these particular figures since in all cases the level of overtime was liable to fluctuation following seasonal and other changes in economic conditions.[1] What is important is that in all groups alike *some* degree of overtime working was accepted as normal, and that, as a result, the main significance of standard hours was often to indicate the point in the working day beyond which higher rates of remuneration became payable.

It is thus important to recognise the fact that the weekly pay-packets of £20 or more that were quite commonly reported by our respondents were usually the achievement of an actual working week of nearer to 50 than to 40 hours. And this may then be set alongside the further fact that the men in our white-collar sample, whose average earnings were at an only slightly lower level,[2] worked a standard week of $38\frac{1}{2}$ hours, with overtime occurring only very sporadically. In other words, it emerges that in order to gain parity in earnings with their fellow employees in clerical grades, the shop-floor men we studied might have to work up to as much as 25% longer. In addition, of course, time spent in the factory is not available for family, friends or leisure activities outside; and, as will be seen in more detail later, the negative effects of regular overtime working on the general quality of social life must certainly be reckoned as another form of deprivation to which our affluent workers were typically exposed.

In much the same way as overtime, shiftwork was for the large majority of our respondents again an integral part of the pattern of their daily

[1] This was particularly so with the semi-skilled men. At the time when our interviews were being carried out, for example, the amount of overtime being worked by the assemblers was at a seasonal low.

[2] I.e. on average around 10*s*. per week less.

lives. Apart from one or two exceptional cases, all the assemblers and process workers in the sample were on shifts and were required to do regular periods of night work, while 80% of the machinists and 90% of the setters worked according to a 'double day-shift' system. Only with the craftsmen was shiftwork not the normal practice, and even then a third of the group was found to be working non-standard hours at the time they were interviewed.

TABLE 3. *Attitudes to shiftwork*

	Skefko workers (craftsmen, setters and machinists) on double day-shift system (N = 67)	Laporte and Vauxhall workers (craftsmen, process workers and assemblers) on shift systems involving nights (N = 109)
	Percentage	
Generally favourable	42	27
Neutral or mixed	16	24
Generally unfavourable	42	50
TOTALS	100	101
Reasons given for favourable attitudes*		
	Times mentioned	
More daytime leisure	25	14
Higher rates of pay	7	10
Other	4	5
Reasons given for unfavourable attitudes*		
	Times mentioned	
Adverse effects on family and community life	21	15
Adverse physical or psychological effects	6	38
Other	14	14

* Includes reasons given by respondents whose attitudes overall were classified as 'mixed'.

As is shown by table 3, shiftwork that did not involve 'nights' was regarded favourably as often as not; but among men from the two plants in which night work took place, negative attitudes were almost twice as often expressed as positive ones. From the way in which these attitudes to shiftwork were explained, it can be seen that the only widely recognised advantages of being on shifts—apart from the 'extrinsic' factor of higher pay—was the increased daytime leisure that was made possible. But for the greater number of workers this advantage was evidently cancelled out where night work was involved by the adverse social, psychological or physical effects that this was felt to produce. And in the light of the findings of detailed investigations of shiftworking which are now available, it is clear that such unfavourable consequences are in no way imaginary: workers on shifts, and especially those on night work or rotating shifts, have been regularly found to have a notably low rate of participation in organised social activities, to encounter characteristic difficulties in performing marital and parental roles, and to suffer from a high incidence of gastro-intestinal and various other bodily disorders.[1]

So far therefore as their typical work experience is concerned, the industrial workers in our sample are still, we would argue, quite significantly differentiated from most varieties of white-collar man: this experience involves stresses and deprivations that are not usually met with in white-collar occupations[2] and is, on the other hand, much less likely to comprise elements that are inherently rewarding. From his study of manual workers who were similarly employed to ours in progressive, high-paying enterprises, Zweig has concluded that industrial work is now far more positively evaluated by those who perform it than ever before, and that the majority of men on the shop floor are 'enjoying or liking, or good humouredly tolerating their job'. This Zweig sees as reflecting a 'changing ethos of work' within the working class which is part of the more general 'move towards new middle class values and middle class existence'.[3] Our findings can lend little support to this point of view.[4] Rather, they lead us to underline the facts, first, that the men we studied *were* affluent because they worked—and for long hours—in large-scale, capital-intensive, manufacturing establishments; and secondly, that in such plants—regardless to some important extent of differing technologies —manual jobs are likely to be appreciably less attractive and more taxing

[1] The most complete study of the problems of shiftworking, which contains a thorough review of previous literature, is Paul E. Mott, Floyd C. Mann, Quin McLoughlin and Donald P. Warwick, *Shift Work: the Social, Psychological and Physical Consequences* (New York, 1965)
[2] In addition to the findings referred to in n. 2, p. 57 above, it may be remarked that among the industrial clerks studied by Dale, the two advantages of clerical work that were most often mentioned were, first, that it was clean and involved no physical strain and, second, that it offered good working conditions and regular hours and entailed no shiftwork. (*The Clerk in Industry*, pp. 19–20).
[3] *The Worker in an Affluent Society*, pp. 79–80, 210–12; cf. also pp. 67–9.
[4] Nor, in our opinion, do Zweig's own.

than in most other work contexts because of the inescapable effects of the fragmentation of work, of standardisation, of 'round-the-clock' production, of bureaucratic administration, and so on.

Thus, what is most obviously illustrated by the evidence we have considered is not any process of generalisation of middle-class attitudes to work, but, we would suggest, a fairly distinctive and widely felt dilemma of working-class occupational life: the dilemma, that is, of having to *choose between* work which offers variety, scope for initiative and relative autonomy and work which, for any skill level, affords the highest going rate of economic return.[1] The men who made up our critical case had opted for this latter alternative, and in what would seem usually to have been a more or less conscious fashion; that is to say, they had opted to give overriding emphasis to the instrumental aspects of work and therefore in effect to *de*value its other aspects. This orientation to work thus underlies the particular nature of their current work experience, and indeed only in terms of such an orientation can the acceptance of this experience make sense either to the observer or to these workers themselves. Moreover, the definition of the activities and relationships of work as being essentially instrumental will obviously carry other important implications for what these men *expect from* the actual work situations in which they now find themselves; and in this respect also, it can be shown, contrasts with the white-collar world of work are often of a revealing kind.

We have argued that among workers in our sample, affluence had generally been gained through these men sacrificing, directly or indirectly, the possibility of a higher level of intrinsic job satisfaction and through their preparedness to sustain various forms of stress and deprivation in work. Their attachment to their present employment—while apparently quite strong—stemmed largely from the purely economic advantages that this was seen to offer: far more so than with their fellow workers in clerical grades or indeed, we would suspect, with various other types of industrial employee.[2] However, over and above this, the findings of our research

[1] The existence and significance of this dilemma has been somewhat surprisingly neglected by industrial sociologists. For an analysis of the economic trends from which it derives, see Clark Kerr, 'The Prospect for Wages and Hours in 1975' in *Labor and Management in Industrial Society* (New York, 1964), pp. 218–23.

[2] See, for example, the various contrasts between the work attitudes and behaviour of our respondents and those characteristic of more 'traditional' industrial workers as noted in *IAB*, pp. 54–5, 74–5, 110–11, 121–3 *et passim*. Cf. also David Lockwood, 'Sources of Variation in Working Class Images of Society', *Sociological Review*, vol. 14, no. 3 (November 1966). In view of the emphasis given to such contrasts in these previous writings (and also in *PAB*) the present volume, being primarily concerned with the *embourgeoisement* thesis, gives greatest emphasis to contrasts between our affluent workers and lower level white-collar groups.

would suggest that our affluent workers are also distinctive in the extent
to which even *within* their present employment non-economic satisfactions
—and in particular those of a 'social' kind—are discounted or disregarded.
Ways and means of making work-tasks less tedious, mechanical or frus-
trating were quite frequently matters of some concern,[1] even though it
was often felt that little could be done; but the possibility of compensating
for inherently unsatisfying work by building up rewarding relationships
with workmates, superiors or other work associates was not one that held
much attraction for the men we studied. In consequence of their view of
employment as essentially a means to extrinsic ends, it would seem that the
work situation could no longer be accepted by these men as a *milieu* at all
favourable or appropriate to the creation of social relationships from which
such rewards as approval, recognition or 'belongingness' might be derived. Rather, work, as the realm of the necessary and instrumental, was
fairly sharply set apart from 'non-work', the realm of relative freedom, in
which the satisfaction of needs of an expressive and affective kind could
be properly pursued.

For example, as we have shown in greater detail elsewhere, the extent
to which our affluent workers had formed close ties with workmates or
associated with them outside the plant was surprisingly limited.[2] From
our observational studies it appeared that tightly knit work groups were
something of a rarity in the shops and departments with which we were
concerned; and this conclusion was supported by the finding from our
interviews that 76% of the more skilled men in our sample and 66% of the
semi-skilled felt that they would be 'not much bothered' or 'not bothered
at all' if moved to another job away from the men they presently worked
with.[3] Furthermore, 60% of the former group and 80% of the latter either
did not claim a single 'close friend' among their workmates or had no
such friend with whom they would arrange to meet for leisure time
activities. For these men, workplace friends—or 'mates'—and friends outside work were largely separate social categories.[4] In contrast, the men in
our white-collar sample, although *less* inclined to describe fellow workers

---

[1] See the analysis of changes that our respondents would like to see made in their present jobs, *IAB*, pp. 20–3.

[2] *IAB*, ch. 3, 'The worker and his work group', pp. 45–63 especially.

[3] In explaining this, respondents frequently made remarks that revealed their narrowly instrumental definition of the work situation. E.g. 'I wouldn't be bothered at all [about being
moved]. The job comes first. Work is what I come here to do.' 'It wouldn't bother me much.
You're here to earn your living.'

[4] Zweig makes a similar observation about the workers in his sample (*The Worker in an Affluent
Society*, pp. 117–18). Cf. also the findings reported by Willmott for workers in Dagenham
(*The Evolution of a Community*, pp. 63–8).

3*

as close friends, typically carried over the work friendships that they did make into their out-of-work lives: friendships between colleagues appeared to lead on naturally to mutual visiting and entertainment between couples. With the white-collar workers, it appeared, no psychological barrier existed against looking to the work situation as a possible source of friends in the fullest sense of the term, nor any obvious dichotomy between workplace 'matiness' on the one hand and the social relationships of 'private' life on the other.

Similarly, the majority of our affluent workers seemed also to be unconcerned with developing more personalised relationships with their superiors.[1] The men interviewed reported for the most part (86%) that they 'got on' with their foreman more or less satisfactorily, but the kind of explanation most frequently given for this was in terms of the small amount of supervisor–worker contact that occurred. Within most occupational groups, it seemed that foremen as far as possible followed a *laissez-faire* style of supervision and that this was generally appreciated by the men in their charge: 'He leaves you alone', 'he doesn't bother you', 'he keeps himself to himself'—these were the terms in which foremen were most often commended. In the case of the white-collar workers, the situation was once again significantly different. To an even greater extent than with the manual workers, favourable relationships with immediate superiors were claimed:[2] however, only a minority explained this as a result of a low frequency of interaction, while the kinds of explanations that were most often advanced referred either to the individual attributes or social skills of superiors, or to the respondent's familiarity or close personal tie with the man directly above him. For these workers, it was evident that what was typically required in the 'good boss' was not simply that he should keep himself out of the way and not interfere but, on the contrary, that he should be 'friendly' and 'approachable', prepared to 'keep you in the picture' and to 'listen to you' and, above all, willing to 'take an interest'.

Thus, what is indicated here is that appreciable differences exist between our affluent manual workers and the men in our white-collar sample not only in their immediate work experience but further, at the normative level, in what they look to their work to provide. Consistently with the findings of other research, the white-collar employees we studied appeared not to define their work in an almost exclusively instrumental way. For these men, certain work associates at least were likely to be

[1] See *IAB*, pp. 63–8.
[2] 94% reported getting on 'very well' or 'pretty well'.

'significant others', and thus the nature of their relationships with these persons was a feature of some importance within the work situation as they viewed it—a source of support or gratification; or if relationships went wrong, of resentment and distress.[1] For our manual workers, on the other hand, and notably for the semi-skilled men, expectations from work were clearly more restricted. The workplace was where they came to earn their living, to sell their labour for the best return they could get; and while shop-floor *camaraderie* and an unobtrusive foreman might in some degree make their jobs less taxing, highly meaningful and rewarding social relationships in work seem rarely to have been anticipated or sought.[2]

Such an outlook may be seen as 'functional' for the workers in question in tolerating and holding down their jobs in the face of technological and organisational constraints that often preclude cohesive work groups or supervision of other than an impersonal character. But it would be a mistake here to think only, or even primarily, in terms of a process of individual adaptation to the conditions of the work situation, objectively considered. For as we have earlier observed, some devaluing of non-economic rewards from employment was implicit in the choice of the jobs that our affluent workers currently held and from which, in fact, their affluence derived. And to this extent, therefore, the narrowing down of work expectations must be regarded not as a product of their in-plant

[1] Evidence on the importance to white-collar employees of interpersonal relationships—with superiors in particular—is contained in several of the studies already referred to. Dufty, for example, reports that fewer rail clerks than clerks in a private firm were favourably oriented towards their employer and explains this as being the result of 'the relatively impersonal administration of a governmental organisation'. ('White Collar Contrasts', p. 70.) Similarly Dale concludes that in creating a favourable office atmosphere 'personalities are all important' and that 'the best personnel policy ever conceived can be rendered useless by poor relations at supervisory level'. (*The Clerk in Industry*, p. 25.) In addition, we may note that on the basis of a number of studies of white-collar workers in France, Crozier has written as follows: 'Les chefs occupent une grande place dans l'univers social de l'employé . . . Le fait d'être accepté ou rejeté par le chef revêt . . . une importance exceptionnelle . . . Il est impossible que son existence *ne concerne pas* l'employé. Ses méthodes, ses manies, ses préférences, sa chaleur humaine et jusqu'à son ton de voix, autant de détails qui touchent l'employé au vif.' See Michel Crozier, *Le Monde des Employés de Bureau* (Paris, 1965), pp. 119-20.

[2] Again an evident contrast exists with more traditional industrial workers whose orientation to work is of a 'solidaristic' kind. But for evidence of other factory employees with a similar outlook to those we studied, see R. Dubin, 'Industrial Workers' Worlds: a Study of the "Central Life Interests" of Industrial Workers', *Social Problems*, vol. 3 (January 1956); Chris Argyris, 'The Organisation—What Makes it Healthy?', *Harvard Business Review*, vol. 37, no. 5 (1958); and G. K. Ingham, 'Organisational Size, Orientation to Work and Industrial Behaviour' (University of Cambridge Ph.D. thesis, 1968). This last study is of particular interest in that it strikingly reveals, within the context of a single town and industry, the contrast between the wants and expectations from work of men employed in large- and small-scale establishments.

socialisation but rather of a prior orientation to work on their part of a decisively instrumental kind.[1]

Furthermore, as well as providing the basis for a number of direct contrasts with white-collar employees, the preoccupation of our affluent workers with the extrinsic 'pay-off' from their employment has implications that are relevant in at least one other important way to the concerns of this chapter; that is, in regard to the possibilities of workers becoming integrated into their employing organisations in the manner that has been regarded by several writers as central to the *embourgeoisement* process. As we noted in chapter 1, this integration has been seen as having two major aspects, both being associated with the development of industrial technology and management: first, the progressive elimination of traditional differences in the conditions of service and status of manual and non-manual employees; and secondly, the greater involvement of members of the rank-and-file in the social life and affairs of the enterprise and their closer identification with their firm and its objectives. However, if the wants and expectations that workers have of their employment are sharply focused on economic returns, with other possible forms of satisfaction in work being accorded relatively little importance, then there are obvious difficulties in the achievement of a high level of employee integration in the sense in question. Such difficulties can be illustrated in several ways from our research findings.

For instance, although in the three firms on which our study was based shop-floor workers generally enjoyed various benefits often reserved for 'staff'—such as pensions and sickpay schemes—one major difference remaining between manual and nonmanual grades was in forms of remuneration. White-collar workers were salaried and were paid on a weekly or monthly basis, while men on the shop floor were paid for particular

---

[1] In this connection we would stress the significance of the lack of variation in attitudes and behaviour among men in our sample with widely differing technological environments and work conditions generally. This finding goes strongly against the idea that our respondents' disregard for 'social' satisfactions in work was a result simply of adaptation, since even in those cases where objective conditions were not in fact particularly unfavourable, neither cohesive work groups nor close personal ties between workmates were any more likely to have formed than in other cases. See *IAB*, pp. 49–54, 56–60. Moreover, it may also be noted that there is no tendency within our sample for instrumental attitudes and behaviour in regard to work to *increase* with length of service—as would be expected if adaptation and socialisation were the crucial processes. If anything, it is the reverse tendency that applies. For example, on the basis of a score of 'instrumentalism' (see *IAB*, pp. 159–62) 40% of men with less than 5 years service in their present firms were classed as 'highly instrumental', 29% as 'intermediate', and 31% as 'less instrumental'; whereas the corresponding figures for men with 5–15 years service were 38%, 27% and 35% and for those with more than 15 years service 23%, 30% and 48%.

amounts of work done, either by the hour or by the piece.[1] In the course of our 'work' interviews, therefore, we asked our respondents by what method they would *prefer* to be paid—by salary, by time-rates or by piece-rates.[2] What emerged, as can be seen from table 4, was that while time-rates were overwhelmingly preferred to piece-rates, there was no generally high enthusiasm for salaries. Among the more skilled men, half would have preferred some form of fixed weekly or monthly payment, but among the semi-skilled men the proportion was only around a quarter, with little variation being revealed by occupational group. From the explanatory comments that were made, the most widely held view appeared to be that hourly rates, like a salary, gave reasonable stability of income ('you know how you stand') while the advantage with a salary of not losing pay for occasional absences was more than offset by the moral pressure on the salaried worker not to take days off and by the loss of overtime earnings. ('I like to be paid for what I do—no more and no less.')

TABLE 4. *Preferred method of payment*

Preferred method	Craftsmen (N = 56)	Setters (N = 23)	Process workers (N = 23)	Machinists (N = 41)	Assemblers (N = 86)	All (N = 229)
			Percentage			
Salary*	50	48	27	24	22	32
Time-rates	46	44	45	61	72	58
Piece-rates	0	4	14	15	2	5
Other, D.K.	4	4	14	0	4	4
TOTALS	100	100	100	100	100	99

* I.e. any form of fixed weekly or monthly payment.

Thus, the *desire* of our affluent workers for white-collar conditions of service was not, in this respect at least, particularly strong. What is significant, rather, is the extent to which the issue was assessed from an 'instrumental' point of view, with some evident dislike of coming under

[1] The assemblers were on straight time-rates; the craftsmen and setters on time-rates plus bonuses; and the machinists on piece-rates also with bonus possibilities.
[2] The exact question was: 'You are paid at an hourly rate/on a piece-rate basis: some workers in other firms are on piece-rates/time-rates and many office workers get paid a fixed salary with nothing extra for overtime. Which method of payment would you prefer?'

any obligations to the firm ('I like the right to a day off when I please') and with little concern for purely status considerations.[1]

One other notable distinction between manual and nonmanual grades which was maintained in our three firms was in canteen arrangements: shop-floor workers had separate facilities from clerical and managerial staff who were in turn segregated according to rank. We asked our respondents whether they approved of there being different canteens for different grades or whether they felt that all canteens should be open to all employees. Again, it proved that there was no very widespread interest in removing 'status barriers'— and again, apparently, because the matter was not primarily considered in status terms. Among men in all occupational groups alike only a little more than a third (35% overall) were against separate canteens, with around a half (53%) approving of existing arrangements and the rest being uncertain or not caring one way or the other. Those men who favoured segregation referred to various practical advantages of this[2] or, more often, stated that they did not *want* to eat in the company of their superiors ('I don't like the idea of the boss breathing down my neck at meal-times'; 'I wouldn't want *them* listening in to my conversation'). On the other hand, those men who objected to separate canteens did so largely on the grounds that the needs they met were ones common to all ('We are all alike when it comes to food and drink') but rarely made any mention of the desirability of breaking down barriers, of workers getting to know managers better or of increasing plant solidarity.

Consistently with this we find (table 5) that if attitudes to canteen arrangements are further analysed in terms of our affluent workers' 'white-collar affiliations', men who dislike segregation tend to be most numerous among those who have the most solidly working-class backgrounds and, conversely, that the minority in the sample with fairly extensive white-collar connections—who might have been expected to be most concerned

---

[1] The status advantages of being salaried were referred to by only 10 respondents (4%), 7 of these being craftsmen. On the matter of wage payment the following question was also put: 'It is possible that at some time in the future workers may get their wages by cheque. How would you feel about this? Would you be generally against, not much bothered, or generally in favour?' With little difference from one occupational group to another, only 33% of the sample welcomed the idea of payment by cheque as against 32% being opposed and 35% indifferent. Once more, status considerations were rarely raised and the matter was discussed very much in terms of what were regarded as the practical advantages or, more often, disadvantages—for example, the need to have a bank account. As we have noted, only 34% of our affluent workers (compared with 89% of the white-collar sample) had a bank account at the time our interviews were carried out.

[2] Most commonly, in preventing tables and chairs from being soiled by men wearing dirty work clothes, or in giving managers privacy for confidential discussions.

about status in the plant—are by far those most likely to *approve* of the existing situation.[1]

Finally in this connection we may note that certain policies specifically followed by the firms in question in part at least to increase employee integration did in fact encounter difficulties in exactly the way that the above discussion would lead one to anticipate. The two most noteworthy examples concern the provision of recreational and 'social' facilities and the policy of 'promotion from within'.

TABLE 5. *Attitudes to canteen arrangements by skill level and by conjugal white-collar affiliations*

Skill level	Conjugal white-collar affiliations*	Approves of segregation	Disapproves of segregation	Other, D.K.		N
					Percentage	
Skilled†	Via family *and* job	78	22	0	100	18
	Via family *or* job	41	38	22	101	37
	Neither	37	50	13	100	24
Semi-skilled	Via family *and* job	72	18	10	100	39
	Via family *or* job	58	34	8	100	64
	Neither	39	46	15	100	46
All		53	35	12	100	228‡

* I.e. through *either* respondent's or respondent's wife's father being of white-collar occupational status; *or* respondent or respondent's wife having at some time held a white-collar job. For further details of this classification, see *PAB*, pp. 51–4.

† Craftsmen and setters.

‡ No information is available on the white-collar affiliations of one respondent. All tables involving this variable are therefore based on an effective sample of 228.

All three firms offered extensive opportunities for their employees to take part in leisure-time activities through work-based clubs and societies. In each case, there was a main 'works club', responsible for general social functions and amenities, to which employees could belong for a nominal sum, and also a wide range of heavily subsidised sports clubs and

[1] From comments made, it would seem that while the men in this latter group tended to have no strong egalitarian views, neither did they wish to regard the way in which they were treated in the work situation as relevant to their social status generally. As we have previously shown (*IAB*, pp. 164–7) a highly instrumental orientation to work was particularly likely to be found among those of our respondents who were in some way or other downwardly mobile. For many of these men, it would appear, factory work was simply a means of securing a relatively high income with which to try to maintain their status position in their out-of-work lives.

'special interest' societies which again had very low subscriptions. The standard of facilities was in general high, and administration appeared usually to be efficient. However, a special investigation that we carried out into the use made of facilities revealed that in each firm alike the majority of clubs and societies had predominantly white-collar member-ships and that the low level of participation by shop-floor workers was a matter of some disappointment and concern to personnel managers and officials. Within our sample of manual workers only a third of the crafts-men and setters and less than a fifth of the process workers, machinists and assemblers belonged to a particular club or society, and a majority of these were irregular attenders if not completely inactive. In fact, 3 out of 4 of the more skilled workers and more than 9 out of 10 of the semi-skilled men could be classed as taking very little or no advantage of *any* of the leisure-time facilities at their place of work, including even the works club bar.[1] As had become commonly accepted within the firms, the problem was not simply one of 'apathy' but appeared to involve also some definite resis-tance on the part of shop-floor workers to having anything to do with their firm after working hours. As one manager put it: 'Even people within easy bus ride don't like coming back to the company. It's their workplace and they don't like it.' But, at least among the men who made up our critical case, such an outlook could scarcely be thought surprising —given what we know about the nature of their work, the length of their working hours, their general orientation to work and the priorities that they had adopted in taking their current jobs.

As regards promotion, all three firms attached importance to providing 'ladders' from the shop floor to supervisory, technical and managerial grades. Assistance was offered in one form or another for training for promotion, and a good deal of attention was given to selection procedures. Moreover, a substantial proportion of existing managers in each firm were in fact men who had 'come up from the bottom' and who could thus illustrate the possibilities open to the rank-and-file employee. Neverthe-less, it was clearly indicated by our interview findings that while the firms' promotion policies might be highly beneficial to certain individuals, they were of little effect in creating interest in advancement within the firm and in encouraging the mass of the labour force to think of themselves as one day likely to become something more than merely wage workers. We asked our respondents if they liked the idea of becoming a foreman (the first major step on the promotion ladder), whether they had ever thought about this seriously and, if so, whether they had taken any action to this

[1] See *IAB*, p. 90.

end. The outcome was that only 20% of the more skilled men and 15% of the semi-skilled were both attracted to the idea of promotion and had given this serious consideration; and that only 9% of the former group and 8% of the latter both wanted to become foremen and had actually done something about this, such as applying for promotion or attending a training course.[1] In brief, for the large majority of the men in our sample the possibility of promotion was of no real significance.[2]

In part, this was certainly the result of workers recognising that, despite their firm's policies, the career possibilities for men on the shop floor were in fact extremely limited; more will be said about this later in the chapter. But at the same time it was equally evident from our interviews that the small amount of interest in promotion was also associated with a feeling that supervisory jobs implied *too great a degree* of involvement in, and commitment to, the firm—and particularly so in view of the often quite modest economic rewards that they offered. In the absence of some very clear financial gain, the workers we studied were unlikely candidates for a job entailing responsibilities and anxieties that it would be difficult to slough off at the end of the day.[3] In other words, in contrast with the majority of white-collar employees, for whom promotion is almost automatically a desired objective[4]—and may well be a moral expectation—the manual workers of our critical case often regarded promotion, if indeed they considered it at all, as a very questionable proposition.

[1] For further details, see *IAB*, pp. 119–20.

[2] In this respect our respondents would seem to have much the same outlook as men in other samples of industrial workers in present-day Britain whose attitudes to promotion have been investigated. See *IAB*, pp. 120–2.

[3] Consistently with this argument, the view that a supervisory job was not worth while was least common among the assemblers and machinists—the men for whom promotion would have meant the greatest increase in wages. See *IAB*, p. 125.

[4] All investigations that have dealt with the matter are agreed that among white-collar workers the desire for promotion is almost universal. E.g. of the rail and other clerks studied by Dufty, 90% stated that they would like promotion ('White Collar Contrasts', p. 69); in an Acton Society Trust study of attitudes to promotion in five industrial firms, 85% of the male office workers interviewed were 'very interested' in promotion and a further 11% 'slightly interested' (*Management Succession* (London, 1956), p. 64); and among the clerks in the sales office of a Scottish iron and steel firm studied by Sykes, 100% said that they wanted promotion ('Some Differences in the Attitudes of Clerical and Manual Workers', *Sociological Review*, vol. 13, no. 1, 1965). In the studies by Walker and Dale, previously referred to, the authors take it as being beyond question that the employees with whom they were concerned thought promotion desirable. Dale adds that 'Advancement tends to be sought not merely for the extra money involved—this is often little enough—but for the prestige it carries and for the opportunity to display initiative and to exercise authority which it brings' (*The Clerk in Industry*, p. 49). Finally, we may record that in our own white-collar sample 87% of the men interviewed said that they would like the idea of promotion 'very much' or 'quite a lot'.

The main conclusion that we would wish to draw from the data reviewed in the foregoing paragraphs is, then, the following: that a factor of decisive importance in determining whether or not industrial workers are likely to become increasingly integrated into their employing organisations is *their own definition* of their work situation and, underlying this, the particular pattern of wants and expectations that they have in regard to their employment. Advances in industrial technology and management may, by design or otherwise, open up new possibilities for the social organisation of the enterprise and for worker participation in its affairs. But it cannot be assumed that industrial workers will react to these changes in ways wished for by management or in fact in *any* uniform manner. Most notably, where the activities and relationships of work are given an essentially instrumental meaning, it is in corresponding degree unlikely that workers will be much concerned with developing solidary ties with workmates or superiors, or at all highly motivated to involve themselves more in the social life or conduct of the enterprise than is directly necessitated by their work-tasks and -roles. And to the extent, therefore, that relatively affluent workers tend to have gained their high rates of pay through opting in effect to forgo intrinsic rewards in work, they may be considered as particularly unsuitable material for the making of 'blue-collar organisation men'[1]—regardless of the technological environment or managerial policies to which they are exposed. In other words, our findings would suggest, in some opposition to the thesis of *embourgeoisement*, that for the industrial worker of the present day, affluence and typically middle-class attitudes towards work itself are in no way directly related; but that, on the contrary, they may often be difficult to reconcile.

Having now examined how our affluent workers experienced their work and the content of their expectations in work, we come finally in this chapter to consider the nature of their work aspirations. What were the long-term objectives that the men in our sample hoped to achieve in the course of their occupational lives, and do significant contrasts yet again

[1] At the same time, it may be observed that just as there is some evidence that our affluent workers were not highly distinctive in their limited outplant association with workmates (see n. 4, p. 65 above) so too there are indications that a lack of interest in purely status issues within the plant, a dislike of work-based leisure, and serious doubts about the advantages of promotion are by no means infrequent among the rank-and-file of large-scale industrial establishments. See, for example, on the first point, Dorothy Wedderburn, 'The Conditions of Employment of Manual and Non-manual Workers', *Proceedings of the S.S.R.C. Conference on Social Stratification and Industrial Relations* (January 1969); on the second, A. Etzioni, 'Organizational Control Structure', in J. G. March (ed.), *Handbook of Organizations* (New York, 1965); and on the third, Acton Society Trust, *Management Succession*, pp. 66–7.

emerge with the corresponding information that we have in the case of white-collar employees?

As we have already seen, one clear-cut difference between our affluent workers and most men in white-collar jobs lies in the fact that among the former, serious aspirations for promotion were held by only a small minority, with one important reason for this being the view that promotion —to supervisory level at least—was simply not worth while. The advantages and disadvantages of a supervisory position tended to be assessed in a highly calculative way, and frequently the demands and strains of the job were felt to outweigh its 'pay off' in economic terms. In addition, though, even where workers favoured the idea of promotion, it was clear from our interview data that aspirations in this direction could often be dulled by recognition of the low chances of their being fulfilled. For example, the finding that those men who were attracted to the possibility of becoming a foreman had only rarely taken any steps to help realise this ambition must be set alongside the further findings that among this same group not a single man was prepared to rate his chances of promotion as being 'very good'; and that the number regarding their chances as 'fairly good' was roughly matched, in the case of the skilled and semi-skilled men alike, by the number who saw their position as 'not too good' or 'hopeless'. In explaining their pessimism, these latter men most often referred to their lack of education and training in a situation in which 'qualifications' were of increasing importance, or mentioned other shortcomings of a personal kind. But many also observed that they were simply members of the mass of shop-floor workers and had no particular way of attracting the attention of management, or that the actual openings for promotion—as determined by the ratio of supervisory to shop-floor jobs— were very few in number in the shops and department in which they were employed.[1]

The extent to which our respondents doubted the objective possibilities of a career from the shop floor upwards is illustrated still further by the material presented in table 6. Even when asked about the promotion prospects of 'a worker of ability' who 'really put his mind to it' over 70%

[1] For further details, see *IAB*, pp. 126-30. Among our white-collar workers, on the other hand, 66% thought that their chances of being promoted were 'very good' or 'fairly good'. A similar picture of quite widespread optimism about promotion emerges from other more extensive investigations. For example, 46% of the industrial clerks studied by Dale believed that their promotion prospects were 'good' or 'fairly good' and only 13% that they had 'none' (*The Clerk in Industry*, p. 53); again, 70% of the rail clerks and 60% of the other clerks studied by Dufty thought that they 'had the chance of being promoted' ('White Collar Contrasts', p. 69); while as many as 91% of the clerks covered in Sykes' enquiry stated that they had 'a reasonable expectation of promotion' ('Some Differences in the Attitudes of Clerical and Manual Workers', p. 299).

in all occupational groups except the assemblers[1] felt that such a person would not get beyond supervisory level. In contrast, when a comparable question was put to the men in our white-collar sample, it can be seen that over half believed that the way would be open as far as middle management and that another quarter made a yet more optimistic assessment.[2]

TABLE 6. *Assessment of promotion prospects of 'a worker of ability, etc.'*

Highest level likely to be reached	Craftsmen (N = 56)	Setters (N = 23)	Process workers (N = 23)	Machinists (N = 41)	Assemblers (N = 86)	White-collar (N = 54)
			Percentage			
Supervisory*	71	74	74	75	19	4
Middle management	16	13	17	12	43	57
Above middle management	9	13	9	10	35	26
Other, D.K.	4	0	0	2	4	13
TOTALS	100	100	100	99	101	100

* Included in the percentages in this row of the table are a number of respondents in each occupational group—ranging from 6% of the assemblers to 24% of the machinists—who doubted the possibility of even supervisory level being attained.

Furthermore, just as they had few illusions about the barriers to advancement within the enterprise, so too were our affluent workers well aware of the difficulties they would face if they sought to escape from the

[1] The marked difference between the response of the assemblers and that of men in the other occupational groups—i.e. Skefko and Laporte workers—is probably to be explained in the two following ways: (i) at Vauxhall, a particularly high proportion of managers had originated in shop-floor or routine office jobs—the firm claimed that this was the case with as many as 40% of the men in executive grades—and thus workers were quite likely to know a manager in their own department who had started at the bottom; (ii) a number of very well-known senior executives at Vauxhall had also 'come up the hard way', and this fact was well publicised through induction courses, 'house' literature, etc. It may still be observed, however, that the Vauxhall men in our sample did not display any similarly distinctive optimism so far as their *own* promotion prospects were concerned. Of those who were attracted to the idea of becoming a foreman, 45% rated their chances as 'not too good' or 'hopeless' as against 52% rating them 'fairly good'.

[2] The exact question posed to the manual workers was: 'If a worker of ability really put his mind to it, how far up this firm do you think he could get in the end?' It might be added here that in comments that were made along with their replies to questions on promotion opportunities our affluent workers showed surprisingly little resentment at the fact that these were now largely blocked; it was usually accepted that men with 'proper qualifications' were needed in modern management and where respondents did reveal a sense of grievance, this tended to be focused on the inadequate educational provision that had existed in their younger days.

role of employee altogether and to go into business on their own account. As we have previously shown, the possibility of doing this had been considered with quite surprising frequency and a number of the men we interviewed had actually made the attempt. But at the same time it was clear enough that, for the large majority, having a business of their own was in fact not so much an aspiration as a 'dream', and one which they knew was unlikely ever to be translated into reality. A shortage of capital would have made any such undertaking hazardous, while on the other hand, as affluent workers, our respondents were far from being in a position in which they had nothing to lose. An unsuccessful venture could quickly have put into jeopardy the relatively high living standards that their labour in the factory had enabled them to build up. Thus, although as many as three-quarters of the workers we studied said that they had at some time or other thought of setting up their own businesses, only 1 man in 5 had either tried to do this or had made serious plans and had discussed the matter with his family.[1]

It can therefore be said that among the workers who made up our critical case, only a very small proportion seriously envisaged advancement of *any* conventional kind in their future occupational lives. For the most part, it would seem, our respondents accepted their position as industrial wage workers as being a more or less permanent one; and indeed, as we have already remarked, most appeared to be fairly firmly attached to the particular jobs that they currently held. The craftsmen apart, between a half and two-thirds of those in each occupational group stated that they had at no time considered leaving their firms, and only around a quarter in each group had ever got to the point of actually investigating other employment possibilities.[2]

What then *did* our affluent workers aspire to in their work, given that they appeared in the main unlikely to change their status as rank-and-file employees or even their present employers? The answer that our interview data would suggest is the following: that instead of aspiring in white-collar fashion to make a 'good career' *within* their firms, these men hoped rather to gain a 'good living' *from* their firms—the typical aim was not a progressive series of jobs but the wherewithal to sustain a progressive advance in the material conditions of their out-of-work lives. Most notably, when our respondents were asked what improvement in their

[1] For further details, see *IAB*, pp. 131–6.
[2] See *IAB*, pp. 25–6. The reasons most frequently given for having thought of leaving concerned the nature of work and unsatisfactory management, supervision or 'shop atmosphere': only 12 men referred to poor promotion chances, 7 to wanting wider job experience and 5 to their plans for starting their own businesses.

way of life they most hoped for over the next ten years, the kinds of aspiration by far most commonly expressed were ones that related to increased consumer capacity and higher standards of domestic living: 3 men in 5 stated simply that they hoped to have more money to spend and more goods and possessions of one sort or another, and 1 in 3 made some particular reference to housing.[1] In contrast, specifically occupational aspirations were mentioned only infrequently—by less than 1 in 5 in the sample; and from a further set of questions it clearly emerged that those of our respondents who believed that their living standards *would* advance —some two-thirds of the total—placed their faith far more in collective than in personal achievement.[2] Only a handful, nine out of 149, related their optimism to their chances of bettering their individual position, whether through promotion, starting their own business or in any other way. The majority looked forward to sharing with their fellow wage earners in the benefits of continuing economic progress, either in the country at large or in the particular industries or firms in which they were engaged.[3]

Moreover, work aspirations structured in such a way fit logically enough into what would appear to be the typical 'project' among the men in question—the attempt that they were making to give some direction and meaningfulness to their lives and those of their families. As we have noted, almost three-quarters were migrants, most of whom, it would seem, had come to Luton specifically in search of higher wages and improved living standards. Again, many had taken up—or at least retained—the jobs they at present held primarily because of the high level of pay that could be earned, even though, as they often knew from previous work experience, this entailed sacrifices in non-economic terms. Thus, given this perspective, it can scarcely be thought surprising that the dominant form of aspiration among these workers should consist in what in effect would often be the vindication of important choices made at some earlier stage in their economic lives. Or, to put the matter somewhat differently, it could be argued that on the basis of what we know about the general pattern of their lives so far—and in particular about their educational and

---

[1] The question put ran as follows: 'Looking ten years ahead, what improvement in your way of life would you most hope for?' For a complete analysis of the results produced, see *IAB*, pp. 136–8.

[2] The questions were: 'How much would you say your standard of living had risen over the last ten years? Would you say it had risen a great deal, quite a lot, not very much, or not at all?'; and 'How about the next five years? Would you expect things to be better, about the same, or worse?' Those respondents whose answers to these two questions together indicated that they expected a rise in living standards in the years ahead were then asked why they viewed the future in the way they did.

[3] See *IAB*, pp. 140–2.

occupational histories[1]—it is difficult to envisage the majority of our respondents having any *other* characteristic set of aspirations in work than ones which related ultimately to out-of-work objectives and which involved group rather than individual ascent.

Once more then, we would claim, the findings of our study are not readily reconciled with the thesis of the worker turning middle-class. Two points of divergence are of particular interest.

In the first place, our affluent workers obviously differ from many white-collar employees in that they lack—and realise that they lack—genuine opportunities for occupational mobility in the form of a career. One recent writer with some degree of sympathy for the *embourgeoisement* thesis—M. M. Postan—has suggested that at least in the most modern or modernised industrial plants a large proportion of manual workers now tend to rate their promotion prospects highly, and that this indicates some shift away from the traditional worker's fatalistic acceptance of existing hierarchies of position and status.[2] However, while one would agree that a decline in working-class fatalism has most probably occurred, it may be doubted whether this change is at all widely reflected in the area in question.[3] The evidence that Postan cites in support of his argument is not entirely well chosen as a basis for generalisation, and is contradicted both by our own findings and by those of other previous enquiries.[4] Moreover, and more importantly perhaps, it is highly probable that, whether industrial workers view their chances of a career favourably or not, these chances are *in fact* being steadily diminished. This trend is

---

[1] The important point as regards education is that 85% of the sample had left school at the minimum age and that only 15% had received any subsequent part-time instruction of a vocational kind; and as regards occupational history, that a relatively high proportion were on a *downward* trajectory in status terms by reference to either their fathers' or to their own previous jobs. See *IAB*, pp. 155–7.

[2] Postan, *An Economic History of Western Europe, 1945–1964*, pp. 323–4.

[3] For further discussion of this point, see pp. 121–2 below.

[4] So far as Great Britain is concerned, Postan refers to studies of coal miners and steelworkers. However, both industries are decidedly atypical so far as promotion prospects are concerned. In coal, there has in the recent past been a shortage of recruits to supervisory positions, chiefly because of the unattractiveness of these, and any coal-face miner able to secure the appropriate statutory qualification (the tests for which are not demanding) can be virtually assured of promotion. At the same time, though, his chances of advancing from a supervisory to a managerial position are very slight indeed. In the case of steel, there exists a hierarchy of manual and supervisory grades—virtually unique in British industry—which makes *some degree* of job advancement almost automatic. For studies which reveal little optimism on the part of manual workers concerning their chances of promotion, see Sykes, 'Some Differences in the Attitudes of Clerical and Manual Workers'; and in a case of workers engaged in a modern (food) process production plant, J. M. Mann, 'Sociological Aspects of Factory Relocation' (University of Oxford D.Phil. thesis, 1968), ch. 4.

indicated by all recent studies of recruitment to managerial and administrative grades in large-scale industry, and what is of further significance is that the extent of recruitment from the rank-and-file is probably *less*, the *more* advanced the technology and the management practices in operation.[1] For in the hyper-modern plant, in particular, promotion chances will tend to be determined by formal qualifications, acquired either during full-time education or through instruction given within the firm to carefully selected trainee entrants. In an earlier paper we argued that:

For those who leave non-selective secondary schools at the age of fifteen for a manual occupation, this kind of work is becoming more than ever before a life sentence. The same factors that are making for more intergenerational mobility —technological progress, increasing specialisation and the growing importance of education in occupational placement—are also operating to reduce the possibility of 'working up from the bottom' in industry, and are thus indirectly re-emphasising the staff-worker dichotomy.[2]

The further relevant information that has become available since we expressed this view has not inclined us to change it; rather, we would regard the process in question as indicating one of the most powerful objections to the idea that we are today witnessing the development of an increasingly homogeneous, 'middle-class' society.

Secondly, the nature of our respondents' aspirations in work represents further grounds for questioning the likelihood of their becoming at all highly integrated into their firms in the manner typical of many middle-class employees. Their concentration on gaining, as wage workers, a steadily increasing 'take' from their firm, rather than on occupational advance within it, underlines the extent to which their relationship with their employer is a purely market or contractual one, containing few of the important moral elements that figure, at least in principle, in the employment relationships of bureaucratic personnel: for instance, the obligation

---

[1] See Acton Society Trust, *Management Succession*, ch. 1; R. V. Clements, *Managers: a Study of their Careers in Industry* (London, 1958), chs. 7 and 8; D. G. Clarke, *The Industrial Manager: His Background and Career Pattern* (London, 1966), chs. 3 and 4; and R. M. Mosson and D. G. Clarke, 'Some Inter-Industry Comparisons of the Background and Careers of Managers', *British Journal of Industrial Relations*, vol. 6, no. 2 (July 1968). See also the data in D. J. Lee, 'Class Differentials in Educational Opportunity and Promotion from the Ranks', *Sociology*, vol. 2, no. 3 (September 1968). Lee points out that a decline in career prospects for rank-and-file workers does not follow *automatically* from greater selectivity in the recruitment of managers—unless certain assumptions are made about other variables that are involved; e.g. the number of managerial vacancies. However, the Census material that Lee analyses (table 8 especially) does suggest that the career chances of the poorly educated are in decline, although never having been very good.

[2] Goldthorpe and Lockwood, 'Affluence and the British Class Structure', p. 137.

of the employee to put his abilities fully and faithfully at the service of the organisation, and of the organisation in turn to guarantee its employees both long-term security and career opportunities. The attachment of the majority of our affluent workers to their firms was, we would argue, very largely a matter of the cash nexus, and their involvement in their employing organisations, of a markedly calculative kind. Thus, while this could apparently produce a tie of some strength (as seen for example, in the low propensity to leave) it implied at the same time not only a low degree of affective identification with the firm but, further, a clear awareness of how in certain basic respects employer and employees were brought into direct conflict. For example, as we have previously shown, a majority of men in all occupational groups except the process workers rated their present firm as 'better than most' as an employer and believed that few other firms could give them comparable employment advantages to those —mostly economic—which kept them in their present jobs. Yet, on the other hand, our respondents very largely took the view that their firms could afford to pay higher wages without damage to their business position, and chiefly substantiated this claim by referring to the sizable profits that their firms were currently making.[1] It is then, of course, in this context that the membership of our affluent workers in trade unions and the nature of their union activity must be considered—aspects of their occupational lives which may be thought of as far more relevant to their aspirations than promotion policies or prospects. However, the significance of unionism is a matter that we shall reserve for discussion later on as part of a more general examination of our respondents' perspective on industrial and political affairs.[2] The point that we wish to stress here is that the affluent worker, as he emerges from our research, is far indeed from being any kind of 'organisation man', bound to his firm by a sense of personal commitment and long-term career expectations. On the contrary, rather than regarding his firm as being to some extent a moral community, he would appear to accept it as an essentially economic form of association,

[1] See *IAB*, pp. 72–3, 80–2, 86–9. On the question of the firm's ability to pay more, the machinists deviated in a revealing manner from the general pattern of response—being almost equally divided on whether or not they though that higher wages could reasonably be demanded. Underlying the doubts expressed was the fact that at the time our interviews were carried out Skefko was currently facing much greater competition in its field than for some time previously, and machinists often referred to the dangers to their jobs and to their long-run wage prospects in pushing the firm too hard at this stage. What is indicated, then, is that our respondents were often willing to accept that to some extent their own fortunes and those of their firms were bound together, even though a situation of economic conflict was seen as co-existing with this interdependence. And such an outlook again implies that between worker and firm an essentially calculative relationship prevails.

[2] See below, pp. 165–70.

within which his hopes for the future must largely rest on the price that he and his fellow workers can collectively obtain for the labour they provide.

In the study we have already cited, Zweig suggests that in the advanced industrial enterprise of the present day the tendency is for the worker to be 'brought nearer to the firm which gives him good treatment, a relatively good livelihood, and a measure of security' and further, as 'perhaps the most significant development', for such a worker in turn to 'loosen the sense of his identity with his own class, to which he is bound no longer by the links of common hardships, handicaps and injustices, and the constant call to arms in class warfare'. In Zweig's view, it is employees of establishments of the kind in question ('large-scale, well-organised, well-conducted . . . and in progressive expanding industries') who are most fully exposed to the new forces of change that are 'potentially at work in every domain of working class existence'.[1]

However, the content of the present chapter should be sufficient to show that, leaving aside for the moment the matter of class identity, little qualitative change at all may have occurred in the *class situation* of the affluent worker—in the sense, that is, of the position he holds within the social organisation of production and the constraints and life-chances that he consequently experiences. The workers who made up our critical case were still men who gained their living through placing their labour power at the disposal of an employer and receiving payment for particular amounts of work done. Indeed, the way in which they had typically become affluent was in effect by devaluing the possibilities of non-economic rewards in employment and by working in jobs that offered a relatively high level of pay in return for a corresponding level of stress and deprivation: in other words, by being prepared to experience their work *as labour and as little else*.

Moreover, we are unable to accept the view that this cost of working-class affluence, as illustrated in our findings, must necessarily be diminished as a result of current 'modernising' tendencies in industrial technology and administration. On the basis of our own investigation and of a now substantial body of other evidence, we would seriously question the idea that these developments automatically transform the nature of industrial work and relationships to the extent that such categories as 'labour' and 'labour force' become no longer applicable.[2] To begin with,

[1] *The Worker in an Affluent Society*, pp. 69, 205.
[2] The work of Naville is of particular significance in this respect; see the items cited in n.2, p.40 above.

the 'objective' consequences of technological progress by no means all run in the same direction of making work less taxing and more intrinsically rewarding, or of lessening functional and status differences between managers and managed: as we have noted, contrary effects to these may well be produced as, for example, through the requirement of shiftworking or by the yet further reduction of career mobility from shop-floor to management grades. Furthermore, the response of rank-and-file workers to greater opportunities for participation in the social life or the affairs of the enterprise, whether resulting from changes in technology or from management policy, need not and will not be invariably positive. Again as our study would indicate, where employees' central life interests are not located in their work, and where work is defined in almost exclusively instrumental terms, little further involvement in the activities and relationships of work may be sought beyond the minimum implied by the employment contract itself.

To generalise from our findings, therefore, we would maintain that so far at least as the world of work is concerned, the thesis of working-class *embourgeoisement* can have little relevance to present day British society. Whatever changes may have been taking place in the sphere of consumption, in the sphere of production a fairly distinctive working class can still be readily identified, even when attention is concentrated on progressive industrial sectors and modern establishments. Moreover, in so far as this last statement might appear in need of qualification, this, we would suggest, is primarily the result of ongoing changes in industry that are affecting *nonmanual* rather than manual workers and are bringing some of the former closer to the position of the latter rather than *vice versa*—for example, the growing scale of units of administration, the spread of office mechanisation and even automation, the increasing recruitment of men destined for senior posts direct from institutions of higher education, and so on. As a result of these various rationalising tendencies, a stratum of white-collar workers has now obviously emerged whose members are dissociated from decision-making or control functions, perform entirely routine and generally unrewarding tasks, and have little more opportunity for career mobility than their blue-collar counterparts.[1]

Even then, the significance of this development, especially in blurring

---

[1] It is in this context, we would believe, that evidence of an instrumental approach to their employment among white-collar employees must be understood. See, for example, Weir and Mercer, 'Orientations to Work among White-Collar Workers'. We would, however, regard such findings as indicating an aspect of 'normative convergence', rather than implying the elimination of all significant differences in the experience and meaning of work between manual and nonmanual grades.

lines of class division in industry, should not be exaggerated. It must be remembered that the new white-collar labour force contains a high proportion of women workers[1] whose employment at a subordinate level improves the chances of male workers occupying higher grade positions. And secondly, it would appear from recent research that the rationalisation of white-collar work does not in fact produce factory conditions in the office nor alienated employees to the extent that has sometimes been supposed.[2] In other words, it is important that the thesis of the white-collar worker becoming 'proletarian' should be regarded as critically as that of the manual worker becoming middle-class. At all events, as we have sought to show in the course of this chapter, fairly marked contrasts still remain between the work experience, expectations and aspirations of most samples of white-collar workers that have thus far been studied and those of the affluent manual workers who were represented in our own enquiry.

[1] For interesting studies of 'white-blouse' labour, see Michel Crozier, *The Bureaucratic Phenomenon* (London, 1964), part 1, and Claudine Marenco, 'Gradualism, Apathy and Suspicion in a French Bank' in W. H. Scott (ed.), *Office Automation: Administrative and Human Problems* (Paris, O.E.C.D., 1965).

[2] See, for example, Weir and Mercer, 'Orientations to Work among White-Collar Workers'; also Enid Mumford and Olive Banks, *The Computer and the Clerk* (London, 1967), and H. A. Rhee, *Office Automation in Social Perspective* (Oxford, 1968).

4. The pattern of sociability

In emphasising the contrasts that exist between the working lives of the men included in our critical case and those of white-collar employees, we have undoubtedly been attacking the thesis of *embourgeoisement* at the point at which it is least well defended. Despite the attention given by certain writers to the impact on the working class of developments in the forces and relationships of production, the claim that the manual worker is being progressively assimilated into middle-class society has been most frequently—and most persuasively—related to changes that have had their effect chiefly in out-of-work life. Indeed, in some more cautious versions of the *embourgeoisement* thesis it has been specifically suggested that today the affluent worker has often a dual social identity: in the context of the industrial plant, he remains a member of a fairly distinctive working class and it is only when his work is left behind that he is able to merge into the broad intermediate strata of modern industrial society. In other words, it is as a consumer and householder, as a family man and member of the local community that he ceases to be recognisably different from his white-collar neighbours and fellow citizens.[1]

So far as *standards* of domestic living are concerned, the above argument is not one that we would wish to question. As we have seen, there is adequate evidence that in this respect a significant number of manual workers have now achieved a position of economic parity with many established middle-class groups in terms of consumption if not perhaps of security. However, the issues that we would regard as being crucial here—and as far more debatable—are ones such as the following. First, do such affluent manual workers and their families also display characteristically middle-class *styles* of social life? Secondly, can, and do, the cultural and social patterns of their lives outside work remain largely unaffected by the nature of their employment—that is, by their acquisition of middle-class living standards through the means of manual wage labour? And thirdly, do they actually associate with persons of white-collar status as frequently and as freely as with persons whose occupational status is the same as their own? In the course of the present chapter,

[1] For examples in the British literature, see the discussion in Klein, *Samples from English Cultures*, vol. 1, pp. 278–9, 422–6.

therefore, as we examine the pattern of sociability of the affluent workers and their wives who form our sample, it is these issues that we shall have particularly in mind.

The salient characteristics of the 'traditional' type of working-class district could be said to derive from the relative stability and the social homogeneity of its population. The tightly knit network of kinship and the close ties of familiarity between neighbours are the products of successive generations of families living out their lives alongside each other; the strong sense of communal solidarity and the various forms of mutual help and collective action reflect the absence of any wide economic, cultural or status differences. Built up from its distinctive ecological and demographic base, the community constitutes a closely defined pattern for social living and one, moreover, which is highly resistant to change on account of the powerful normative controls that it is able to impose upon its members.[1]

Some proportion of the affluent manual workers with whom we were concerned had no doubt past experience of community life of a kind which approximated to this pattern: but, as we have described, the communities—or more accurately, perhaps, the residential areas—in which the men in our sample currently lived were far removed from the traditional type. Most were of quite recent origin and, we may surmise, their inhabitants included many families which, like our respondents' own, had no roots in the locality and were widely separated from the majority of their kin.[2] Furthermore, in the private housing developments at least, a notable degree of occupational as well as of regional diversity appeared to exist: for example, we find our affluent manual workers living next door to clerical and sales workers, schoolteachers, and even departmental managers, industrial chemists and professional engineers. Thus, we would argue, traditional working-class influences on these men and their families were likely to be at a minimal level. Whatever their previous community experience may have been, they were now largely free from

[1] Empirical findings from an appreciable number of studies of working-class communities of a traditional type have been usefully synthesised in Klein, *Samples from English Cultures*, vol. 1, ch. 4. It is at this juncture perhaps worth underlining the point we have made before (Lockwood, 'Sources of Variation in Working Class Images of Society', p. 250, and also *PAB*, p. 74) that such concepts as the 'traditional worker' or 'traditional working-class community' must be understood as tools of sociological and not historical analysis. Their use, for example, contains no implication that at some period of time all or even most of the members of the working class displayed social characteristics, or lived in communities with characteristics, of the kind that are labelled as 'traditional'.

[2] Cf. the demographic data for Luton referred to above, pp. 38 and 43–4.

the continuous and essentially conservative social pressures exerted by the extended family and by established neighbourhood custom. At the same time, one may suggest, their exposure to the innovatory influences of the mass media was thereby increased and, in addition, they often had white-collar models of social life immediately before their eyes. If then, as the *embourgeoisement* thesis claims, such models are today being widely emulated by manual workers who have the financial means to do so, one would certainly expect to find the process under way among the sample we studied. Whether or not this was the case may best be assessed if we consider first the data we collected on the leisure-time social relationships of our workers and their wives, and then secondly, the further information that we possess on their characteristic modes of sociability.

In the course of the 'home' interviews that we held with the couples in our sample, we asked three sets of questions aimed at discovering who were the people with whom our respondents most frequently associated in their out-of-work lives. The first set, which we addressed to husbands and wives separately, began with the question: 'Who would you say are the two or three people that you most often spend your spare time with—apart from your wife/husband and children?' We then went on to ask for various details about each of the persons mentioned. The second set of questions was intended for wives only and concerned the day-time visits that they had made and had received during the week immediately preceding the interview.[1] The third set, put to husband and wife jointly, then asked about couples whom our respondents might from time to time 'have round' for the evening and about how often this kind of entertainment took place.[2] Table 7 brings together the material that was produced by these questions so as to show the relative importance of the social sources of the relationships that were reported; comparable information for our sample of white-collar workers is also presented.[3]

[1] We asked: 'During the last week, did you happen to visit anyone in the daytime?' and 'Did anyone come to see you?' If the answer to either of these questions was 'Yes', we then asked, 'Who was that?'

[2] We asked: 'We've been talking about your friends and your spare-time activities—how about having other couples round, say for a meal, or just for the evening: how often would you say you do this, on average?' If couples were entertained in the way in question, we then asked: 'When did you last do this?'; 'Who is it you have round—are they friends, relatives, or who?'; and 'What is it you do when they come round?' It is of some substantive interest to note that it emerged from our pilot interviews that our respondents could specify with no great difficulty the couples, if any, with whom they had a home entertaining relationship—i.e. that such couples almost invariably formed a fairly well-defined, and generally small, set. One would guess that for most couples of professional or managerial status at least, this would not be the case and that asking them 'Who is it you have round?' would scarcely be meaningful.

[3] In classifying these relationships, difficulties occasionally arose through certain of them having more than one possible source. In dealing with such cases, kinship was always given precedence, and we sought in general to classify according to the initial source.

TABLE 7. Leisure-time social relationships

	Manual couples							White-collar couples					
	Percentage					Total mentioned	Average per respondent/couple	Percentage					Total mentioned	Average per respondent/couple
	Kin	Neigh-bours*	Work-mates†	Others				Kin	Neigh-bours*	Work-mates†	Others			
People with whom spare time is most often spent														
Reported by husband only	23	22	35	21	101	156	0·68	21	0	36	42	99	66	0·61
Reported by wife only	34	51	10	6	101	218	0·95	22	34	19	25	100	32	0·59
Reported by husband and wife	37	33	16	14	100	263	1·15	38	18	19	26	101	85	1·57
All	32	37	19	13	101	637	2·78	31	17	23	29	100	150	2·78
Wives' visiting partners	37	41	22		100	383	1·68	26	44	30		100	88	1·66
Couples entertained at home	57	12	11	20	100	542	2·36	47	17	13	24	101	184	3·41

* Includes ex-neighbours. For the purposes of our interviews and in subsequent analysis, 'neighbours' were defined as persons living within ten minutes' walk of the respondent.

† Includes ex-workmates.

In view of what we have said earlier about the degree to which the couples in our manual sample were physically removed from their kin, the point that is initially striking about the data of table 7 is the quite large part that parents, siblings and in-laws still play in our respondents' lives.[1] The figures given conceal some appreciable variations in this respect since, as one would imagine, these relatives tended to be of greater prominence to the extent that couples did have them within easy reach. Nevertheless, even in the case of those couples whose kin were for the most part located outside Luton (49% of the sample) kin still accounted for 22% of their most frequent leisure associates, for 20% of the wives' visiting partners and for over half—58%—of the people they entertained at home.[2] What these findings suggest, therefore, is that for our affluent workers and their wives those of their kin who were *reasonably* available represented a major source of friends and companions, despite the fact that these kin rarely lived in such close proximity that contact could be maintained with them in a largely casual and unplanned way.[3]

At the same time, it remains obvious that no matter how intensively available kin were drawn on,[4] the importance of kinship among the men and women we studied was inevitably limited by their frequent separation from their kinship 'homes'.[5] As can be seen in table 7, so far at least as spare-time activities and wives' visiting are concerned, *neighbours*— broadly defined as persons living within ten minutes' walk—are of comparable importance to kin in our respondents' associational patterns, and are generally more important for the couple than friends made through work or in any other way. Moreover, and more significantly, the further analysis of table 8 reveals that, in cases where kin are for the most part physically distant and are thus removed from our respondents' day-to-day

[1] In principle, 'kin' in table 7 covers all persons claimed as kin by respondents: in fact, these persons were to a quite overwhelming degree immediate kin of the kind referred to in the text.
[2] In the case of couples whose kin *were* largely resident in Luton, the corresponding proportions of kin were 41% (leisure associates), 52% (wives' visiting partners) and—again—58% (people entertained at home). The effects of mobility are brought out somewhat more strongly if we consider those couples (25% of the sample) a majority of whose kin lived outside Luton and more than fifty miles from the town: in their case, the figures for kin were 22%, 16% and 48% respectively.
[3] See above, p. 38.
[4] In fact, evidence of some degree of 'selectivity' in kinship relations can be produced. See below, p. 104.
[5] We take this notion from Jane Hubert, 'Kinship and Geographical Mobility in a Sample from a London Middle-Class Area', *International Journal of Comparative Sociology*, vol. 5 (March 1965). It is interesting to note that while for the majority of our respondents such a kinship 'home' could be readily identified, this was not so with Hubert's samples of London middle-class couples.

social lives, it is the importance of neighbours, rather than of any other category of friend, that chiefly increases. In other words, it would seem that for the two forms of sociability in question, neighbours are the preferred *substitutes* for the kin that are missing.

TABLE 8. *Sources of regular spare-time companions and of wives' visiting partners by location of majority of couple's kin*

	Location of majority of couple's kin*	Kin	Neigh-bours†	Kin plus neigh-bours†	Work-mates‡	Others		Total men-tioned
				Percentage				
Spare-time companions	In Luton§	41	27	68	19	13	100	235
	Outside Luton	22	47	69	19	11	99	296
Wives' visiting partners	In Luton§	52	27	79	21		100	147
	Outside Luton	20	54	74	26		100	175

* 35 couples were unclassifiable.
† Includes ex-neighbours.
‡ Includes ex-workmates.
§ 'Luton' refers to the area covered by the town boundaries plus contiguous built-up areas.

Reverting to table 7, this propensity of our affluent workers and their wives to limit their friendship relations largely to kin *or* neighbours is further brought out through the comparison that can be made with our white-collar sample. In regard to each of the three kinds of relationships on which data are given, it may be observed that the white-collar couples draw more heavily on friends made through work and, in particular, on friends who are neither kin, neighbours nor workmates. It may also be noted that in the case of spare-time associates and wives' visiting partners, the number of persons mentioned per couple does not differ between the two samples. Thus, it would appear, it is not merely a matter of the white-collar couples having just as many friends as the manual couples who are kin or neighbours and then other friends *in addition* to these: different patterns of preference are almost certainly involved.[1]

[1] In the case of spare-time associates we were of course asking about the 'two or three people' with whom husbands and wives most often spent their spare time. But it was evident in our interviews that we were not in this way unduly restricting our respondents' enumeration of their regular companions. Only 16% of the manual and 15% of the white-collar couples mentioned five or more persons *between* them. See further below, p. 103.

The findings set out in the foregoing paragraphs are then already suggestive of one general conclusion: namely, that the couples who figured in our critical case, despite their affluence and the characteristics of their community setting, remain in fact largely restricted to working-class styles of sociability, and in the formation of their friendship relations are for the most part neither guided by middle-class norms nor aided by middle-class social skills.[1] To the extent that kinship could not provide the foundation of their social life, these couples turned most readily for support and companionship to those persons who, as it were, formed the next circle of immediate acquaintance—that is, to persons living in the same neighbourhood. Thus, in much the same way as working-class people in more traditional contexts, they would appear to build up their friendship relations largely on the basis of social contacts that are in the first instance 'given'. Actually *making* friends—through personal choice and initiative—from among persons with whom no structured relationships already exist could not be regarded as at all a typical feature of their way of life.[2]

Furthermore, the view that our affluent workers and their wives do not greatly share in middle-class styles of sociability can be supported by several other results that emerged from our interviewing programme. To begin with, the material contained in table 7 itself enables us to make at least two more points that are of relevance.

First, the data on leisure associates reveal that although, as we have observed, our manual and white-collar couples claim the same average number of relationships overall, the former report fewer *joint* relationships and more companions of the wife alone—these being overwhelmingly kin or neighbours, while white-collar wives' associates come almost as often from other sources.[3] At the same time, it can be seen that the white-collar

---

[1] In making statements of this kind, we are all well aware of the fact that detailed studies of the life-styles and sociability of the British middle class are unfortunately few, and thus that attempts to assess the degree to which our affluent workers and their wives approximate middle-class patterns cannot always be as well-grounded empirically as would be desirable. However, as will be evident from subsequent references, there is not such a complete dearth of relevant material that comparisons are impossible. It is incidentally worth noting that proponents of the *embourgeoisement* thesis have themselves rarely been inhibited in their claims by our limited knowledge of middle-class social life.

[2] The way in which, among the traditional working class, friendships tend to be inextricably bound up with kinship and neighbour relations is well described in Michael Young and Peter Willmott, *Family and Kinship in East London* (London, 1957), pp. 81–4. For arguments similar to our own on the contrasts between working and middle-class styles of sociability, see J. M. Mogey, *Family and Neighbourhood* (Oxford, 1956), ch. 5; Margaret Stacey, *Tradition and Change: a Study of Banbury* (Oxford, 1960), pp. 114–15, 155; and Willmott and Young, *Family and Class in a London Suburb* (London, 1960), pp. 127–9.

[3] This difference is reduced but not eliminated if we control for wives working.

husbands have *no* regular companions drawn from among their neighbours whom they do *not* share with their wives. Considered together, therefore, these two findings would indicate that among our manual sample there is still maintained, although in some obviously attenuated form, the traditional working-class pattern of wives having important sets of friendship relations based essentially on family and neighbourhood and largely segregated from their husbands' networks;[1] while in turn the latter, unlike the white-collar workers, still sometimes find it possible to have a number of 'mates' recruited from the locality, as well as from work, with whom they typically associate independently of their wives.

Secondly, table 7 shows that as regards 'having couples round' our affluent workers and their wives claimed significantly fewer couples whom they invited to their homes than did our white-collar respondents, and also that they had a stronger tendency to restrict such entertaining to members of their kin. Further analysis of the data in fact reveals that as many as 42% of the manual couples (compared with 24% in the white-collar sample) reported entertaining at home *only* couples who were kin—if indeed they 'entertained' at all—and that another 33% mentioned no more than one other couple apart from kin whom they would meet with in this way. Further still, it should be said that social occasions of the kind in question were not, in the main, particularly frequent occurrences in these respondents' social lives—taking place on average somewhat less than once a month.[2] Thus, couples who entertained at home a good deal, and who also might bring into their homes numbers of friends who were not 'family', constituted only a quite small minority within our total sample.[3] Such a situation, then, can scarcely be taken as demonstrating the spread of typically middle-class friendship relations and modes of sociability. On the contrary, it would more obviously suggest the persistence of the long-established working-class belief that the home is a place reserved for kin and for very 'particular' friends alone.[4]

[1] For accounts of this pattern in different types of traditional working-class community, see, for example, Young and Willmott, *Family and Kinship in East London*, pp. 31–3, 44–6; N. Dennis, F. Henriques and C. Slaughter, *Coal is Our Life* (London, 1956), chs. 5 and 6; and Stacey, *Tradition and Change*, pp. 101–5, 112–14.

[2] In the case of our white-collar couples, the average was clearly more than once a month. However, there is a lack of other 'middle-class' data on this point and it may well be that it is in the style rather than in the frequency of home entertaining that class differences are most marked.

[3] Thus, for example, only 17% of our manual couples (as compared with 31% in the white-collar sample) reported that they had couples round for the evening at least once a month on average *and* mentioned two or more couples who were so entertained and who were not kin. It should be noted that our data do not enable us to say how frequently any *particular* couple, or *type* of couple, were entertained.

[4] For accounts of this, see, for example, E. W. Bakke, *The Unemployed Man* (London, 1933), pp. 153–5; Young and Willmott, *Family and Kinship in East London*, pp. 84–5; Richard

Lastly, there is one other set of data that we can refer to in assessing the extent of our affluent workers' acceptance of middle-class patterns of social life: this concerns their participation in formal associations. Numerous investigations in Great Britain and elsewhere have shown that membership in such associations is more frequent among middle-class than among working-class groups, and that middle-class persons are also more likely to hold official positions within the associations to which they belong.[1] If then *embourgeoisement* is a reality, we would expect the couples in our critical case to have a level of participation in clubs, societies and other organisations which is, at all events, higher than that generally reported for manual workers and their wives.

TABLE 9. *Participation in formal associations*

Number of associations belonged to*	Manual couples			White-collar couples		
	Husbands	Wives	All	Husbands	Wives	All
	Percentage			Percentage		
None	52	63	58	33	46	40
One	33	26	29	28	20	24
Two or more	14	11	13	39	33	36
	99	100	100	100	99	100
Committee members and/or office-holders†	9	4	6	35	13	24

* Excluding trade unions and general works club memberships, but including membership in works club *sections* with additional membership fees.
† Including trade union offices.

Such an expectation is not in fact borne out by the relevant results from our interviews. Apart from their membership in trade unions and in works clubs—the former being sometimes involuntary and the latter, as we have

Hoggart, *The Uses of Literacy* (London, 1958), p. 21; and M. Kerr, *People of Ship Street* (London, 1958), pp. 101-6. It may also be noted that when our affluent workers and their wives did have other couples round for the evening, the style of the entertainment that typically occurred differed somewhat from that reported by our white-collar couples. Playing cards and listening to records and tapes were clearly more common activities among the latter, and watching television and going out for a drink among the former.
[1] For Great Britain, see the studies already cited by Mogey, Young and Willmott; and also T. Cauter and J. S. Downham, *The Communication of Ideas* (London, 1954), pp. 66 *et seq.*; T. B. Bottomore, 'Social Stratification in Voluntary Associations', in D. V. Glass (ed.), *Social Mobility in Britain* (London, 1954); and Colin Rosser and Christopher Harris, *The Family and Social Change* (London, 1965), p. 107.

seen, being often merely nominal—our affluent workers prove to have very limited associational attachments. As is shown in table 9, 52% belong to *no* other associations at all; and the average number of memberships per man works out at 0·9. Even if we count in union membership, this figure rises to no more than 1·8. Not surprisingly, then, the number of men who were in any way involved in the running of an association was very small indeed—amounting to less than 1 in 10 of the sample as a whole even when union offices are included. Furthermore, our workers' wives are revealed as even less enthusiastic 'joiners' than their husbands: 63% belonged to no association and the average number of memberships per wife fell to as low as 0·5, with only 1 in 25 being a committee member or official. Given such findings, therefore, we can certainly claim that the couples in question show no greater degree of associational participation than do the working-class men and women in samples previously studied: rather, the similarities that emerge are the striking feature of comparisons on this basis.[1] At the same time, we may note that the data for our white-collar couples, also presented in table 9, point once again to important differences in the organisation of sociability across the manual–nonmanual line, and to ones which, we would suspect, still persist over a wide range, regardless largely of whether differences in incomes and living standards have been eliminated or not.[2]

Table 10, which lends support to this point of view, may serve to complete the argument of this section of the chapter. From the table it can be seen that on a number of indicators of style of sociability derived from the preceding discussion, those of our affluent workers and their wives with the most extensive white-collar connections are, with some regularity,

[1] For example, if we consider the study with data most comparable to our own—that by Cauter and Downham—we find that the figures given for men and women of manual status (Derby, 1952) are exactly the same as ours—i.e. 58% with no associational memberships, 29% with one only, and 13% with two or more. Moreover, for skilled manual workers the corresponding figures were 43%, 37% and 20%. In the other British studies the percentage of respondents of manual status with no memberships is generally reported as being somewhat higher than in our case—usually in the range of 60–80%. However, in these studies *church*, as well as trade union, memberships were not counted, while our practice was to regard belonging to a church as a membership in a voluntary association wherever it was claimed as such. If we were to discount the church memberships of our sample, then the percentage recorded as having no memberships would certainly increase to well within the range in question. Our respondents were, of course, almost all in the age group 21–46, and it might be claimed that this covers a phase of the life-cycle in which participation in associations tends to be at a low. But this point is one that is very much in dispute in the literature. See, for example, M. Hausknecht, *The Joiners* (New York, 1962), pp. 32–6 especially. Within our sample there were no significant differences in associational memberships according to whether or not couples had children under school age, or none at all.

[2] We would attach particular significance here to the marked differences between our manual and white-collar samples in the proportion taking some part in the running of associations.

TABLE 10. *Indicators of style of sociability by conjugal white-collar affiliations*

Conjugal white-collar affiliations*	% of regular spare-time companions not kin, neighbours or work-mates	Ratio of non-joint to joint friends		Couples entertained at home: average number mentioned		% entertaining couples at home at least once a month on average and reporting entertaining non-kin	Average number of memberships in formal associations†	
		All	Non-kin	All	Non-kin		Husbands	Wives
Via family *and* job (N = 57)	16	1·4	1·5	2·79	1·46	44	1·12	0·58
Via family *or* job (N = 101)	12	1·5	1·5	2·33	0·90	36	0·91	0·56
Neither (N = 70)	11	1·3	1·7	2·00	0·77	34	0·83	0·37
White-collar couples (N = 54)	29	0·8	1·0	3·41	1·83	52	1·72	1·04

* Unless otherwise indicated, the N values in this column apply in all other tables involving this variable.
† Excluding trade union and general works club membership.

the most comparable with our white-collar couples; while, on the other hand, those with the most solidly working-class backgrounds show the greatest degree of contrast. The implication we would draw from this is, therefore, the following: that in so far as some degree of subcultural similarity is in evidence between our samples, this results less from their economic homogeneity than from the existence within the manual sample of couples in which at least one spouse has experience of white-collar *milieux* from family or occupational life. Moreover, to the extent that these couples may be regarded as having been in some way or other *downwardly* mobile,[1] the phenomenon to which the data of table 10 most obviously point is not that of *embourgeoisement* but rather that of a 'submerged' middle class of fairly sizable proportions.[2] And, as will in due course emerge, this same conclusion is suggested by several further features of our interview material.

With the possible exception, then, of this *déclassé* element within our sample, it would seem difficult to sustain the idea that the affluent workers we studied typically possessed dual social identity—still working-class in their role as rank-and-file production employees but in their out-of-work roles indistinguishably part of middle-class society. Furthermore, this idea is also controverted by other of our data which enable us to argue that our respondents' objectives as producers and the conditions of work they experienced did in fact carry implications for their lives outside work, and ones which, in general, appeared more likely to inhibit than to promote their assimilation into middle-class cultural and social patterns. Rather than such assimilation, our findings would indicate as the most probable concomitant of these workers' orientation to work and of their present type of employment what we have earlier referred to as *privatis-*

---

[1] If we assume that the status of a couple is primarily determined by the position of the husband, downward mobility of some kind could be said to have occurred in the case of all the couples in question except where *both* family and occupational white-collar ties came via the wife. Such instances numbered 18 (32%) out of the total of 57 couples. Of the remainder, 30 (53%) were cases where the husband had a white-collar father (12 husbands also having white-collar work experience and 25, a wife with such experience); and 9 (16%) were cases where the husband had held a white-collar job but where the white-collar family links were only through the wife.

[2] The sociological significance of a downwardly mobile middle-class element among the mass of manual wage workers has been previously recognised by a number of writers. So far as the British case is concerned, there are many insightful comments in the work of George Orwell— see, for example, *The Road to Wigan Pier* (London, 1937), ch. 13—while more recent discussion is to be found in Brian Jackson and Dennis Marsden, *Education and the Working Class* (London, revised ed., 1966), pp. 67–70, especially; and Rosser and Harris, *The Family and Social Change*, pp. 93–9.

ation[1]—a process, that is, manifested in a pattern of social life which is centred on, and indeed largely restricted to, the home and the conjugal family.

For example, one can in the first place point to a fairly obvious relationship between the fact that the men in our sample are engaged in relatively high-paying jobs and the fact that a majority are physically removed from the centres of their kinship networks. As we have already noted, virtually all the couples who had migrated to Luton had done so specifically in search of better living standards;[2] and, whether directly or indirectly, job opportunities such as those offered by Vauxhall, Skefko and Laporte were clearly a major factor in the town's attractiveness. Couples had no doubt often approached the move with misgivings about its effects upon their social lives, and from our interviews we know that some remained much aware of what they had lost in this respect.[3] But generally, one may infer, staying near their kin had not appeared to these migrants as being compatible with achieving the material standards to which they aspired. To break away from their existing pattern of sociability had been, in other words, a prerequisite of their becoming affluent; and this, despite the possibility of social isolation, was the course of action that they had chosen to follow.

Furthermore, for couples separated from their kin especially, but in some degree for all those we studied, an active and varied social life within their present community was, we would suggest, made difficult to establish because of the exigencies experienced by our affluent workers in the daily performance of their jobs. In the preceding chapter we have seen that in the plants in which these men were employed overtime working was the normal practice, and that the majority were required to work according to some form of shift system. Consequently, leisure hours were frequently curtailed and occurred at unusual and often varying times of day; in addition, energy and what could perhaps be termed 'social vitality'[4] were likely to be unduly sapped. In these ways, therefore, obstacles must inevitably have been created not only to the acceptance of distinctively middle-class styles of sociability—such as, say, evening parties or extensive participation in clubs and societies—but indeed to *any* kind of frequent and regular association with persons outside the immediate family group. Analysis of our interview data does in fact provide various

[1] See Goldthorpe and Lockwood, 'Affluence and the British Class Structure', pp. 150–5.
[2] See above, p. 38 and *IAB*, pp. 152–3.
[3] *IAB*, pp. 153–4.
[4] Cf. Wilensky, 'Orderly Careers and Social Participation: the Impact of Work History on Social Integration in the Middle Mass'.

4*

results that are strongly supportive of this conclusion. For example, among couples where the husband reported working up to three hours overtime per week, the proportion saying that on average they entertained at home less than once a month was 37%; this figure then rises steadily with the amount of overtime worked to 69% in the case of couples where the husband was working upwards of 15 hours overtime per week.[1] Similarly, where husbands were on shiftwork, the proportion of couples entertaining at home less than once a month was 50% as against 32% for couples where the husband did not work shifts. Moreover, if we consider those couples who in this respect appeared particularly privatised (i.e who entertained friends at home less than four times a year) we find that they account for 40% of those who had to contend with shiftworking but for only 16% of the remainder of the sample.[2]

Finally in the present connection it may be added that among the wives of our affluent workers almost all who did not have young children were themselves in gainful employment, and that so too were a number of those still in the period of active motherhood. In total, 32% worked, slightly more than half (17%) full-time and the rest on some kind of part-time basis. Where, then, wives sought in this way to raise family incomes to a still higher level, further limitations on the couple's social life were the probable outcome: most obviously, through time in the evenings and at weekends having to be given over to housework, shopping and other chores, but here again, one would suspect, also as a result simply of physical fatigue.[3]

To illustrate the argument of the foregoing paragraphs and also to show just how privatised the social lives of our couples were, we may turn now to the more detailed information that we acquired on the actual use that was made of leisure or, rather, of non-working time. In the course of our 'home' interviews, we asked husband and wife separately to give an account of the main spare-time activities that they had engaged in on the

[1] Where husbands are working no overtime at all, the figure in question was 49%. This seemingly anomalous result is probably to be accounted for by the fact that almost all these men were on shifts and most were doing night work.

[2] The majority of men not working shifts were craftsmen (see above, p. 62). However, it seems unlikely that the differences in the amount of home entertaining that are shown can be explained in terms of skill level alone. Inspection of the cases of those craftsmen who were regularly on shifts indicates a frequency of entertaining closer to that of other men on shifts than to that of other craftsmen.

[3] The wives of men in our white-collar sample were still more likely to go out to work (24% full-time and 26% part-time). But in the case of our manual couples the effect of wives working must of course be appreciated as operating cumulatively with the effects of overtime and shiftworking.

two week-days preceding the day of the interview and during the preceding Saturday and Sunday;[1] we also recorded any overtime work
which extended into what was usually a leisure period and any substantial
amount of housework done in the evenings or at week ends.

To begin with, we reproduce below the data collected for four of our
couples, these being selected so as to represent types of situation that were
fairly commonly found.

Use of 'leisure' time : four cases

COUPLE A   Migrated from Scotland seven years previously; husband a setter at Skefko; one
daughter aged three; wife pregnant and not working; have recently bought a new semi-detached
house.

	HUSBAND	WIFE
Week-day 1		
Evening	Worked on building a garage to adjoin house	Did housework
Week-day 2		
Evening	Fitted new cupboard and shelves in kitchen	Watched TV
Saturday		
Morning	[Worked overtime]	Went shopping in Luton with daughter
Afternoon	[Worked overtime]	Did housework
Evening	Drove to other side of Luton to collect cement for use on garage	Watched TV
Sunday		
Morning	[Worked overtime]	Did housework
Afternoon	Laid linoleum in kitchen	Played with daughter
Evening	Watched TV	Watched TV and knitted

[1] The actual questions were: 'Now I know it's difficult, but could you try to think back and
tell me what were the main things you did in your spare time last weekend?' and then 'And
what were the main things you did in your spare time on [last two week-days]?' We explained
that by 'main' activities we were thinking of ones lasting roughly an hour or more. After
respondents had given their accounts we also asked: 'Would you say that is typical of the
way you spend your spare time? Is there anything else that you usually do?' Over 80% of
both husbands and wives gave answers to these last two questions indicating that their accounts
were typical, and in the remaining cases the tendency was, if anything, for accounts to be
thought atypical in the direction of *exaggerating* the extent of respondents' spare-time activities and social contacts—as, for example, when the days in question fell in a holiday period.

COUPLE B Migrated from London area five years ago, wife Irish; husband an assembler at Vauxhall on shiftwork; two boys aged twelve and nine; wife working part-time as shop assistant; live in a council house but are planning to buy their own shortly.

	HUSBAND	WIFE
Week-day 1		
Evening	[Worked overtime]	Went 'bulk' shopping in Luton
	Read stories to younger son	
	Played guitar with elder son	Watched TV
Week-day 2		
Evening	Gardened with elder son	Knitted
	Played guitar with elder son	Wrote letters to relative in London
	Watched TV	
Saturday		
Morning	[Worked overtime after night shift]	Did housework
Afternoon	Went shopping for gardening supplies with sons	Did housework
Evening	Went to bed	Watched TV and knitted
Sunday		
Morning	Read papers	Went to Mass
		Did housework
Afternoon	Visited by wife's sister and husband (also living in Luton)	(see husband)
Evening	Went to 'local' for a drink with brother-in-law	Watched TV

COUPLE C Husband a Lutonian, wife from Lancashire; husband a craftsman at Skefko; three children, eldest twelve; wife not working at present; have bought their own house.

	HUSBAND	WIFE
Week-day 1		
Evening	Watched TV	Watched TV
Week-day 2		
Evening	Went for walk with wife and children	(see husband)
	Watched TV	Knitted
Saturday		
Morning	Went shopping with wife and children in Luton	(see husband)
Afternoon	Went for car ride into country with wife and children	(see husband)
Evening	Went to 'local' for a drink with wife	(see husband)
Sunday		
Morning	[Worked overtime]	Did housework
Afternoon	Watched TV	Watched TV
Evening	Went to 'local' for a drink with wife	(see husband)

COUPLE D Have lived in Luton for seventeen years, originally from the Midlands; husband a process worker at Laporte on shiftwork; two teenage sons; wife works full-time at a dry cleaner's, also on shifts; now buying their own home.

	HUSBAND	WIFE
Week-day 1		
Afternoon	Helped elder son to paint his motor scooter	Did housework
Week-day 2		
Afternoon	Went shopping for provisions	Did housework
	Worked on repairs to car	Watched TV
Saturday		
Morning	Did housework with wife	(see husband)
Afternoon	Went shopping in Luton with wife	(see husband)
Evening	Watched TV	Watched TV
Sunday		
Morning	Stayed in bed	Did housework
Afternoon	Visited for lunch by a couple of 'old friends'	(see husband)
Evening	Watched TV	Went to bed early

In these specific cases, one has clearly revealed the variety of ways in which both previous occupational mobility and the demands of their present jobs can shape the pattern of our respondents' out-of-work lives. For example, it may be observed that extra-familial kin figure very little in the spare-time activities that are reported; and that the only mention made of an arranged meeting with friends is by couple D, who had lived longest in the Luton area. The impression conveyed is very strongly one of husband, wife and children forming together a highly 'individuated'[1] and self-reliant group, with couples A and C demonstrating such home- and family-centredness in an extreme form. At the same time, though, the intrusiveness of working life is in all cases apparent, and there are illus- trations of the taxing effects of overtime and shiftwork when combined with extensive domestic and family duties—as, for instance, the husband of couple B retiring to bed on a Saturday evening. Indeed it becomes evident that a further possible source of privatisation lies in the fact that the couples we studied might often have only very limited time at their disposal which could be regarded as 'spare' or 'free' in any genuine sense; that is, which was not taken up either with work outside the home— including preparing for and recovering from this—or with the multi- farious activities required to keep a house, garden, car and so on in a

[1] Cf. Elizabeth Bott, *Family and Social Network* (London, 1957), pp. 100-1.

minimum state of order and repair. Interviewers noted that after relating their recent activities, respondents quite frequently made somewhat embarrassed and apologetic remarks such as 'We don't seem to do very much at all, do we?' or 'You must think we lead very dull lives';[1] yet many spoke also of being very busy, of 'never having a minute' and of being 'always on the go'. Such remarks were not necessarily contradictory: what seemed often to happen was that after finishing work and carrying out their various chores and familial obligations, our affluent workers and their wives wanted only to 'take it easy' and 'relax' before the daily round began again.[2]

The qualitative insights gained from examining particular illustrations of our respondents' privatised style of life can be backed up by quantitative analysis of data collected from our sample as a whole. This confirms that the cases presented above are in no way atypical in the degree of home- and family-centredness that they display. For example, of all the spare-time activities that our affluent workers and their wives reported for the two days and the weekend prior to being interviewed, 62% prove to be activities that took place in and about the home itself. Among the husbands, the two types of activity that figured with greatest prominence could be described as 'chores and odd jobs'—including gardening—and 'home-based leisure', most notably watching television. Among the wives 'home-based leisure' was the most important category but often leisure of this kind appeared to be combined with some more utilitarian activity— 'watching television and knitting' being the classic formula. Again, three-quarters (74%) of all activities reported were ones carried out either by husband and wife alone or together with other members of the household.[3] Almost a quarter of our couples (23%) had engaged in *no* activity in company with persons from outside the household, and 60% mentioned

[1] Contrary to initial expectations, it was a fairly common experience of interviewers to find that the leisure questions constituted a more 'difficult' part of the interview schedule than, say, the questions on money, politics or conjugal relationships.

[2] Probably the main source of the difficulty that our respondents experienced in giving accounts of what they did in their spare time was that for much of it they were often not engaged in any well-defined or sustained activity at all. They were just 'sitting around' or 'doing this and that'. Thus, in between their reportable activities—i.e. those lasting approximately an hour or more—there would be large 'gaps' of time that could not be accounted for in any very specific way. If the cases presented above are at all unrepresentative, it is in not sufficiently displaying such gaps.

[3] In all but 3% of cases, 'household' can be equated with 'conjugal family'. In answer to further specific questions, the bulk of couples with children (72%) reported having 'family outings' between once a week and once a month in frequency, while in regard to couples having 'evenings out' alone, a bimodal distribution emerged: 59% of all couples said they did this, if at all, less than four times a year but 31% reported such occasions as occurring at least once a month.

no more than two such persons with whom they had shared their spare time during the periods in question. Overall, the average number of such persons mentioned per couple worked out at 2.4.

Findings of this nature, one may add, are strongly corroborated by certain of the data that we have already presented in table 7. When respondents were asked about friends with whom they spent their spare time, it will be recalled that husband and wife were both invited to name their 'two or three' most frequent companions. However, as is evident from table 7, the number of such friends who were actually mentioned is well below the maximum possible, the average for husband and wife *together* being less than three. Indeed, further analysis of the data discloses that 7% of the couples in the sample could name no regular leisure companions at all, and that a further 36% shared only one or two between them.

We have, then, a variety of evidence to show that for the majority of our affluent workers and their wives time outside work was time devoted overwhelmingly to home and family life rather than to sociability of any more widely based kind. And, as we have earlier argued, this pattern can be seen as one associated both with our respondents' dominant orientation to work—their emphasis upon the economic 'pay-off'—and with constraints and pressures in their working lives that this overriding concern with economic rewards has led them to accept. From this point of view, therefore, a privatised style of life can best be understood not as a sign of incipient 'middle-classness', in the way it seems often to have been interpreted, but rather as reflecting the adaptation of long-standing working-class norms of sociability to new economic and social conditions —those created by mobility and separation from kin, by employment in modern, large-scale plants and by the possibility of attractive housing and high standards of domestic living. And at the same time, one is led back to the contention that if distinctively middle-class norms *had* been widely adopted among the couples we studied—and the corresponding social skills acquired—then the expected outcome would have been a *less* privatised mode of existence than that we observed, involving appreciably higher levels of social participation of both a formal and informal kind.

However, before concluding this examination of the prevailing style of life within our sample of affluent workers, there are at least two further points that need to be made by way of qualification and in order thus to put the foregoing discussion in proper perspective.

First, it must be emphasised that our arguments concerning the relationship between our respondents' working and non-working lives should not be taken to imply that their degree of privatisation was *entirely* the un-wanted and unwelcome consequence of their quest for affluence—that, for example, those couples who had become isolated from their kin and now lived among people who were largely strangers *always* regarded this as yet another cost of achieving material prosperity. That this is unlikely to have been the case is indicated by two aspects of our interview data.

On the one hand, it is clear from our findings that our affluent workers and their wives, whether migrants or Lutonians, did not invariably main-tain close relationships with all those of their kin who *were* living within easy reach: on the contrary, a considerable degree of selectivity appeared to occur. Following criteria suggested by Bott, we classified our respon-dents' relations with their more immediate kin as 'intimate', 'effective', 'non-effective' and 'unfamiliar',[1] and it was then found that while re-lationships with parents resident in the Luton area were generally of an 'intimate' kind, this was not so with relationships with siblings. For example, although overall 35% of the husbands' siblings and 40% of the wives' were living in the Luton area, only 11% and 20% of the respective totals were accounted for by kin who qualified as 'intimate'; that is to say, kin with whom there was frequent visiting and mutual aid when necessary. In other words, close ties did not exist in the case of at least two-thirds of the siblings readily available to the husbands, nor in the case of at least half of those available to the wives.[2] The possibility has therefore to be recognised that for some proportion of the couples we studied, being separated from the body of their kin or living in a community in which kinship ties were of slight importance was actually experienced as an advantage in that it made it easier to restrict or to discontinue kinship relations that were found not to be rewarding.

Furthermore, we may record—more impressionistically—that our respondents often made remarks which revealed that their home- and family-centred existence was something that in many ways they positively valued. Most notable, perhaps, was the frequency with which in both the 'work' and 'home' interviews the men in our sample emphasised the

---

[1] See Bott, *Family and Social Network*, pp. 119–21. In the course of the 'home' interviews, details of our respondents' kin were collected by means of the extremely useful 'family tree' method devised by Professor J. P. Martin, to whom we are much indebted. After the tree had been constructed, we asked our respondents about the nature of their relationships and their social contacts with each of the living adults named on it. The material thus gathered enabled Bott's classification to be followed with only minor modifications.

[2] It is of course conceivable that in some cases visiting with siblings was infrequent as a result less of choice than of the exigencies of work or of conjugal family life; but the fact remains that such exigencies seem rarely to have prevented the maintenance of 'intimate' relationships with parents.

central place that 'the wife and kids' held in their lives and their approval of this state of affairs.[1] Although we have no systematic material through which the extent of such feelings can be directly demonstrated, we can nevertheless point to two features of the general pattern of our couples' family lives which confirm that familistic values are of some importance; namely, that in comparison with what is known of the more traditional worker, the amount of time spent by the men in our sample on leisure pursuits with 'mates' outside the home is very small; and that within the home many appear to take part in—or indeed to have taken over—activities which in the traditional view would be usually regarded as 'women's work'.

As to leisure spent with mates, much of our material that is germane has already been presented.[2] By way of adding to this, we may note simply that on the question concerning spare-time activities only 16% of

TABLE 11. *Participation of husbands in various domestic and family activities*

Activity	% of husbands taking main responsibility	% of husbands sharing in responsibility	% of husbands participating in some degree (total of first two columns)
Doing main shopping	5	19	24
Washing up	3	38	41
Putting children to bed*	10	38	48
Reading to children and telling stories†	22	45	67
Taking out younger children and babies*	7	73	80

* Percentages refer only to cases where couples had at least one child (N = 210).
† Percentages refer only to cases where this activity occurred or had occurred in the past (N = 170). To a base of 210 the corresponding percentages would be 18, 37 and 55.

the activities reported by husbands were *both* 'extra-mural' and extra-familial (which includes activities engaged in alone); and that in naming their most frequent leisure companions apart from members of their family, 47% of our affluent workers did not mention *any* friend whom

[1] In the course of the work interviews, we asked respondents if they could think about other things while doing their jobs: 160, or 70%, said they could (see *IAB*, pp. 18–19) and in the case of these men the things they reported thinking about most were the following (number of times mentioned in brackets): wives and families (57); sports, recreations, etc. (37) and holidays and weekends (30).
[2] See pp. 90–2 above.

they did not share with their wives.[1] As to husbands' participation in 'women's work', the relevant data are given in table 11. It is interesting to observe from this that while in the case of shopping and washing-up some degree of segregation of conjugal roles is certainly still in evidence, a majority of husbands, or at any rate of those who are fathers, are likely to be involved in activities that are in some way concerned with children.[2] It could of course always be claimed that what is reflected here is not so much the free expression of values as the force of various exigencies in the lives of our respondents—ones resulting, say, from their social isolation, from wives going out to work and so on. But in fact further analysis of our data provides only limited support for such an argument,[3] and, moreover, the distinction that is involved is not a clear-cut one. It is not difficult to imagine how family arrangements of the kind in question—and especially those involving children—might perhaps have been born of exigencies but, once established, provided relationships that were valued for their own sake.[4]

The second point that should be made by way of completing the discussion of this section is one that follows on from the foregoing remarks when they are considered together with the data assembled in table 12. From this table, it would appear that while our affluent workers are, as husbands, as family-centred as the white-collar workers we studied, the white-collar couples are on a number of counts little or no less privatised in their social lives than are our affluent workers and their wives. Although in several respects the white-collar couples clearly reveal more middle-class traits in their styles of sociability, it is equally evident that they too

[1] This excludes the 30 men who could mention no regular spare-time companion at all. Our findings generally in this connection may be contrasted with those reported by Rich for a working-class sample based on a traditional Black Country community. Rich demonstrates the considerable extent to which the leisure patterns of husbands and wives were segregated, and in particular in consequence of the husbands' extra-mural activities—chiefly drinking and sport—either alone or more probably in the company of mates. See D. Rich, 'Social Relationships in Leisure Time' (University of Birmingham Ph.D. thesis, 1951); and 'Spare Time in the Black Country' in Leo Kuper (ed.), *Living in Towns* (London, 1953). For a similar, though more impressionistic, account see also ch. 4, 'Leisure', in Dennis *et al.*, *Coal is Our Life*.

[2] In this latter respect, it may well be that our respondents' behaviour is comparable to that of fathers generally in the more skilled or higher income groups, though not in the lower strata, of the present-day working class. See the data presented in J. and E. Newson, *Infant Care in an Urban Community* (London, 1963), chs. 6 and 12.

[3] For example, husbands whose wives work differed appreciably from the rest only in being more likely to help with shopping and washing-up.

[4] For further discussion of this issue and for more detailed analysis of our findings on conjugal roles, see Jennifer Platt 'Some Problems in Measuring the Jointness of Conjugal Role-Relationships', *Sociology*, vol. 3, no. 3 (September, 1969).

are not involved in any very intensive social round of visits, mutual entertainment and other shared activities with a wide circle of friends, such as
might be observed in the case, say, of couples of higher managerial or
professional status.[1]

TABLE 12. *Indicators of privatisation and home- and family-centredness*

	Manual couples	White-collar couples
% of couples reporting no more than two regular spare-time companions	43	50
% of couples entertaining other couples at home less than once per month on average	46	37
Average number of formal associations belonged to:		
husbands	0·95	1·69
wives	0·52	1·03
% of reported spare-time activities occurring in and about the home	62	60
% of reported spare-time activities carried out by husband and wife alone or with other members of household	74	73
Average number of spare-time associates mentioned per couple who were not members of their household	2·38	3·04
% of reported spare-time activities of husband that were 'extra-mural' *and* extra-familial	16	17
% of husbands participating in care of children:		
putting children to bed*	48	51
reading and telling stories†	67	78
taking out younger children and babies*	80	71

* For manual couples, N = 210; for white-collar couples, N = 37 (see table 11).
† For manual couples, N = 170; for white-collar couples N = 31 (see table 11).

There is here, then, some possible support for the idea that we previously advanced of a process of 'normative convergence' between
affluent manual and lower-level white-collar groups—one focal point
of this being an overriding concern with the economic fortunes and social
relationships of the conjugal unit. Although, as we have described, the
worlds of work of the men in our two samples show notable contrasts, and
although with the manual workers at least work exerts a clearly restrictive
influence upon the pattern of non-working life, it would seem that the
majority of our manual and white-collar couples do have in common a
propensity to devote their spare time overwhelmingly to home and family
and to limit their wider social contacts even to the point at which the
family is in a state of near isolation.[2]

[1] Cf. Willmott and Young, *Family and Class in a London Suburb*, chs. 8 and 9.
[2] It may be added in this connection that while, as we have seen, those affluent workers and
their wives with relatively extensive white-collar affiliations were distinctive in coming closest
to our white-collar couples in their style of sociability, they do *not* differ significantly from the
rest of the sample on our various indicators of privatisation.

How far and in what ways this might represent a new pattern of white-collar sociability is difficult to say for want of comparative material;[1] but the differences between the social life of the privatised and the traditional manual worker are fairly obvious. The extent to which these differences are attributable directly to normative shifts must not be exaggerated; as we have earlier argued, the degree of normative continuity under much changed external conditions is often a significant feature of new working-class life-styles. Nevertheless, at least among the couples included in our critical case, it would certainly appear that some of the values that sustain the communal, kin-based sociability of the traditional type of working-class community were no longer dominant. Specifically, on the evidence we have been able to present, one could assert that primacy was clearly given to the material well-being, the social cohesiveness and the autonomy of the conjugal family over against the demands or attractions of wider kinship or community ties; and one could at least suggest that probably the one most important concomitant of this changed emphasis was the acceptance among these workers and their wives of the ideal of the 'companionate' marriage.[2]

So far, then, we have shown that, rather than displaying recognisably middle-class characteristics in their style of sociability, our affluent workers and their wives for the most part lead a notably circumscribed kind of social life in which their main associates are members of their own immediate family. Our findings in this respect thus go contrary to the *embourgeoisement* thesis even in the form in which the assimilation of the industrial worker into middle-class cultural and social patterns is seen as limited to the out-of-work sphere. At the same time, though, we have observed that a relatively privatised style of life is also prevalent among the lower-level white-collar couples whom we included in our study; and while it would most probably be mistaken to suppose that the sources of privatisation were entirely comparable in the two cases, some degree of similarity in underlying social norms may reasonably be inferred.

[1] In any case, so far as the idea of normative convergence is concerned it should be remembered that the major implication of this for white-collar groups is a change not in their pattern of sociability but rather in the means that they typically rely on in advancing their economic interests, and at the same time in their social perspectives and ideologies. See Goldthorpe and Lockwood, 'Affluence and the British Class Structure', pp. 152–4.

[2] The changing pattern of marriage is one topic which has been curiously neglected in recent research into working-class social life. While our own study cannot help much to fill the gap, it does serve to indicate that the development of new normative expectations in regard to marital relationships may well be of major importance in understanding new working-class life-styles in general.

This being so, a further possibility arises of which we must take note: namely, that on the basis of some measure of normative convergence between more 'advanced' manual and lower-level white-collar groups, a process of genuine social fusion may be occurring across the marked status division that has hitherto been generally found between manual and non-manual strata. While *embourgeoisement* in the sense of industrial workers becoming directly absorbed into middle-class society may be a mis-conceived, or at any rate a premature, notion it could still be the case that a new social stratum is currently being formed in between the working and middle classes as these have been conventionally delineated. So far as the couples in our critical case are concerned, this possibility can best be investigated through considering the extent to which, in the course of their leisure and other non-work activities, our respondents came into regular contact with persons of white-collar status: that is to say, the extent to which they interacted with white-collar persons on what could be assumed to be usually terms of social equality.

On a number of the more important items in our interview schedule that were concerned with our affluent workers' patterns of sociability, we collected information about the occupational status of the associates to whom respondents referred. On the basis of this information, we can in fact show that in so far as the couples we studied spent their spare time with persons outside their immediate family circle, the persons in question were to a preponderant extent *other* manual workers and their wives.

To begin with, and perhaps most importantly, we find that in the case of our couples' most frequent spare-time companions, 75% of the total number of individuals who were named were of manual status, as against only 17% who were unambiguously white-collar—the remaining 8% falling into our 'intermediate' category.[1] Moreover, it is relevant to add that of these white-collar contacts, almost a third (31%) were kin rather than friends who had in some way been 'made'. Alternatively put, this means that in total our 458 affluent workers and their wives reported only 73 white-collar persons who were not their kin but with whom they regularly associated in out-of-work contexts. In fact, 66% of the couples in our sample reported no white-collar companions at all, and 76% none apart from kin. On the other hand, there were only 17 couples (7%) whose regular spare-time associates, leaving kin out of account, were entirely white-collar persons; and only 25 (11%) whose companions included no-one other than kin of manual status. Here, therefore, we have evidence which goes strongly against the idea either of '*embourgeoisement*

[1] For details of the occupational classification used throughout our research, see appendix A.

through assimilation' or of the emergence of a new social stratum which effectively obliterates the manual–nonmanual division. Rather, our findings would indicate that whatever the degree to which the couples in our critical case have come closer to certain white-collar groups in the normative basis of their social lives, they are still largely set apart from white-collar persons in terms of actual relationships.[1]

It might conceivably be suggested that while such segregation is evident enough so far as our respondents' most frequent spare-time companions are concerned, they could at the same time still have, as it were, a toehold in middle-class society through certain 'special' friends with whom they associated somewhat less often but more formally. In order to check on the likelihood of this being so, we can turn to the data that we have on the occupational status of those couples whom our respondents entertained in their homes. What we find is that, of the couples who were referred to in this connection, 68% were of manual status as compared with 9% of 'intermediate' and 23% of white-collar status; and further that of the latter number, 59% were kin. The majority of the couples we studied—66%—did not report entertaining *any* white-collar couple, while as high a proportion as 82% did not entertain any such couple who were not kin. Thus it would seem that, if anything, white-collar friends were even *less* likely to be entertained in white-collar style than to be associated with in other ways; at all events, the effect of these findings is to reinforce the impression that our affluent workers and their wives were quite sharply cut off from white-collar worlds.

As one final indication that this is indeed the case, we may revert to our data on our respondents' participation in formal associations. This, it will be recalled, was not at a high level: 52% of our affluent workers and 63% of their wives had no associational memberships at all. Furthermore, though, if we examine the character of those associations to which our respondents did belong, we find that they were largely of two kinds: ones that were likely to be almost entirely working-class in membership, such as working men's clubs, angling or allotment societies; or, if somewhat more mixed in their social composition, ones which had some fairly specific function—religious, charitable, sporting—and also some formalised internal hierarchy in which our respondents rarely held superior

[1] It may be of some interest to add here that in the case of our sample of white-collar couples, 40% of the regular leisure companions named were of manual status, as against 53% being white-collar and 7% 'intermediate'. However, further analysis reveals that 52% of persons in the first-mentioned category were kin (with 46% of our white-collar couples, either husband or wife was the child of a manual worker). Excluding kin, the figure for companions of manual status falls to 28%, with 64% being white-collar and 8% 'intermediate'.

positions. What was particularly lacking among the couples we studied was participation in associations with probably substantial white-collar memberships, other than ones with limited functions; or in associations with some white-collar membership and primarily diffuse 'social' functions and a non-hierarchical structure—for example, drinking clubs or clubs in which recreational or cultural activities were chiefly occasions for sociability *per se*. Of a total of 321 associational memberships claimed by our affluent workers and their wives, only 46 (14%) were in associations that could be regarded as being of the type in question.[1] We may therefore reasonably conclude that participation in formal associations was unlikely to provide more than a very small number of our respondents with opportunities for meeting and interacting with white-collar persons on an essentially egalitarian basis.

Given, then, that for the large majority of the couples in our critical case regular contacts with white-collar persons were not a feature of their pattern of sociability, the one remaining matter of interest, so far as our examination of the *embourgeoisement* thesis is concerned, is to investigate the composition of the minority who *were* apparently to some extent involved in middle-class society.

One fairly obvious possibility is that this minority was largely made up of those couples in our sample who had bought their own homes on private estates or who had otherwise come to live in predominantly middle-class localities. Whether this is so or not can be adequately tested on the basis of our classification of our respondents' area of residence within Luton in terms of 'residential status'.[2] The relevant data are set out in the first section of table 13. From this, it can be seen that couples who lived in middle-class areas did in fact have appreciably more white-collar contacts than those living on council estates. Moreover, further analysis of our data suggests that one way at least in which this was brought about was through our affluent workers' wives forming friendships with 'white-collar' wives among their neighbours. As regards spare-time companions, for example, it is the social composition of *wives'* friends, and to a lesser degree of joint friends, that gives rise to the overall difference in white-collar contacts between couples resident in middle-class areas and the council estate dwellers; and the white-collar friends of wives living in the

[1] For full details of our classification of associations and of respondents' membership patterns, see appendix B.
[2] This classification we take from Timms, 'Distribution of Social Defectiveness in Two British Cities'. The items on which the classification is made are: distance of the area from the town centre; rateable value per house; age of housing; land-use characteristics; rateable value per elector; net population density; and the 'jurors' index.

A and B grade areas are, apart from kin, very largely neighbours. Thus, it would seem that 'ecological' factors can in some degree be effective in reducing status segregation and in encouraging social mixing across the manual–nonmanual division.

TABLE 13. *White-collar contacts by status of area of residence and conjugal white-collar affiliations*

		% of regular spare-time companions of white-collar status		% of couples entertained at home of white-collar status	
		Including kin	Excluding kin	Including kin	Excluding kin
Status of area of residence*					
A 'Middle-class'		20	20	29	30
B 'Lower middle-class'		22	22	27	18
C Council estate		10	11	11	11
Conjugal white-collar affiliations					
Via family *and* job		28	28	33	23
Via family *or* job		15	14	23	23
Neither		8	7	12	17
Conjugal white-collar affiliations	Status of area of residence				
Via family *and* job	A	30	29	39	31
	B	48	58	48	50
	C	20	22	15	11
Via family *or* job	A	19	20	36	46
	B	15	10	22	21
	C	9	10	13	6
Neither	A	12	12	13	19
	B	7	0	24	8
	C	4	5	7	16

* 18 of our couples living in D and E grade areas—rated as inferior to council estates in residential status—are excluded from this table. The numbers of couples living in A, B and C grade areas was 84, 42, and 85 respectively.

However, before too great an importance is given to this conclusion, two further points need to be made. First, it should be recognised that even among those of our couples resident in A and B grade areas, white-collar contacts were still not particularly extensive.[1] And secondly, it

[1] Among such couples, still as many as 62% reported *no* person of white-collar status among their regular spare-time associates, and 73% no white-collar couple among those they entertained in their homes.

proves to be the case that the connection between area of residence and white-collar contacts to some extent results from the operation of another factor—that of our couples' white-collar affiliations via their families of origin or their occupational histories. As is shown in the second section of table 13, this variable is also clearly related to differences in the number of white-collar associates.[1] Moreover, when the effects of residence and white-collar affiliations are considered together, as in the third section of the table, it is the latter which would appear to exert the stronger influence, at any rate in regard to the status of spare-time companions; and this one could reasonably regard as being the more significant of the two items that are considered.[2]

Again, then, our findings would suggest that in so far as our critical case does contain manual workers and their wives who move in white-collar worlds, these couples are to an important extent ones whose white-collar connections cannot be seen as being, at least in any direct way, the *result* of their affluence, and who could often in fact be regarded as being on a downward rather than an upward path of social mobility. If we consider the 57 couples in our sample—25% of the total—who have *both* family and occupational links with white-collar society, we find that they account for 45% of all reported leisure companions of white-collar status and for 42% of all white-collar couples entertained in our respondents' homes. On the other hand, in the case of the 70 couples—31% of the total—who have no white-collar affiliations of this kind at all, the corresponding figures are 15% and 14%.[3] Thus, where no family or occupational 'bridges' to white-collar society existed—or at least none of the kind we recorded—it could be said that sustained 'social' ties with white-collar persons were almost entirely lacking among the couples we studied. One final statistic may be quoted which brings out this point most strikingly. If we leave

---

[1] As might be expected, a tendency existed—although not a very strong one—for those couples with more extensive white-collar affiliations to be found more often in A and B grade areas. Full details are given in *PAB*, table 32, p. 61.

[2] Substantively, because in the case of home entertaining a large minority of the couples in our sample (42%) restricted this to kin (if they entertained at all) and because, in general, its occurrence was not very frequent; and statistically, because the numbers involved in the last column of table 13 in particular are often small and because, as earlier noted (n. 3, p. 92 above) we do not know the relative frequencies of the entertainment of kin as opposed to non-kin or of white-collar as opposed to manual couples.

[3] A similar, though slightly less marked tendency is also evident if we examine the memberships claimed by our affluent workers and their wives in formal associations of a kind which would appear likely to lead to interaction with white-collar persons on a basis of equality (types 1, 2 and 4 in appendix B). We find that those couples who make up the quarter of our sample with relatively extensive white-collar affiliations account for 37% of such memberships, while those comprising the third with no comparable affiliations are responsible for only 17%.

aside all relationships with kin, it proves that the 140 husbands and wives in our sample who were of solidly working-class background named as friends with whom they most often spent their spare time only eleven individuals who were of 'intermediate' status and only *nine* who were white-collar quite unambiguously.

From one point of view, the findings that we have reported on in the above paragraphs may appear surprising, even to the extent, perhaps, of inciting disbelief. Given the affluence and the other distinctive social characteristics of the couples in our sample and given the nature of their community setting, it might well be thought remarkable that their pattern of sociability should remain so overwhelmingly based upon relationships with persons of similar occupational status. Certainly, the majority of commentators on current changes in working-class life—and not only proponents of the *embourgeoisement* thesis—have tended to assume that where manual workers and their families have the economic means and the social opportunities to gain an entry into white-collar society, this is something that they will for the most part seek to achieve (although perhaps being resisted through various forms of middle-class exclusiveness). For example, such an assumption underlies the distinction, made initially by Mogey and then taken over by Klein and several other writers, between manual workers who are 'status assenters' and those who are 'status dissenters'—the former readily accepting the traditional way of life and social position of the working class, the latter being led by changing external conditions to aspire to new life-styles and experiences dependent upon both material and status advancement.[1] Thus, it is supposed, for 'status dissenters' white-collar strata within their local communities will constitute important reference groups and, in addition, membership groups to which they would like to belong.

However, as we have earlier argued, to suppose that the less traditional, more forward-looking sections of the working class *do* generally regard white-collar groups in this way is to decide a crucial issue on a very inadequate empirical basis. Neither Mogey's pioneering study of a 'new' working-class community nor any similar study made thus far has in fact documented a concern for status enhancement specifically focused on white-collar models: consequently, 'status dissenters' remain a largely hypothetical category. Indeed, as we see it, the relevant evidence would rather suggest that there persists within the working class an element of status dissent in a much more radical sense than that intended by Mogey:

[1] See Mogey, *Family and Neighbourhood*, ch. 8; Klein, *Samples from English Cultures*, pp. 238–46

that is, dissent from the middle-class conception of the status hierarchy, from the values of 'status striving', and in particular from the idea that white-collar jobs confer upon their occupants any degree of social or moral superiority that might make such persons fit objects for the manual worker's deference and emulation.[1]

Moreover, if *this* interpretation is the more generally valid one, our own findings are surprising no longer. From this point of view, there is no reason to anticipate that manual workers and their families who have succeeded in achieving high incomes and living standards will be at all motivated to detach themselves from social relationships with other persons of manual status in favour of white-collar friends and companions: in other words, there is no reason why the drive to material improvement should be linked with aspirations defined in status terms. On the contrary, a sharp dissociation between the two is possible and indeed likely. Changes in working-class ways of life are certainly to be expected in consequence of affluence, better housing and so on—but *not* changes in specifically middle-class directions.

We have come, therefore, to the point at which our understanding of the pattern of sociability among the couples included in our critical case can only be completed by taking our analysis one whole stage further: that is to say, by examining directly the way in which our respondents themselves expressed their aspirations, and by examining also the nature of the 'images' of society within the context of which these aspirations were typically developed. It is to this that we turn in the chapter that follows.

[1] See further below, pp. 140–4. Of particular interest in this connection is Willmott's study of working-class life on the Dagenham estate, forty years after its inception. Willmott concludes that, in the main, people on the estate appeared to view their neighbours not as adversaries but as allies in a collective advance; social comparison did not lead to status competition, and concern and anxiety over differences in consumption patterns were far less marked than in either the middle-class suburb or the recently built working-class estate which Willmott (with Young) had earlier studied. See *The Evolution of a Community*, pp. 98–100 esp. Klein attempts to explain away the absence of 'status dissent' and status striving among the relatively prosperous workers of Dagenham in terms of this being a stable and highly homogeneous working-class community whose inhabitants tend thus to lack directly available models of white-collar life and white-collar reference groups. (*Samples from English Cultures*, pp. 259–61, 271, 277, 288.) However, as will emerge in the next chapter, there is a broad similarity between Willmott's findings for Dagenham and those from our own sample—one drawn, that is, from a community to which Klein's arguments would certainly not apply.

5. Aspirations and social perspectives

The assumption that members of the new working class will aspire not only to higher standards of domestic living but further to participation in distinctively middle-class life-styles and society is, as we have observed, a large and by no means well-founded one. It begs a number of questions that are of basic importance. None the less, it is an assumption that has been frequently made by recent analysts of the British class structure and it is thus of some interest to consider briefly, at the outset of this chapter, why this should have been the case.

As we have earlier indicated, some part of the explanation is certainly to be found in confused notions of what constitutes 'middle-classness' and in the consequent failure of many of those who have taken up the theme of working-class *embourgeoisement* to distinguish and to examine separately what we have referred to as the economic, normative and relational aspects of the problem.[1] Again, it may well be that with some writers at least, middle-class bias has simply prevented them from even conceiving of the possibility that working-class aspirations might be focused on something other than their own cultural and social standards. In addition, though, there is a third source of possible error to be noted and one that is of particular interest in the present connection; namely, certain fairly general shortcomings in the design and interpretation of the sociological studies that have thus far been made of various kinds of non-traditional working-class community.

Contrary to what might be supposed from the conclusions that have been commonly drawn from such studies, their authors have in fact only rarely been concerned with collecting data on 'new' working-class aspirations in any systematic way; and still less have they attempted to investigate the social and conceptual contexts within which such aspirations are formed.[2] Where in these studies information on aspirations has been

---

[1] See above, p. 24.

[2] Several of the studies in question have already been referred to—e.g. those by Mogey, Young and Willmott, and Zweig. Others are L. Kuper, 'Blueprint for Living Together' in Kuper (ed.), *Living in Towns*; the two studies contained in E. I. Black and T. S. Simey (eds), *Neighbourhood and Community* (Liverpool, 1954); and Hilda Jennings, *Societies in the Making* (London, 1962). None of these accounts in fact offers other than quite fragmentary data on the aspirations of the working-class families studied; yet all claim, or assume, that some significant proportion of these families were concerned with status enhancement.

obtained, this has for the most part been of either an impressionistic or piecemeal kind, and has been presented without any indications of how respondents envisaged the social order that provided the framework of their ambition or of how the nature of their aspirations might be linked with their typical social experiences and life situations. Consequently, it has not been within the scope of such enquiries to bring out at all fully or reliably the actual meanings *for respondents themselves* of the aspirations that they expressed, usually in answer to somewhat isolated questions. The tendency has rather been for the investigators, or for other commentators, to impose their own preconceptions in this respect. Thus, it is not perhaps surprising to find that almost any aspiration for a better life that has been admitted to by members of new working-class communities has at some point or other been represented as evidence of status striving or of a desire to achieve a middle-class position. For example, the aspiration to own a house, to live in the suburbs, to have a car, to be able to afford various other consumer durables, to see one's child in a selective secondary school or nonmanual occupation—all these have been interpreted as signs of at least incipient *embourgeoisement*. Yet it has scarcely ever been known whether or not those having such aspirations did in fact think of them primarily as entailing status enhancement, or indeed held to conceptions of the class structure in terms of which becoming 'middle-class' would be at all a likely objective.[1]

In reaction against writers who were prepared to argue in this way, our own concern, as we have already made clear, was to stress an alternative possibility: that is, that manual workers and their families might expand their social horizons considerably, and notably in the sphere of consumption, *without* either the structure or the content of their aspirations becoming middle-class in any meaningful sense of the term. Thus, in designing our own study, we gave the investigation of our affluent workers' aims and hopes for the future a central place, and tried to ensure that we would be able to form some understanding both of the particular significance that our respondents themselves attached to their aspirations and of the relationship between their aspirations and the characteristic patterns of their social lives.

Furthermore, it was evident to us from our reading of previous studies

---

[1] As was observed in an early paper: 'What is a status symbol for whom depends entirely on the social universe to which a person orients himself, and this is not a simple function of the size of his pay packet. It is, in any case, sociology gone mad to assume that because people want goods of this kind [i.e. consumer durables] they always want them as status symbols. A washing machine is a washing machine is a washing machine.' (Lockwood, 'The "New Working Class" ', p. 253.)

that in evaluating data on aspirations in relation to the issue of *embourge-oisement*, the view taken of the essential points of difference between traditional working-class and middle-class social perspectives was a matter of crucial importance. In order, therefore, to make our own ideas in this respect as clear and explicit as possible, we attempted, in the light of available empirical material, to represent these two perspectives in ideal-type form as a preliminary to the analysis of our research findings. Before, then, we go on to review the data produced by our interviews, it will be appropriate to define here the benchmarks in relation to which, in our view, the findings in question can be most usefully assessed.[1]

First, we set out our conception of the traditional working-class perspective for which there is by now, we believe, a quite substantial basis in British sociological literature.[2]

Traditional working-class perspective

(i) The basic conception of the social order is a dichotomous one: society is divided into 'us' and 'them'. 'They' are persons in positions in which they can exercise power and authority over 'us'. The division between 'us' and 'them' is seen as a virtually unbridgeable one; people are born on one side of the line or the other and very largely remain there. The social circumstances an individual faces are thus 'given' facts of life and, apart perhaps from exceptional strokes of luck, these facts have to be accepted and 'put up with'.[3]

(ii) Consistently with this view of social circumstances as being more or less immutable—or at any rate as being unlikely to change much for the better—wants and expectations are themselves relatively fixed. The major economic concern is with being able to *maintain* a certain standard and style of living, not with the continuous advancement of consumption norms and widening of cultural experience. In a traditionalistic context, as Max Weber has written, 'A man does not "by nature" wish to earn

---

[1] The ideal-type constructions which follow may be regarded as developments of those essayed in Goldthorpe and Lockwood, 'Affluence and the British Class Structure', p. 147.

[2] As pointed out in a previous paper (Lockwood, 'Sources of Variation in Working Class Images of Society'), it is in fact important to distinguish *two* main types of working-class traditionalism—the 'proletarian' and the 'deferential'; here it would appear appropriate to concentrate on the former.

[3] Cf. Bott, *Family and Social Network*, ch. 6; and Hoggart, *The Uses of Literacy*, ch. 3. For comparable accounts from other societies, see O. E. Oeser and S. E. Hammond (eds.), *Social Structure and Personality in a City* (London, 1954), chs. 20–3; H. Popitz, H. P. Bahrdt, E. A. Jures and H. Kesting, *Das Gesellschaftsbild des Arbeiters* (Tubingen, 1957); and A. Willener, *Images de la société et classes sociales* (Berne, 1957).

more and more money, but simply to live as he is accustomed to live and to earn as much as is necessary for that purpose.'[1]

(iii) Complementary to the idea of 'putting up' with life is that of 'making the best of it'; that is, of living in and for the present. As Hoggart observes, 'working-class life puts a premium on the taking of pleasures now, discourages planning for some future good'.[2] This emphasis on the present and the lack of concern for 'planning ahead' are moreover encouraged by the view that there is in fact little to be done about the future, that it is not to any major extent under the individual's control. Fatalism, acceptance and an orientation to the present thus hold together as a mutually reinforcing set of attitudes.[3]

(iv) In so far as it is felt that purposive action can be effective, the emphasis is placed on action of a *collective* kind aimed at the protection of collective interests—trade unionism being, of course, the most developed form. A prime value is that set on mutual aid and group solidarity in the face of the vicissitudes of life and the domination which 'they' seek to impose. This value in turn confirms the shared, communal nature of social life and constitutes a further restraint on attempts by individuals to make themselves 'a cut above the rest'. Such attempts, in the form, say, of conspicuous consumption or occupational advance, are likely to be interpreted by the community as threats to its solidarity, as expressions of group or class disloyalty.[4] Even in the case of children, parental concern that they should 'do well' is confined to achievement within the context of working-class values and life-styles—as, for example, in becoming established in a 'trade' or a 'steady' job. Aspirations do not extend to levels of education and types of job which would result in children being taken away from their family and community in either a geographical or a social sense.[5]

In specifying the corresponding ideal-type for the middle class we have far less research material to guide us. However, that which is available

---

[1] *The Protestant Ethic and the Spirit of Capitalism* (trans. T. Parsons, London, 1947), p. 59. Cf. F. Zweig, *The British Worker* (London, 1952), ch. 8, 'The Traditional Standard of Living'; also Dennis *et al.*, *Coal is Our Life*, pp. 137–40, and Hoggart, *The Uses of Literacy*, p. 58.

[2] Hoggart, *The Uses of Literacy*, p. 105.

[3] *Ibid*, pp. 109–11; see also Zweig, *The British Worker*, ch. 17, and the several studies referred to in Klein, *Samples from English Cultures*, vol. I, pp. 193–7.

[4] Cf. Dennis *et al.*, *Coal is Our Life*, pp. 31–2, 79–82; and Hoggart, *The Uses of Literacy*, pp. 64–5. There are a number of accounts of reluctance among industrial workers of a traditional type to take up supervisory positions because of the disloyalty this would imply. Cf. the discussion in *IAB*, pp. 121–2.

[5] Cf. F. M. Martin, 'Some Subjective Aspects of Social Stratification', in D. V. Glass (ed.), *Social Mobility in Britain* (London, 1954), pp. 68–70.

suggests, with some consistency, a configuration of beliefs and values that is in almost point by point contrast with the working-class pattern.

Middle-class perspective

(i) The basic conception of the social order is a hierarchical one: society is divided into a series of levels or strata differentiated in terms of the life-styles and associated prestige of their members. The structure is, however, seen as a relatively 'open' one: given ability and the appropriate moral qualities—determination, perseverance, etc.—individuals can, and do, move up the hierarchy.[1] What a man achieves in the end depends primarily on what he 'makes of himself'. Moreover, it is felt that the individual has an obligation to assume responsibility for his own life and welfare and to *try* to 'get on in the world' as far as he can.

(ii) Consistently with the notion of a social ladder that all have opportunity to climb, wants and expectations are, from a middle-class standpoint, capable of continuous enlargement. The typical objective is to keep up a progressive improvement in consumption standards and, correspondingly, a steady ascent in terms of prestige and the quality of lifestyle. From the point of view of the individual or family, it is in fact a key expectation that such an advance *will* occur—that careers will progress, seniority grow, incomes rise, and so on.[2]

(iii) The emphasis placed on 'getting on' and the expectation that over time advancement will in some degree occur together imply, on the part of the individual or family, a marked orientation towards the future. Major importance is attached to looking and planning ahead and, where necessary, to making present sacrifices in order to ensure greater advantages or benefits at a later stage. Such deferring of gratification—say, in the furtherance of a career or business undertaking—is approved of as a matter of morality as well as of expediency.[3]

(iv) The middle-class social ethic is thus an essentially individualistic one: the prime value is that set on individual achievement. Achievement is taken as the crucial indicator of the individual's moral worth. However, achievement is also regarded as a family concern: parents feel an obligation to try to give their children a 'better start in life' than they them-

[1] Cf. Bott, *Family and Social Network*, ch. 6; and Willener, *Images de la société et classes sociales*, pp. 170-4.
[2] For an analysis of the development of such normative expectations among the nineteenth-century urban middle class, see J. A. Banks, *Prosperity and Parenthood* (London, 1954); and for a discussion of the idea of 'career advance' which 'permeates the whole middle-class life style' see Colin Bell, *Middle Class Families* (London, 1968), pp. 13-20.
[3] Cf. Martin, 'Some Subjective Aspects of Social Stratification', pp. 73-5.

selves enjoyed, and then anticipate that their offspring will in turn attain to a still higher level in the social scale. In other words, the expectation is again that advancement will be continuous—between generations as well as in the course of individual lifetimes.[1] Indeed, through parental aspirations for children, it is possible for desires and hopes for the future to become virtually limitless.

As ideal types, the two perspectives we have outlined do of course involve exaggerations and thus overstate the degree of divergence that may often in fact be found as between specific working-class and middle-class groups. For example, within the traditional working class one could point to the 'respectable artisan' who sets great store on a well regulated existence and on looking ahead, and who has white-collar ambitions for his children; or, on the other hand, to the lower middle-class 'ritualist'—to use Merton's term—who has drawn in his horizons and has in effect rejected the obligation to continue to strive for material success.[2] Nevertheless, the empirical evidence that is reflected in the ideal types makes it clear enough that quite basic class differences in aspirations and in their conceptual contexts do exist; and, on our reading of this evidence, the models that we have formulated bring out the major dimensions on which these differences occur.

From material that we have already presented, it is evident that in one important respect at least the social perspectives of our Luton couples were some way from conforming to what we had depicted as the traditional working-class outlook. Our findings reveal that, far from their material wants and expectations being relatively static, the concern of our respondents to advance their living standards was in fact a key motivation in their lives. It is primarily in terms of this concern, it would seem, that we must understand their geographical and occupational mobility, their typical orientation to work and the kind of industrial employment in which they were currently engaged. We know that in order to have a better job or housing opportunities many of the couples we studied had been prepared to move away from their communities and families of origin; and that in order to increase their earnings many of our affluent workers had abandoned work that they had found relatively rewarding in itself for jobs that were highly paid largely as compensation for their inherent stresses and deprivations. Thus, we would argue, the individuals

[1] Cf. Bell, *Middle Class Families* and also 'Mobility and the Middle Class Family', *Sociology*, vol. 2, no. 2, (May 1968).
[2] R. K. Merton, *Social Theory and Social Structure* (Glencoe, 1957), pp. 149–53.

included in our critical case may be regarded as having exceptionally powerful aspirations in the sphere of consumption, even in comparison with other samples from the new working class that have been described in previous enquiries. In particular, they would appear distinctive in the extent to which they have declined to view the future in a fatalistic way but have rather formed projects for their material advancement which have entailed such initiatives as migration and job changes aimed at 'following the money'. In fact, as a result of the way our study was designed, we have a sample that is in some degree self-selected on the basis of such initiatives.

Given, then, that in terms of their aspirations as consumers, at any rate, the couples we interviewed were largely free from traditionalistic restraints and had moreover been often prepared to pursue new goals and standards in a purposive manner, the crucial question can now be broached of the typical concomitants of these attributes. Were expanded economic aspirations—and the actual achievement of these to some extent—usually associated with some more general shift in social values and norms, and one involving the acceptance of specifically middle-class models and reference groups? Or, to put the most sharply opposing view, had the quest for affluence resulted in little more than the adaptation to changed economic and physical conditions of what was still a recognisably working-class outlook?

In the main, as we shall now seek to show, our findings bring us closer to the second of these alternatives than to the first. The social horizons of the members of our Luton sample certainly prove to be wider than those we have taken as characteristic of the traditional worker, and in other respects apart from material standards of living. However, it is also evident from the results of our enquiry, first, that the aspirations of our respondents were still in important ways shaped and defined by the social realities of their position as manual wage workers—that is to say, by their distinctive class situation; secondly, that their more 'middle-class' aspirations were often not held with any great belief in the possibility that they would be realised or were not associated with attitudes and behaviour most conducive their realisation; and thirdly, that only very rarely were aspirations specifically focused on status enhancement in the sense of there being a desire to emulate, and to gain the acceptance of, persons regarded as belonging to a superior status group. In sum, our findings again point to the inapplicability of the *embourgeoisement* thesis to the case we studied.

In substantiating the above claims, we can usefully begin by referring back to the data on our respondents' aspirations in work which we have already considered in chapter 3. In the present context, these data have a twofold significance.

On the one hand, the nature of our affluent workers' response to the idea of promotion—or of starting their own businesses—brings out well both the way in which certain aspirations may be held with relatively little conviction as to their plausibility and, more importantly, the way in which aspirations can be thus weakened, or indeed inhibited altogether, by the severity of the objective barriers to advancement that the individual faces. As we earlier argued, on the basis of marked contrasts in the attitudes of our manual and white-collar samples towards promotion, the middle-class conception of 'getting on' through a career can be of little relevance in relation to the typical life-chances of largely unqualified rank-and-file industrial workers employed in modern, large-scale plants.[1]

On the other hand, the very general and frequently optimistic aspirations of our affluent workers for yet greater consumer power and higher living standards undoubtedly testify to some sort of 'revolution of rising expectations' but, at the same time, also reveal the extent to which these men still envisage material advancement as an essentially collective rather than individual process. Although many of them had at some point in the past taken action as individuals to improve their economic position—and with some success—they gave little emphasis to self help of this kind so far as their future progress was concerned. One statistic that we have given previously will bear repetition in this connection: that is, that of those men in our sample who anticipated a rising standard of living in the years immediately ahead (two-thirds of the total) only *nine* saw this as resulting from any form of improvement in their individual situation. The importance attached by the majority to the economic fortunes of the country as a whole or of their particular firms or industries reflects the fact that for these workers generally, as they themselves largely recognised, the influence that they could personally exert over their own economic futures, though not perhaps insignificant, was none the less strictly limited.

The further implications of this situation become evident if we move our attention from our respondents as wage earners in industrial enterprises and consider them rather as members of families, understood as

[1] Moreover, it may be added that among those of our respondents who were attracted to the idea of promotion, some sizable proportion appeared not to see this as a means of 'getting on' in career terms so much as a way of escaping from the dilemma of having to forfeit immediate satisfactions from work in order to obtain a level of earnings appropriate to their out-plant objectives. (See *IAB*, pp. 125–7.) In other words, even where manual and white-collar workers are alike in wanting promotion, the meanings of their aspirations may differ significantly.

decision-making units in the field of spending and saving. As consumers, it would seem that our affluent workers and their wives often held aspirations of a virtually open-ended kind: certainly, in this respect they cannot be thought of as any less ambitious than the couples in our white-collar sample. However, there are a number of further findings that emerge from our research which suggest that, as regards the *manner* in which the economic goals of the family are actually pursued, appreciable differences remain between white-collar norms and practices and those exhibited by many of the manual couples in the case we studied. In part, such differences may no doubt be attributable to the persistence among these couples of traditional attitudes and associated 'lags' in social and economic skills; but in part too, we would argue, they must be related to other abiding and more fundamental differences between manual and white-collar workers that are of a specifically class kind.

To begin with, we may observe that, in comparison with our white-collar sample, our affluent workers and their wives were clearly less likely to discuss their family finances together and to try to plan these over time. In view of their affluence and the degree of confidence they felt in the security of their employment,[1] these couples were obviously under little pressure to follow the day-to-day pattern of family economy often imposed upon manual workers whose incomes are low and uncertain: in fact, 60% reported that they saved regularly—the same proportion as in the white-collar sample—and, as we have noted, there were few differences between the two samples in the numbers having accounts with building societies or savings banks.[2] Nevertheless, in the case of our manual couples it appeared that regular saving was not at all closely associated with financial planning in the sense of considering saving and spending decisions in a relatively long-term way.

As one of a set of questions on household financial arrangements, we asked our respondents: 'Do you and your wife discuss together how you should spend the money?' Where an affirmative answer was given, we then asked further: 'What sort of thing do you discuss?' and probed specifically to try to establish the degree of planning and kind of time perspectives that were involved. The data that were obtained are summarised in table 14. The most notable facts that emerge from this table are that only a quite small minority of our affluent workers and their wives attempted to plan their domestic expenditure in more than a short-term manner—that is, for more than three to four months ahead;

[1] See above, pp. 37–8.
[2] See above, p. 37.

and that more than half engaged in virtually no planning at all. On the other hand, in the case of our white-collar couples, the proportion of non-planners was appreciably less than the proportion reporting financial planning which entailed time perspectives of longer than three to four months. Relating our respondents' answers on planning to those they gave on saving, it would seem that among the manual couples saving was mainly undertaken in order to meet regular, usually weekly or monthly, commitments such as tradesmen's bills or hire purchase payments, or in a more or less *ad hoc* fashion with a view to the purchase of particular items —clothing, household equipment, leisure goods and so on.[1] In contrast, a sizable proportion of the white-collar couples appeared to think not simply in terms of 'what to buy next' or of 'what to do with the money in hand' (phrases which were often used by our affluent workers) but to be concerned rather with deciding on some overall order of priority in their various consumption wants and on a way of allocating their resources accordingly over a quite lengthy time scale.[2]

TABLE 14. *Planning of family finances*

	Manual couples	White-collar couples
	Percentage	
No planning other than to provide for payment of regular bills or for holiday expenses	55	29
Short-term planning: usually with purchase of only one or two items in mind; time-perspective of up to 3–4 months	19	17
Long-term planning: usually with a number of possible purchases or commitments in mind; time-perspective of longer than 3–4 months	13	42
No information	13	13
TOTALS	100	101

[1] The only form of more obviously long-term saving that seemed of any importance among our manual couples was saving for retirement or for a 'rainy day'—mentioned by 41%; the sums involved, however, were usually small.

[2] In this connection it may be added that, in general, our white-collar couples appeared to manage their financial affairs on a 'joint' basis to an appreciably greater extent than did our manual couples. Taking into account their practices concerning housekeeping money, use of wife's earnings (if any) and the payment of bills and accounts, we classified 72% of the latter couples as having more or less 'segregated', and 28% more or less 'joint', financial arrangements; whereas with the white-collar sample, the corresponding figures were 56% and 44%. At the same time, though, it is evident that only a minority of our affluent workers and their wives managed their family finances on the extremely segregated basis that has been regularly described in studies of traditional working-class life. See, for example, Zweig, *The British Worker*, pp. 72–5; Dennis *et al.*, *Coal is Our Life*, pp. 186–90; and Michael Young, 'Distribution of Income Within the Family', *British Journal of Sociology*, vol. 3, no. 4 (December 1952).

Divergences in characteristic attitudes and behaviour of the kind in evidence here cannot be separated, we believe, from differences which still widely persist between the conditions of service and occupational opportunities of manual and white-collar employees: most notably, from the fact that the latter are far more likely to have genuine career chances or at any rate to be able to look forward to steadily rising incomes from salary increments quite apart from any general wage and salary movements. Such prospects encourage and facilitate the adoption of a relatively long-term financial outlook much more than do those of the rank-and-file manual worker, who is primarily dependent upon general wage increases for his material advancement and whose further income will tend thus to be less progressive and also less certain and predictable—even assuming that his continuity of employment is unbroken. The orientations individuals have towards the future may be expected to display a certain degree of consistency; and it would thus be surprising if the differing perspectives associated with 'careers' and 'jobs' in the world of work did *not* have their counterparts, in terms of differing approaches to saving and spending, within the context of the family economy.[1]

One other important way in which we can show that the family 'policy' of our affluent workers and their wives remains distinguishable from that characteristic of lower middle-class groups concerns the limitation of family size. It now seems fairly well established that in Great Britain, as in most other advanced industrial societies, lower white-collar strata have particularly low rates of fertility—lower than those of either manual workers on the one hand or of superior administrative, managerial and professional grades on the other.[2] The explanation of this phenomenon that has found widest acceptance is that lower white-collar couples tend to be highly status-conscious and thus restrict the size of their families stringently in order to conserve their resources for forms of consumption consistent with their status aspirations, and also to give the children they do have the best possible chances for achieving further mobility.[3] Con-

---

[1] It is interesting to note that as regards the planning of family finances we do not find the usual tendency for those of our manual couples with the more extensive white-collar affiliations to come closer than the rest of our sample to the white-collar pattern of behaviour. This would support the idea that what is important in this connection is not so much subcultural influences as the 'logic' of existing class situations.

[2] See Dennis H. Wrong, 'Class Fertility Differentials in England and Wales', *The Millbank Memorial Fund Quarterly*, vol. 38 (January 1960) and D. V. Glass, 'Fertility trends in Europe since the Second World War', *Population Studies*, vol. 12, no. 1 (March 1968).

[3] Cf. Charles F. Westoff, 'The Changing Focus of Differential Fertility Research: the Social Mobility Hypothesis', in J. J. Spengler and O. D. Duncan (eds.), *Population Theory and Policy* (Glencoe, 1956).

sequently, if affluent manual workers of the type we studied are also powerfully motivated by status considerations, we might expect this to be revealed through reproductive behaviour that approximates the lower middle-class pattern. Zweig has, in fact, singled out the tendency to have smaller families as a distinctive feature of the new working class which, in his view, is now moving towards the acceptance of middle-class values and social norms. 'Family planning', he writes, 'is a firmly established and widespread practice ... Once the worker has discovered that he can control the size of his family, the conflict between his desire for children and the fear of being over-burdened assumes its full force.' And he goes on to assert that 'family planning seems to be one of the most important vehicles of prosperity in the working classes, or at least it is so regarded by workers'.[1] However, we know of no evidence—Zweig himself does not produce any—to show that in the recent past family planning among the more prosperous sections of the working class has resulted in their fertility being brought closer to the level of lower white-collar strata. Furthermore, the relevant information that we obtained from our sample of manual couples does not indicate that in their case such a reduction in fertility was taking place.

Table 15 gives data on size of families among both our manual and white-collar couples, as related to duration of marriage. It can be seen that the former have clearly more children than the latter, and that, in particular, they do not restrict their fertility nearly so tightly during the first decade or so of marriage.[2] By the time all the wives concerned have completed their reproductive periods it may well be that the fertility gap between the two samples will have narrowed somewhat as a result of the white-collar couples having more children later on in their marriages. But this of course in no way detracts from the significance of the current differences that the table reveals. Moreover, it must be thought very likely that even in terms of completed family size an appreciable gap will remain: for the further important point that emerges from table 15 is that, on the figures given, our affluent workers and their wives show no sign of being any less fertile than couples of skilled or semi-skilled manual status in the country at large. Indeed, the indications are, if anything, to the contrary, in so far as close comparisons with Census data can be made.[3]

[1] *The Worker in an Affluent Society*, p. 14.
[2] Even though on average the white-collar couples had married at a later age than the manual workers and their wives. It may also be added here that the differences in family size between the two samples still persist when current income is held constant.
[3] Compare the data given in the 1961 Census (England and Wales), *Fertility Tables* (London, H.M.S.O., 1966), table 10.

TABLE 15. Family size by duration of marriage

Duration of marriage* (completed years)	Manual couples							White-collar couples						
	Number of couples	Number of children					Average per couple	Number of couples	Number of children					Average per couple
		Percentage							Percentage					
		0	1	2	3+				0	1	2	3+		
0 – 5	36	17	50	30	3	100	1·21	12	50	25	25	0	100	0·75
6 – 11	76	7	21	42	30	100	2·18	18	33	39	11	17	100	1·20
12+	117	8	25	38	29	100	2·16	24	21	33	25	17	100	1·77
All	229	9	28	38	25	100	2·02	54	32	33	20	15	100	1·35

* With a negligible number of exceptions, wives were still in the reproductive period: i.e. when interviewed their years of married life were virtually all years 'at risk'.

We can, then, at all events claim that the workers in our Luton sample did not display any *particularly* marked concern to restrict the size of their families in the interests of increasing their consumer power; and that in the matter of family planning their norms and practices were still apparently at some variance with those typical of lower white-collar groups.

The major consequences of differences in fertility, as regards the family economy, were undoubtedly those felt through the relative ability of wives to contribute to income. Our affluent workers' wives had tended to leave gainful employment fairly early in married life in order to start their families and were thus faced with lengthy periods of active, if not necessarily intensive motherhood, during which full-time work at least was difficult to maintain. On the other hand, the lower fertility of the wives of our white-collar workers meant that they were much freer to work, especially in the early years of marriage, and it would in fact seem that the wife's ability to supplement her husband's earnings during these years was often crucial in enabling a couple to sustain a middle-class way of life.[1] The contrasts in family policy that are evident here can therefore be regarded as illustrating further the greater propensity of our white-collar couples to take the long-term view and to organise their lives consistently with an ordered set of objectives. However, it must be noted that the kind of policy which these couples favoured can be seen as one closely geared to the expectation that the husband's income will rise appreciably over time, and that the rationality of such a policy would be far less apparent in cases where, as with most manual couples, the early years of marriage coincide with the husband's peak earning capacity. Again, we would argue that it is mistaken to think simply in terms of our affluent workers and their wives having had as yet insufficient time to learn middle-class habits of prudence and foresight: the implications of their class situation as rank-and-file wage earners also remain of major relevance.

Following on this discussion of consumer aspirations and related issues of 'family planning'—in both the more general and specific senses—we may now move on to consider a further important aspect of our respondents' orientation to the future; namely, the aspirations that they held for their children, educationally and occupationally.

In the course of our 'home' interviews, we asked all couples with one or more children not yet at secondary school about what type of secondary

---

[1] As noted earlier (n. 3, p. 98 above) at the time of our interviews, the wives of our white-collar workers were more likely to be working, and to be doing so full-time, than wives in the manual sample. It was the wives' contribution that accounted for the slightly higher average family income of the white-collar couples.

school they would best like a child of theirs to attend. Where couples had one or more children already at secondary school, we also investigated the kinds of occupation that parents hoped their children would enter.[1] The main results that were thus produced are given in table 16.

From this table it is fairly apparent that the aspirations that our affluent workers and their wives held for their children were at only a slightly lower level than those of the white-collar sample. To a preponderant extent their preferences were for selective secondary schools—mostly, in fact, for grammar schools—and nonmanual occupations were clearly favoured over manual ones. Moreover, if we compare our findings in this respect with those of earlier studies that have reported on working-class parental aspirations, the ambitiousness of our Luton couples is further underlined.

For example, in Martin's enquiry into parental preferences in secondary education, carried out in a prosperous part of Hertfordshire in 1952, only 48% of parents of skilled manual status wanted a grammar school education for their children, as against 23% preferring technical schools and 17% modern schools; while for parents of semi-skilled or unskilled status the corresponding figures were 43%, 19% and 24%.[2] The results of more recent work by Douglas (1958) would suggest that, as might be expected, working-class aspirations in this area are rising; but even so, the proportion of mothers in a national sample who hoped for a grammar school place for their children was no greater than 58% among those graded as 'upper working class' (largely the wives of skilled workers) and 49% among the residual 'lower working class' group.[3] Thus, even if it is accepted that working-class parents are now generally widening their educational horizons, the couples we studied must still be seen as being well in the lead of this movement. Furthermore, as regards occupational aspirations, our Luton workers would appear to be yet more clearly drawn from a 'vanguard' population. Another of Martin's investigations, made in Greenwich and Hertford in 1950, showed that only 31% of manual

[1] Each of these questions was asked, where appropriate, about only one child per couple: i.e. the first about the oldest boy (or girl if no boy) not yet at secondary school; the second about the oldest boy (or girl if no boy) still at secondary school.

[2] F. M. Martin, 'An Inquiry into Parents' Preferences in Secondary Education', in Glass (ed.), *Social Mobility in Britain*, table 3, p. 163. A further enquiry a year later in the Middlesbrough area revealed grammar school preferences on the part of 53% of parents of skilled status and 48% of those of semi- or unskilled status. See J. E. Floud, A. H. Halsey and F. M. Martin, *Social Class and Educational Opportunity* (London, 1957), p. 82.

[3] J. W. B. Douglas, *The Home and the School* (London, 2nd ed., 1967), p. 75. If we divide our affluent workers in terms of skill, so as to make possible somewhat closer comparisons with Martin's and Douglas' data, we find that the proportion of parents hoping for their children to go to grammar (or private) school is 83% among the craftsmen and setters and 59% among the semi-skilled men.

TABLE 16. Parental aspirations for children

Manual couples

Preferred type of secondary school

Percentage

Preferences expressed for	Private	Grammar	Technical	Modern	Other D.K.		N
Boys	4	69	14	6	8	101	80
Girls	7	55	22	10	7	101	60
All	5	63	17	8	8	100	140*

Preferred type of occupation

Percentage

Preferences expressed for	Higher professional, managerial, etc.	Other white-collar	Intermediate	Skilled manual	Semi-skilled manual	None, D.K.		N
Boys	16	35	3	26	0	19	99	31
Girls	0	56	15	7	4	19	101	27
All	9	45	9	17	2	19	101	58†

White-collar couples

Preferred type of secondary school

Percentage

Preferences expressed for	Private	Grammar	Technical	Modern	Other D.K.		N
Boys	5	79	5	5	5	99	19
Girls	0	71	14	14	0	99	7
All	4	77	8	8	4	101	26

Preferred type of occupation

Percentage

Preferences expressed for	Higher professional, managerial, etc.	Other white-collar	Intermediate	Skilled manual	Semi-skilled manual	None, D.K.		N
	17	50	0	8	0	25	100	12‡

* By error, data were not obtained from 29 couples whose children were all under the age of five.
† By error, data were not obtained for 5 couples.
‡ Preferences expressed for 3 boys and for 9 girls.

workers would like to see their sons in white-collar jobs; comparably Swift reports that in an enquiry in the North of England in the early 1960s the 'occupational horizons' of 60% of working-class parents with sons were limited to the idea that their children should 'get a trade'; and among a sample of manual workers in the Medway Towns studied by Toomey as late as 1967, still only 35% wanted their sons to go into non-manual work on leaving school.[1]

What then are the conclusions that we should draw from our findings on parental aspirations? This is again an area in which, obviously, the perspectives of our affluent workers and their wives diverge notably from the traditional working-class pattern: but what precisely is the meaning that these aspirations carry? Do they in fact reflect fading or thwarted ambitions for white-collar status on the part of parents which are now being displaced onto their offspring; or is their significance one that can be explicated with little reference to status consciousness in any form?

In attempting to decide this issue, we can turn to the further information that we collected on the reasons that parents gave for the educational and occupational preferences that they expressed. In the case of secondary school preferences, the material is not in itself particularly helpful: those parents who wished for their children to attend selective schools predominantly explained this in terms of the better education, the higher level of qualifications and the greater opportunities for advanced education that could thus be obtained.[2] One point of interest is that only four couples out of a total of 140 made any mention of considerations of prestige. Much more revealing, however, are the reasons that were given for occupational aspirations. Most frequently, these related to two aspects of the job or type of job that was preferred: its economic rewards and prospects, and its inherent attractions either in general or to the particular child in question. Of the couples who had formed fairly specific occupational

---

[1] Martin, 'Some Subjective Aspects of Social Stratification', table 15, p. 69; D. F. Swift, 'Social Class, Mobility–Ideology and 11+ Success', *British Journal of Sociology*, vol. 18, no. 2 (June 1967); Derek Toomey, personal communication about work in progress at the University of Bradford. It should be noted that the studies in question here differ in their focus and methods and most importantly perhaps in regard to the ages and school career stage of the children about whom parents were asked. Nevertheless, taken together their results make it fairly clear that the aspirations of our respondents, for their sons at least, were of a relatively elevated kind. The findings which come closest to matching ours are those reported by Runciman for a national sample (1962) in which, among manual workers and their wives aged 21–45, 47% said that they would prefer a son of theirs to choose a nonmanual rather than a manual job. However, the question was not apparently limited to those couples who were parents or who had sons. See W. G. Runciman, *Relative Deprivation and Social Justice* (London, 1966), pp. 233–5.

[2] Such reasons accounted for 68% of all reasons given.

aspirations for their offspring, 41% explained these by reference, in part at least, to considerations of the first kind, and 38% by reference to considerations of the second kind.[1] In contrast, a concern with prestige or status enhancement was, as in the expression of school preferences, relatively little in evidence—being discernible in only 19% of the answers given.[2] What was apparently being emphasised, in other words, was not the social importance of getting into white-collar employment but rather the importance to the child as an individual of having work which would be as rewarding as possible to him, whether economically or otherwise. Indeed, the specific jobs that were most often mentioned were ones that were approved of on grounds of *both* their economic *and* their inherent attractions. For example, in the case of boys, clerical and administrative work was little favoured, and the jobs that were most often singled out were ones such as 'electronics engineer', 'industrial designer' and 'draughtsman'—jobs, that is, which were seen as guaranteeing a sound economic future 'in the scientific age' (as one man put it) and which at the same time were thought to be 'worth while', to 'give scope for ability' and 'enable you to really accomplish something'.[3]

In general, then, in the way in which they discussed their aspirations for their children, the couples in our sample did not give the impression that vicarious status striving influenced their hopes and preferences to any great degree. Indeed, in so far as any connection may be traced between their own life experiences and their ambitions for their offspring this would appear to be of a clearly different kind. The relevant experience in this respect, we would suggest, was not the failure of our affluent workers to secure white-collar status, but rather their confrontation with the distinctively working-class dilemma that we stressed in chapter 3: namely, that of having to choose between work which provided them with some degree of intrinsic satisfaction and work which afforded the highest going rate of economic return.[4] If one accepts the subjective significance of this dilemma in the case of a sizable proportion of our respondents, then it is readily understandable that, for their children, they should hope

[1] It is possible that this underestimates somewhat the real concern with economic rewards, since there was some tendency for references to the suitability of the job to the child to be made more often in the case of younger children; i.e. those furthest from the actual point of choice.

[2] Since only 47 couples are involved here, numbers are too small for much to be said about whether aspirations for manual and nonmanual jobs were explained differently; but some tendency existed for the latter to be associated more with status advantages.

[3] In the case of girls, the kinds of job most often referred to were quasi-professional ones, such as nursing or (chiefly junior school) teaching.

[4] See above, p. 64.

for occupations that offered a high level of material reward *and* of inherent attractiveness, and for the type of education that is generally necessary in order to open the way into such occupations. While our interview findings cannot demonstrate the actual extent to which our respondents' parental aspirations were thus shaped, they do at least provide instances in which parents themselves spelled out the logic of their aspirations much on the lines that we have indicated.[1] Moreover, the essential point is in any case clear enough: that for workers such as those we studied, there are adequate reasons for seeing many 'middle-class' occupations as highly desirable for their children (just as there are for wanting many kinds of consumer goods) that have little at all to do with prestige or with status implications. And in attempting to account for such aspirations, the hypothesis of vicarious status striving is neither the most economical nor the best supported one.

In addition to raising the question of the meaning of our affluent workers' ambitions for their children, it is also relevant to enquire to what extent these ambitions appeared likely to be fulfilled. Was the relatively high level of aspiration on the part of parents in fact being matched by a correspondingly high level of achievement on the part of their offspring in the educational and occupational fields? The best basis for an answer is provided by the data of table 17, which shows the record of those of our respondents' children who had reached secondary school age or who had already taken up full-time employment.

The information presented is sufficient to establish that these children at least have *not* performed at all exceptionally. Indeed the proportion having gained entry into grammar schools is somewhat *lower* than one would expect on the basis of results from national surveys.[2] Thus, as a comparison of tables 16 and 17 makes evident, the discrepancy between parental aspirations and children's performance is often quite striking. For instance, more than 6 out of 10 of the couples we interviewed expressed a preference for grammar school education, but so far less than 1 child out of 10 has achieved this. Again, half the couples wanted to see their sons in white-collar jobs and only a quarter limited their aspirations to manual work; yet among those of their sons who have entered the

[1] For example: 'I'd like a job in engineering [for son] because it's got good money and a future, and it's work worth doing. Not like me earning my money on a job I'm glad to get away from.' 'I'd to give up the job I liked because there wasn't the money in it. I want him [son] to have a job that's right for him [designing] and one he can get a good living from.'

[2] Cf. the data brought together in Alan Little and John Westergaard, 'The Trend of Class Differentials in Educational Opportunity in England and Wales', *British Journal of Sociology*, vol. 15, no. 4 (December 1964).

TABLE 17. Children's educational and occupational achievement

Children of manual couples

Type of secondary school attended

	Private	Grammar	Technical	Non-selective	Other		N*
			Percentage				
Boys	0	6	10	79	4	99	67
Girls	0	13	12	74	2	101	69
All	0	9	11	77	3	100	136

Type of occupation entered

	Higher professional, managerial etc.	Other white-collar	Intermediate	Skilled manual	Semi- and unskilled manual		N†
			Percentage				
Boys	0	18	7	57	18	100	28
Girls	0	58	15	0	27	100	26
All	0	37	11	30	21	99	54

Children of white-collar couples

Type of secondary school attended

	Private	Grammar	Technical	Non-selective	Other		N*
			Percentage				
Boys	0	33	11	44	11	99	9
Girls	8	33	0	58	0	99	12
All	5	33	5	53	5	101	21

Type of occupation entered

	Higher professional, managerial etc.	Other white-collar	Intermediate	Skilled manual	Semi- and unskilled manual		N†
			Percentage				
All	57	14	14	14	0	99	7

* N = all children of secondary school age or over.

† N = all children who have left full-time education.

labour market, under a fifth have secured white-collar employment and manual work is the lot of three-quarters.[1] In the case of our white-collar sample, we find that discrepancies of the kind in question also exist, but that they are clearly less extreme; in the educational field at least, it can be seen that our white-collar workers' children are appreciably more successful than those of our manual couples in living up to what their parents hope for them, even though they too will—inevitably—disappoint to some extent.

Why then, we may ask, should our affluent workers' ambitions for their children appear so unlikely to reach fulfilment? Is it that the aspirations they express—like, say, their aspirations for promotion—are often not very serious ones; or is the explanation to be given more in terms of the ability—or rather lack of ability—of the couples we studied to help bring about that which they hoped for?

As regards the first of these possibilities, we have some evidence of a directly relevant kind. Following on our questions on parental aspirations, we asked our respondents how they rated the chances that their children would get the sort of education or occupation that they wished for.[2] For the most part, the answers given proved to be of a not unhopeful kind. For example, among those parents who stated a preference for a selective secondary school a majority of 65% put the chances of their children gaining admission to such a school at 'about fifty-fifty'—this being perhaps the 'easy' answer to give; but, more significantly, only 16% believed that there was 'not much chance' while 19% thought their child's success in this respect was 'more or less certain'. In the case of occupational aspirations, none of the couples wishing for their children to achieve higher grade white-collar jobs was confident that this would

---

[1] In the case of daughters, the gap between levels of occupational aspirations and actual achievement is clearly less than with sons, but at the same time it is more than it appears from tables 16 and 17: within the 'other white-collar' category, the kinds of occupation most frequently hoped for were, as we have earlier noted, quasi-professional ones, whereas those that had been obtained were in fact mostly secretarial or other office jobs.

It should be said that the children represented in our information on educational and occupational achievement are not, of course, the same ones as those concerned in our data on aspirations; but even making all reasonable allowance for the fact that the latter children may do somewhat better at school or in work than their older brothers and sisters, it is still highly probable that a considerable discrepancy between aspirations and achievement will remain.

[2] The exact questions were: 'What sort of chance do you think there is that [name of child] will get to a [preferred type] school: would you say it was more or less certain, about fifty-fifty, or not much chance?'; and 'What sort of chance do you think there is that [name of child] will get that sort of job [i.e. sort preferred by parents]: would you say it was more or less certain, about fifty-fifty or not much chance?'

happen; but, on the other hand, among those parents whose sights were set on other white-collar or 'intermediate' occupations, only 20% took the clearly pessimistic view and as many were highly optimistic.

Thus, it would appear that in the main the high aspirations for their children that our affluent workers and their wives expressed were not, in their view, merely wishful thinking, but were held with some belief in the possibility that they could be realised. We may also note that other data from our interviews indicate that these aspirations were serious in the further sense that parents were for the most part ready to accept certain probable conditions or consequences of their offspring being successful— such as their having to spend three years at a university or to move away from their home and family in order to advance their careers.[1] The view one is led to is, therefore, that what was chiefly missing in the case of the couples we studied was neither seriousness of intention in their parental aspirations nor willingness to support their children's efforts, but rather certain dispositions and capacities necessary to make such support really effective. Such a conclusion can be strongly supported through a comparison of the answers given by our manual and white-collar couples to questions which we put to them with the aim of investigating the nature of their involvement in their children's education.

The first question was: 'Do you [i.e. husband and wife] discuss the children's education together?'; those couples who said that they did were then asked: 'What sort of things is it you talk about?' Later, we also asked: 'Do you think there is anything parents can do to help children do well in school?', and again parents who answered affirmatively were invited to elaborate on their replies.[2] In addition, in the course of enquiring into parental aspirations, we ascertained whether or not couples had ever discussed their hopes for their children with any of their teachers; and we also asked couples to pick out from a list of twelve school subjects the three which, in view of their aspirations, they regarded as being most

---

[1] When asked: 'Would you be prepared for [name of child] to spend three years at university if this was necessary for him/her to become a [preferred occupation]?' *all* couples with white-collar occupational aspirations for their children answered positively. All couples with a child at secondary school were further asked: 'Supposing you knew of a better job than he/she could get in Luton going in another part of the country, would you want him/her to go and take it, or would you rather he/she stayed in Luton?' Of those answering for sons, 80% were for taking the better job as against 7% for staying in Luton with 13% uncertain; while with those answering for daughters, the corresponding figures were 40% as against 28% with 32% uncertain.

[2] The first set of questions was put to all couples with one or more children at school (N = 203 manual; 35 white-collar); the second to all couples with children of whatever age (N = 210 manual; 37 white-collar).

important for their children.[1] In table 18 we provide a summary of the
responses that these several questions elicited.

From the data presented, a number of contrasts between our affluent
workers and their wives and the couples in our white-collar sample are at
once apparent. To begin with, it can be seen that among the white-collar

TABLE 18. *Parents' involvement in children's education*

	Manual couples Percentage	White-collar couples Percentage
Discuss children's education regularly—'how they are getting on', etc.	40	66
Believe they can do something to help children 'do well' in school		
in regard to school work specifically	54	70
in other ways	75	89
Have discussed aspirations for children with teachers*	27	45
Emphasise 'academic' rather than 'vocational' subjects as important for children to learn†	37	56

* In 16 cases this question was omitted by error in interviews with manual couples.

† In 10 cases this question was omitted by error in interviews with manual couples. The twelve
subjects, from which respondents were asked to choose three, were made up as follows.
'Academic' subjects: English literature, French, history, geography and science; 'vocational'
subjects: technical drawing, woodwork, typing, needlework and domestic science; and two
'intermediate' subjects: mathematics and art. Parents were classed as favouring an 'academic'
rather than a 'vocational' combination of subjects if they chose two or more 'academic'
subjects or one 'academic' subject plus the two 'intermediate' ones.

couples, two thirds reported regular discussion of their children's educational progress, whereas this was the case with only two-fifths of the
manual parents. Again, a large majority of the former couples believed that
they could help their children to 'do well' in school both through giving
assistance with school work and in less direct ways. But among the couples
in our manual sample, half felt unable to help with school work, and it may
be added that of the larger number who believed that they could help in
other ways, most referred simply to giving encouragement or to 'taking an
interest'. The white-collar parents, on the other hand, more often mentioned more specific forms of aid such as providing the right conditions

[1] These two questions followed those on parents' educational and occupational aspirations for
their children and were asked in regard to the same children (see note 1, p. 130 above). However, information on discussions with teachers was only sought in cases where parents had
expressed some fairly specific aspiration (N = 144 manual; 23 white-collar). The question on
school subjects was suggested to us by Professor Basil Bernstein, to whom we are duly grateful.

and atmosphere for study or fostering appropriate attitudes of respect for knowledge, curiosity about things and so on. What one may infer, then, is that the white-collar parents are, or at least feel, generally more familiar —more ' in touch '—with what is going on in their children's education and are thus more likely to think that they can play some positive part in increasing their children's chances of success. Similarly, the white-collar couples' greater readiness to consult with teachers on questions concerning their parental aspirations may be taken as further suggesting their closer identification with the school, and also their greater ability to make use of its services as an advisory agency. Finally, the fact that the white-collar couples did actually have a better understanding than our manual respondents of how the educational system works and of the connections between education and occupation is well brought out by the data on which school subjects were regarded as important.

As can be seen, in comparison with white-collar parents, our affluent workers and their wives were appreciably less likely to stress 'academic' subjects—English literature, French, history, geography or science—and were more likely to include in the subjects they picked out as important such more directly 'vocational' ones as technical drawing, woodwork, typing, needlework or domestic science. Moreover, this tendency persisted even where parents hoped for a grammar school education for their children or for a white-collar occupation which would normally call for a university or other higher-level academic training. In other words, there was frequent evidence of a lack of appreciation of the way in which types of secondary school differed in their functions and in the opportunities they offered, and of the nature of the educational requirements of particular kinds of job. For example, couples who were concerned that their daughters should win grammar school places quite often included among the subjects they thought it important for them to learn, typing or domestic science; and among parents who favoured careers for their sons in the field of electronics, technical drawing was in some cases regarded as an important subject while natural science was not. In the answers of our white-collar couples, it was notable that inappropriate choices of this kind were far less commonly encountered.

In sum, then, we may say that looking simply at the level of our affluent workers' aspirations for their children, and setting these alongside the findings of previous studies of working-class samples, there is an apparent indication of considerable normative convergence with white-collar groups. However, examination firstly of the motives and values that would seem to underlie these aspirations and, secondly, of the adequacy of our respondents' attitudes and actions in relation to their achievement is sufficient to show that highly significant normative differences still remain. And it is, of course, in the nature of differences of the kind in question that they tend to perpetuate themselves from generation to generation.[1]

Finally in this examination of the pattern of aspirations of our affluent workers, we may consider the results produced by several sets of questions in our interview schedule which were designed to bring to light any aspirations that our respondents might hold specifically for raising their status through greater contact with members of groups regarded as socially superior. We recognised that respondents might well be inhibited from expressing such ambitions in any outright manner (and might even be reluctant to admit them plainly to themselves) because of doubts about their own motives or fears of appearing 'snobbish'. Consequently, we adopted an oblique approach and at different points in the interview raised a number of topics in the discussion of which status aspirations, if they in fact existed, appeared likely to be revealed or at least suggested.

For example, after collecting information from respondents about their actual friendship relations, as reported on in the preceding chapter, we asked: 'Given a free choice, which of these kinds of people would you most like to have as your friends?' Respondents were then handed a card containing the following five descriptions:

People with a good education
People who have a bit of class about them
People with a similar background and outlook
People who are good company even if they can be a bit common at times
People who do interesting and responsible work.

What emerged was that a clear majority of the sample—59%—made the same choice: 'people with a similar background and outlook'. Moreover, the next most frequent choice, made by 26%, was 'people who are good company even if they can be a bit common at times'. In contrast, only 9%

[1] As would be expected, there is in all the data we have presented on parents' involvement in their children's education a tendency for those manual parents with extensive white-collar affiliations to come closer than the rest of the sample to the white-collar pattern. E.g. among the 57 couples with both familial and occupational white-collar connections, 50% discuss their children's education regularly; only 25% believe they can do nothing to help with school work (and 21% nothing to help in other ways); 34% have discussed their aspirations for their children with teachers; and 47% emphasise 'academic' rather than 'vocational' subjects. Furthermore, it is striking that of the children of these couples who have reached secondary school age, 19% have got to grammar school as compared with 11% of children of parents with either a familial or an occupational tie, *and no children at all* of parents with no white-collar affiliation.

of the sample favoured 'people who do interesting and responsible work'; only 6%, 'people with a good education'; and no more than 1%, 'people who have a bit of class about them'. In other words, there was little indication of any tendency among our affluent workers to regard as particularly desirable friends persons with superior status attributes.[1] On the contrary, they were far more likely to prefer persons who were much the same as themselves—meaning, it would seem, chiefly persons who were subculturally working class—or indeed individuals who might behave in ways actually unhelpful to status improvement.[2] We have previously shown that the friendship relations of the couples in our Luton sample were to a notable extent confined to other manual workers and their wives. It can now be seen as inappropriate to think of this situation as being primarily the result of white-collar exclusiveness. For little basis can be found for assuming that to gain a wider range of friends, including ones of middle-class status, was a goal that aroused any widespread interest or concern among the couples we studied.[3]

A similar attempt to unveil possible status aspirations was also made following on the questions contained in our interviews on membership of formal associations. We asked respondents: 'Are there any clubs or

[1] We would attach particular importance to the fact that such small numbers within our sample chose 'people who do interesting and responsible work' and 'people with a good education'—since these would appear very acceptable choices for respondents with covert or latent status ambitions.

[2] When respondents were asked to say why they made the choice they did and what kind of people they had in mind, the majority opting for 'people with a similar background and outlook' or 'people who are good company...' overwhelmingly referred to the importance of similarity in such respects as 'interests', 'the things you talk about', leisure pursuits, educational level and jobs; or to the importance of friends being 'sociable' and 'easy to get on with'. The people they had in mind they characterised in such terms as 'ordinary working men', 'the sort of people we live with every day', 'people at our level—not highbrows'.

Directly after this last item, we also asked respondents: 'And which of these kinds of people would you be most likely to be put off making friends with?'—offering a set of descriptions closely related to those used in asking about people who would be preferred as friends. Our analysis above is largely confirmed by the fact that the three descriptions which accounted for three-quarters of the sample were: 'people who talk about things I don't understand' (31%); 'people with a very different background and outlook' (22%) and 'people who live in a way that I'd find it hard to keep up with' (22%). In contrast, only 13% picked out 'people who're a bit common'. The least chosen description, however, was 'people whose work puts them in a different class' (10%). In so far as this result can be taken to mean that our respondents did not accord much salience to occupation *per se* as a determinant of lines of class division, it is of interest in relation to the discussion below (pp. 145–9) of their images of the class structure overall.

[3] Moreover, though, in this respect again it may be observed that systematic variation occurs within our sample in terms of couples' white-collar affiliations. Most notably, couples with both familial and occupational white-collar connections were twice as likely as couples with no such ties to prefer friends on grounds of their 'interesting and responsible work', 'good education' or 'bit of class'.

societies that you have ever wanted to join, but didn't?' Those answering 'yes' were then asked about the nature of the association or associations in question, and about why they did not become members. In fact, only 46 (20%) of our affluent workers and 33 (14%) of their wives reported unfulfilled ambitions in this respect. Furthermore, of the clubs and societies to which they referred less than a third were ones which, in terms of their social composition and functions, appeared at all likely to have status attractions; that is to say, ones with a sizable proportion of middle-class members and engaging in chiefly 'social' activities.[1] Consistently with this, among respondents' explanations of why they never came to join no more than nine cases could be found in which status uncertainty or status exclusiveness were as much as hinted at; and consistently with arguments previously advanced, the barriers to participation that were almost invariably mentioned were ones associated with work and family commitments—shifts, overtime, children, housework and so on.

As one other probe into the extent of specifically status aspirations among our affluent workers, we may turn to the set of questions that we put to them concerning their area of residence. To begin with, we asked our respondents to say which of the following descriptions best fitted the area they at present lived in:

A pretty rough area
An ordinary working-class area
A very mixed area
A nice quiet and respectable area
A rather select area.

It can be seen from table 19 that while a majority of respondents living on council estates—85%—see themselves as living in 'an ordinary working-class area' or 'a very mixed area', there is little tendency for those living in areas of middle-class status (largely private housing developments) to regard these as 'rather select'. A half still describe them as 'ordinary working-class' or as 'mixed', and most of the remainder opt for 'a nice quiet and respectable area'. Also shown in the table are the further results which were produced when respondents were asked: 'Do you like this part of Luton or would you like to live somewhere else?' First, it emerges that the council estate dwellers are no more likely to want to move than

---

[1] In terms of the classification of voluntary associations previously established (see appendix B) only 5 of the 83 associations mentioned in total were of type 1, 8 were of type 2 and 13 of type 4.

the couples living in the A and B grade areas: a large majority in both groups reported that they liked the part of Luton in which they presently lived. Moreover, it may be added that in explaining such a preference

TABLE 19. *Description given to present and desired areas of residence by status of present area**

| Description given to present area of residence | Status of area of residence | | | |
	A and B 'middle class' (N = 126)	C council estate (N = 85)	D and E inferior areas (N = 18)	All (N = 229)
	Percentage			
'A pretty rough area'	0	1	0	1
'An ordinary working-class area'	26	47	28	34
'A very mixed area'	25	38	28	30
'A nice quiet and respectable area'	43	14	44	32
'A rather select area'	6	0	0	3
TOTALS	100	100	100	100
% wishing to move	21 (N = 27)	18 (N = 15)	39 (N = 7)	21 (N = 49)

Description given of area of residence preferred†	Percentage			
'An ordinary working-class area' *or* 'A very mixed area'	22	27	0	20
'A nice quiet and respectable area'	37	60	100	53
'A rather select area'	22	13	0	16
D.K.	19	0	0	10
TOTALS	100	100	100	99

* For details of this classification, see n. 2, p. 111 above.
† No respondent described the area of residence he would have preferred as 'a pretty rough area'.

couples in the latter group were in fact little more inclined than those in the former (26% as against 20%) to refer to status considerations[1] and that reasons of this kind which were given were very largely ones that turned on contrasts between 'rough' and 'respectable' rather than between 'working class' and 'middle class'. Similarly, when those respondents who wanted to move were asked which of the previously supplied

[1] In both groups a large majority explained their preference for their present area of residence in terms of its physical characteristics—'away from the centre of town', 'near to the open country', 'plenty of space for the children', etc.

143

descriptions they would give to the area they aspired to, it can be seen that only 8 out of the 49 (16%) chose a 'rather select area', and that 'respectability' was again the major concern.

So far, then, as we can tell from a variety of questions included in our interviews, our affluent workers and their wives were not for the most part highly status-conscious and, more specifically, appeared only rarely to have adopted white-collar or other middle-class reference groups as the basis of 'social' aspirations. In so far as status concerns were apparent, they seemed most likely to involve a negative rather than a positive reference group—namely, that of the lower strata within the working class. However, such an outlook was not strongly in evidence, and it must in any case be remembered that distinctions such as that between 'rough' and 'respectable' are in no way new but have rather been observed in a variety of traditional working-class communities.[1]

Thus, from these and from our other findings reviewed earlier in this chapter, we can only conclude that among the sample we drew from our critical case there was in fact little sign of Abrams' 'middle-class' workers, of Crosland's workers with a 'middle-class psychology' or of Lipset's 'aspiring workers' who 'identify with the upper strata'.[2] If therefore the possible importance of these social types is still to be taken seriously, the onus is, in our view, now squarely with the writers in question to do what they failed to do in the first place: that is, to indicate in what social *milieux*—for example, in precisely what work and community settings— and in what numbers these workers are to be discovered.

For our own part, the matter that remains of major interest is to try to take our understanding of our affluent workers' aspirations another

---

[1] See, for example, Hoggart, *The Uses of Literacy*, pp. 58–60; Jennings, *Societies in the Making*, pp. 55–7; R. Firth, *Two Studies of Kinship in London* (London, 1956), p. 60; and Kerr, *People of Ship Street*, pp. 101–6. It may be observed that in most existing accounts of new working-class communities, the emphasis on the 'rough–respectable' distinction (on the part of 'respectables') appears much more marked than among the workers we studied. Cf. especially Kuper, 'Blueprint for Living Together', pp. 66–82; and Black and Simey (eds.), *Neighbourhood and Community*, pp. 39–68, 105–23. It may also be noted here that the findings reported above are not, in general, supportive of the view advanced by Runciman that status aspirations are now heightening among manual workers and their families and are thus giving rise to an increased sense of relative deprivation in this regard—greater, in fact, than in regard to economic inequalities. See *Relative Deprivation and Social Justice*, chs. 5 and 11 especially. As Runciman recognises, his argument rests very largely on data on (sometimes hypothetical) parental aspirations, and in this respect our findings, as we have seen, would certainly confirm his. But the further relevant material we have collected—on attitudes and behaviour in relation to friends, associations, area of residence, etc.—leads us to an interpretation of high parental aspirations (pp. 132–4 above) which does not entail the assumption that these are shaped by acceptance of middle-class notions of the status hierarchy.

[2] See references cited above, n. 2, p. 22 and n. 2, p. 23.

step further by considering the social perspectives, and more particularly the images of the social order, within which these aspirations were conceived. We have argued that powerful economic aspirations—and the at least partial realisation of these—are not associated among the majority of our respondents with any general normative shift towards distinctively middle-class orientations to the future nor with any widespread desire to gain 'middle-class' status. Rather, the quest for, and achievement of, affluence would appear to have had only a limited effect in modifying what often remain recognisably working-class norms and practices, even though in certain specific respects both aspirations and expectations have quite clearly surpassed traditional standards. It may be that this somewhat complex pattern can be elucidated if we now examine how our respondents themselves envisaged the structure of the society in which they formed and pursued their goals, how they understood the logic of this structure, and how they saw their own position within it.

In the ideal-type characterisations of working- and middle-class social perspectives with which we began this chapter, we tried to bring out how these perspectives can each be seen as developing from a particular conception or image of the social order: the former from a basically dichotomous image, the latter from a more complex hierarchical one. Closely associated with the way in which the salient features of the social order are represented, there are, we imply, distinctive assessments of life-chances and of possible life objectives, and in turn related social values and ideologies. Given this point of view, therefore, the images of society held by our affluent workers were obviously a matter of major interest to us as providing a possible framework for understanding the more general significance of the various different types of aspiration that they expressed in reply to specific questions. In the course of our interviews we thus devoted a good deal of time to investigating respondents' social imagery, especially in regard to the class structure, and a large amount of relevant information was gathered. Details of the method of 'unstructured' interviewing that was used and of the way in which our material was subsequently analysed are given in appendix C. Here it will be sufficient to say that the findings to which we attach most importance are ones of a relatively gross kind which are least likely to be affected by the distortion inevitably involved in reducing a mass of rich and complex data of the kind in question to a quantifiable form.[1]

---

[1] Some further analysis of the data will be presented in a forthcoming paper: John H. Goldthorpe, 'Images of Class among Affluent Manual Workers'.

The main importance of the material we collected on our affluent workers' images of society lies, in our view, in the way in which at a number of points it shows notable differences from the findings of other investigations. To begin with, it is evident from our data that very few indeed of the workers in our sample had formed their images of the class structure on what, following earlier studies, we have taken to be the traditional working-class pattern; that is to say, few saw society as being divided into two confronting classes on the basis of the possession or non-possession of power and authority. To be sure, as many as 76 of our respondents (33%) distinguished no more than two major classes in present-day Britain; but, of this number, only two men advanced quite explicit 'power' models of society (both had some obvious acquaintance with Marxist ideas) while the images of a further eight could be regarded as implying such models in that the two classes were described as 'bosses and men', 'employers and workers', 'the employing class and the rest of us', or in some similar manner. In the main, though, the striking feature was undoubtedly the infrequency with which the language of 'us' and 'them' was used—the language which, one may note, has been represented by writers such as Ossowski and Dahrendorf as common to men who experience their position in society as one of subjection and exploitation.[1]

On the other hand, however, it is also apparent from our findings that no very large proportion of our respondents held elaborate hierarchical images of society based upon the idea of differential prestige. Of those not adhering to two-class models, the large majority—amounting to 48% of the total sample—distinguished only three major classes, and only 11% of the sample had multi- (i.e. more than three) class models. More-over, while respondents who distinguished three or more classes were more likely to think in terms of status levels than those who recognised only two, only 19 men, or 14% of the former group (as against 7% of the latter), did in fact regard aspects of life-style, social 'background' or social acceptance as being the crucial determinants of class. In other words, then, only a quite small minority among our affluent workers approximated to what has been seen as the characteristic middle-class conception of society:[2] so far as the bulk of our sample were concerned, the social

[1] See Stanislas Ossowski, 'La vision dichotomique de la stratification sociale', *Cahiers Internationaux de Sociologie*, vol. 20, 1956; and *Class Structure in the Social Consciousness* (London, 1963), ch. 2; Ralf Dahrendorf, 'Bürger und Proletarier: Die Klassen und ihr Schicksal', in *Gesellschaft und Freiheit* (Munich, 1961).

[2] Cf. the references cited in n. 1, p. 120 above. Consistently with the findings of these studies, only 13% of the men in our white-collar sample operated with two-class models, as against 50% distinguishing three classes and 30% four or more.

order was to be envisaged neither as a system of power nor as a pyramid of prestige.

What indeed could be said in general about our respondents' images of social class is, in the first place, that they exhibited a considerable amount of diversity. To attempt to account for them exhaustively on the basis of a relatively small number of categories, following the practice of most other studies, would be a difficult and most probably a dubious undertaking. In addition, it should be noted that respondents were sometimes rather vague and confused in their formulations, and that with 7% of the sample it was not in fact possible to establish any image at all as a result of the uncertain, contradictory or eccentric nature of the views they expressed. However, this does not mean that among our data no central tendency of any kind was to be found: on the contrary, one certainly existed and is, in our view, both interesting and important. Despite the diversity we have referred to, there was within our sample of affluent workers a marked propensity to regard social class as being primarily a matter of *money*; or, to be more precise, of differences in the incomes, wealth and material living standards of individuals and groups.

Of all respondents who possessed some communicable image of the class structure, as many as 61% (56% of the total sample) regarded 'money' in the above sense as being the most important determinant of class.[1] Furthermore, virtually all those who held this idea were also alike in one other respect: that is, in seeing as a major feature of present-day society a large 'central' class which embraced the bulk of wage and salary earners and to which they themselves felt that they belonged. In other words those of our affluent workers who regarded 'money' as the basis of class almost invariably discounted the manual–nonmanual distinction as a significant line of social cleavage, and tended in fact to expand the boundaries of their own class so as to take in all but a number of 'extreme' groups. And this pattern was maintained, it may be noted, regardless largely of the number of classes that individuals recognised or of the names they gave to classes, their own included.

[1] While differences in method preclude any very close comparisons, this would appear to represent a clearly greater emphasis on 'money' as determining class position (rather than, say, on occupation, aspects of life-style, education, relationship to means of production, etc.) than that revealed by any similar study. See Bott, *Family and Social Network*, p. 172; Oeser and Hammond, *Social Structure and Personality in a City*, pp. 283–4; Willener, *Images de la société et classes sociales*, pp. 167–9. Compare also Martin 'Some Subjective Aspects of Social Stratification', pp. 58–61; Richard Centers, *The Psychology of Social Classes* (Princeton, 1949), pp. 89–93; and Kaare Svalastoga, *Prestige, Class and Mobility* (Copenhagen, 1959), p. 179. Within our white-collar sample, only 35% regarded 'money' as the most important determinant of class differences as against 24% stressing aspects of life-style, 11% occupation and 17% other factors; the views of 13% were indeterminate in this respect.

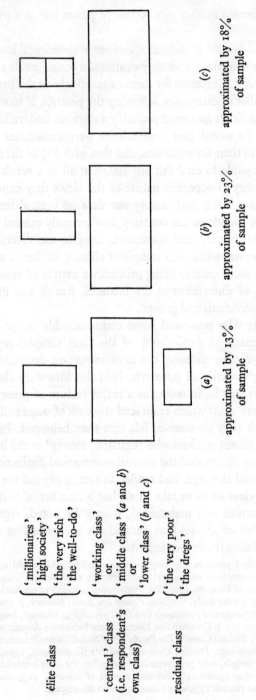

élite class
{ 'millionaires' / 'high society'
  'the very rich' / 'the well-to-do' }

'central' class
(i.e. respondent's own class)
{ 'working class' or
  'middle class' (*a* and *b*) or
  'lower class' (*b* and *c*) }

residual class
{ 'the very poor' / 'the dregs' }

(*a*) approximated by 13% of sample

(*b*) approximated by 23% of sample

(*c*) approximated by 18% of sample

Fig. 1. 'Money' models of class

To illustrate, perhaps the clearest examples of what we may call the 'money' model of the social order were to be found among those men (13% of the sample) who placed themselves in a broadly defined inter-mediate class—called either 'working' or 'middle'—within a three- or possibly four-class 'money' hierarchy; the upper class or classes then being represented as élite strata whose economic superiority was such as to give them a qualitatively different position, and the lower class[1] as a residual one made up of deprived, undeserving or disadvantaged persons (fig. 1*a*). At the same time, though, those further respondents who, while emphasising 'money' as the main determinant of class, distinguished only *two* main classes (23% of the sample) in fact appeared to accept essentially the same model as the former group, but *minus* the bottom stratum. For the lower class to which all these men claimed to belong— under the name of 'lower', 'working' or 'middle'—was invariably ex-panded at least to the extent of embracing some administrative, managerial and professional grades (fig. 1*b*). Finally, among those men (18% of the sample) who held three-or-more class 'money' models and who placed themselves in the bottom class—called 'lower' or 'working'—we again find adherence to the basic 'money' model; but modified in this case both by the exclusion of the residual class and by the inclusion of more than one division towards the peak of the hierarchy. Once more the respondent's own class, even while situated at the base of the hierarchy, is regularly conceived on generous lines—that is, as including the large mass of the working population, manual and nonmanual alike (fig. 1*c*).[2]

In sum, therefore, we may say that only a small fraction of our affluent workers presented either the 'power' or 'prestige' models that have figured prominently in the findings of earlier studies; that around a third held images of the class structure of a degree of diversity that made useful categorisation virtually impossible—or had no communicable image at all; but that still more than half the sample can be regarded as sharing in some degree in a fairly distinctive 'money' model of the class structure of a

---

[1] Where more than three classes were distinguished, the respondents in question invariably placed themselves in the next-to-bottom class.

[2] One other quite common feature of 'money' models as expressed by our respondents was that the large central class in which they claimed membership was seen as being a newly emergent one, resulting from the fusion of the more distinctive working and middle classes of an earlier period. Hence, one may add, the variability of class 'self-ratings' among these men who held to essentially the same view of the class structure: 10% labelled their own class 'lower', 65% 'working' and 14% 'middle', while 11% said that 'working' or 'middle' were equally appropriate terms. For further discussion of 'self-rating' generally, see below, pp. 174–6.

kind that has hitherto been little noted.[1] This situation is represented in table 20. How, then, do these findings help to advance our understanding of the pattern of aspirations among our affluent workers that we have previously considered?

To begin with, they are, in our view, of value in understanding why among our respondents powerful economic aspirations were generally to be found, but unaccompanied, apparently, by any correspondingly marked concern for status ascent. Most obviously, if the social order is not usually envisaged as comprising a gradation of status levels within which upward movement is in principle desirable, then specifically status aspirations will not readily be formed or will at all events be unlikely to

TABLE 20. *Images of class structure*

	N	Percentage
Approximate 'power' model—i.e. two major classes, differentiated in terms of possession and non-possession of power and authority	10	4
Approximate 'prestige' model—i.e. three or more classes, differentiated in terms of aspects of life-style, social background or acceptance	19	8
Approximate 'money' model—i.e. one large central class plus one or more residual or élite classes differentiated in terms of wealth, income and consumption standards	124	54
Other images not approximating above models	59	26
No communicable image	17	7
TOTALS	229	99

have any great saliency. For example, higher standards of consumption may be strongly desired for the various benefits and pleasures that they can directly bestow; but they are unlikely to be much thought of as carrying prestige implications—and to be pursued for this reason—unless individuals recognise, and are impressed by, the existence of some 'social

[1] The tendency for individuals to define the class with which they identify in generous terms has been earlier observed by, among others, Oeser and Hammond (*Social Structure and Personality in a City*, p. 281), who refer to it as the 'expansion effect'. However, the association of such a tendency with an emphasis on 'money' as the chief determinant of class has been no more than hinted at. The findings which most interestingly foreshadow our own are those reported by Martin, 'Some Subjective Aspects of Social Stratification', pp. 58–64. Although commenting that 'it is interesting to see how few people, in plotting their map of all the classes, make explicit use of a simple income scale', Martin notes that manual workers (Greenwich and Hertford, 1950) who rate themselves as 'middle class' specify classes by reference to incomes and living standards more often than any other group, and also that their most popular definition of the middle class is 'everyone who works for a living'. He concludes that 'when a manual worker assesses himself as middle class he is not merely asserting his personal superiority; he carries with him a large proportion of his compeers, and in so doing, he shifts the boundaries of the classes'.

scale' in which they can rise by acquiring the appropriate material symbols. Similarly, our affluent workers' lack of any particular interest in forming sociable relationships with recognisably middle-class persons ceases to be surprising once it is accepted that our respondents did not typically think in terms of a hierarchy of status groups which, as it were, constituted the 'course' for social advancement. For in the absence of such a conception of the social order, there is no reason why association with middle-class persons *should* in itself be regarded as particularly attractive and desirable. In this connection, it is worth adding that a large majority within our sample believed that only rarely were individuals in fact able to move up from one class to another during their adult lives; upward mobility was not usually seen as something that could be realistically striven for. The significantly exceptional group was that of the 19 respondents who adhered to a 'prestige' model of society—11 of whom (or 58%) thought that such mobility occurred quite frequently. In contrast, however, among the 124 men who subscribed to some kind of 'money' model, this view was taken by only 25 (or 20%).[1]

It may of course be argued that in so far as they remained insensitive to differences in life-styles and associated prestige rankings and status group structures, our respondents interpreted the social order in a way that was seriously incomplete and indeed unrealistic—for such phenomena are quite objective social facts which cannot be simply defined away. Such an argument is, without doubt, a largely valid one; but at the same time at least three further points need to be made.

First, the discrepancy that clearly exists between our affluent workers' images of their society and the 'reality' of this society—as seen, say, by the sociologists—may *also* be of relevance in understanding their aspirations in certain respects. This is most notably the case in regard to parents' exaggerated hopes for their children's careers, which had evidently been conceived with little appreciation of the subcultural and social barriers that were likely to stand in the way of their realisation.

Secondly, it is important to note that in some cases, and quite often where 'money' models were advanced, respondents did not so much neglect the prestige and status aspects of social stratification as deny their validity—pointing in particular to what they saw as the hollowness and absurdity of lower middle-class 'pretensions' and 'snobbism'; that is to

---

[1] And by only one (10%) among the ten respondents whose images of the class structure approximated 'power' models. It should be borne in mind that for adherents of 'money' models, mobility between classes would tend to require some quite dramatic change of circumstances: e.g. to move up out of their own class, as they typically observed, would mean 'inheriting a fortune', 'winning the pools', etc.

say, the images of society they adhered to had a critical function. For example, attacks were regularly launched against the idea that having a nonmanual rather than a manual job provided grounds for any claim to social superiority; and special scorn was directed at attempts by white-collar families to maintain such a claim—to 'keep up appearances'—when their economic superiority had largely vanished. 'It's all a sham—all on the surface; often they're as poor as church mice'; 'They give themselves airs but there's nothing behind it—we've got much more than most of them have'; 'It's all lace curtains at the window and nothing on the table'—in these and similar phrases revealing contrasts between white-collar 'appearances' and economic realities were frequently asserted.[1]

Thirdly, it must be observed that while our respondents' refusal to be impressed by prestige and status differences may appear unrealistic and tendentious in relation to certain known facts of British society at large, it appears a good deal less so in relation to what we know about the more immediate social world in which these men lived. As we have seen, their characteristic style of life was a privatised one involving very few group affiliations; they were not typically implicated in status systems of an interactional kind; and they were not therefore greatly exposed to possibilities of social exclusion and rejection. At the same time, in the more visible aspects of their social lives, they could quite reasonably regard themselves as being in a broadly comparable position to that of many, if not most, of the white-collar persons they saw around them; they owned similar goods and possessions, housing standards differed little, they could afford much the same sort of outings and holidays, and so on. In other

---

[1] The notably critical attitude of many of our respondents towards 'snobbism' was also brought out in the answers given to two other questions which we put to them in discussing their social lives. We asked: 'We all know that there are some kinds of people we feel completely at ease with, while with others we feel a bit awkward. Could you say what sort of people you feel completely at ease with?'—followed by: 'And what sort of people would you feel a bit awkward with?' In reply to the first question, 58% referred to people who were similar to themselves in socio-economic or other terms; and a further 36% explicitly to persons who were 'sociable', 'easy to get on with', 'not stuck up' or 'not snobbish'. In reply to the second question, people who were 'snobs', or who were referred to by some equivalent term, were mentioned by 30% of our respondents—far more often than any other comparable category. It might, perhaps, be argued that what is indicated here is in fact a considerable degree of status consciousness among our respondents, manifested in status *conflict* with white-collar, or other groups. But this interpretation is difficult to sustain in view of the lack of any evidence of our affluent workers and their wives being involved in such conflict in actual social situations —as, for example, in community or associational contexts. As Rex has pointed out, ideological differences in this respect may concern more than merely the criteria whereby status is assigned: they may be more fundamental in that some groups are inclined to reject the entire idea of a generalised status hierarchy. See John Rex, *Key Problems of Sociological Theory* (London, 1961), pp. 144–53.

words, if attention is concentrated on the local situation, then the distinctive tendencies that occur in the way our affluent workers view the class structure can in fact be seen as linking in a fairly logical manner the nature of their everyday social experience and their preoccupation with economic rather than status advancement. Moreover, in this perspective we may confirm the view that our respondents' economic aspirations are unlikely to be status aspirations in disguise: for the importance attached to 'money', together with the conception of a large central class, implies in effect an emphasis on social equality rather than inequality. As argued in an earlier paper, in 'money' models of society, in contrast with 'power' and 'prestige' models, inequalities are not expressed through social relationships at all:

Income and possessions may be the marks of persons, but unlike power and status they do not involve persons in relationships of inequality with one another. Inequalities take on an extrinsic and quantitative, rather than intrinsic and qualitative form. In fact, compared with power and prestige, money is not inherently a divider of persons at all; it is a common denominator, of which one may have more or less without its thereby necessarily making a difference to the kind of person one is.[1]

As well as throwing light on the formation and focus of our respondents' aspirations, consideration of their images of the social order is also helpful in understanding their view of the possibilities and means of actually achieving their objectives. So far as aspirations for economic advance were concerned, we have drawn attention to the large proportion of our affluent workers who were optimistic that these would, in some degree at least, be fulfilled; and we have stressed the way in which these men placed their faith overwhelmingly in advance of a collective rather than an individual kind. However, there is in this connection one other point that is worthy of note: that is, the extent to which this optimistic majority within our sample envisaged their material advancement as resulting in some more or less automatic way from the continuation of economic growth, and made relatively little mention of the part to be played in this respect by collective *action*.[2] In other words, these men looked forward to being the collective beneficiaries of a developmental process rather than seeing their yet more affluent future as dependent upon the outcome of social struggles in the industrial or political arenas.

[1] Lockwood, 'Sources of Variation in Working Class Images of Society', p. 261.
[2] The minority who were relatively pessimistic about their future also explained their point of view chiefly in terms of economic trends and circumstances. The findings in question are not, however, to be taken as implying that collective action was in *all* respects regarded as being of little consequence. See below, pp. 167–8, 169–70.

6+

The prevalence of an outlook of this kind is, in our view, both confirmed and elucidated by the fact that among the workers we studied the idea of society as fundamentally divided into opposing classes was only very rarely advanced. The class structure was not, as they described it, a historically created system of domination which had to be overthrown, or at any rate combatted, in order for men such as themselves to achieve their legitimate objectives. More usually, one could say, it was represented as a basic *datum* of social existence—as a natural rather than as a man-made phenomenon, which individuals had in the main to accept and adapt to. As corroboration of this, it may be noted that of those respondents who were able to present some definable image of the class structure, the large majority—69%—believed that a structure of the general kind they had outlined was a *necessary* feature of society—either because of certain inherent aspects of human nature or because of the basic prerequisites of any organised form of social life.[1] Given such an interpretation, therefore, it is scarcely surprising that our respondents should tend to think far more of advancing their welfare within the existing order of society, and as part of its general evolution, than of pursuing their goals through action directed against this order.

Here once more, questions may well be raised concerning the objective 'correctness' of our affluent workers' understanding of their society: for example, questions of the extent to which they may be the victims of a 'false' consciousness. Such questions are often posed in a way that makes them virtually impossible to answer on any empirical basis; but certainly one argument could be reasonably advanced. This is that certain important features of our respondents' actual position in society—ones of which they were not in fact unaware—were only rarely seen by them *as aspects of social class*, and tended thus not to be incorporated, or at least not centrally, into their conceptions of the class structure and of their own place within it. One would cite, for instance, the fact that as manual workers they performed entirely subordinate roles within their employing organisations and, in society at large, tended to belong to the stratum of those who regularly received orders but who seldom gave them; or that, as representatives of wage labour they stood always in a relationship of at least potential conflict with their employers over economic and authority issues.

[1] In more detail, of the 146 men in question, 8% explained the necessity of class in terms of a human propensity to evaluate ('the need to have a pecking order') and 14% in terms of inherent inequalities ('differences in the old grey matter'), as against 21% referring in some way to the need for social incentives and 27% to the need for a hierarchy of authority. A further 8% gave other explanations, and the remaining 22% offered no coherent or adequate explanation.

Again, however, examination of the likely sources of our respondents' seemingly distorted view is worth while. The men who made up our sample, it must be remembered, had for the most part given high priority to raising their material standard of living and had moreover achieved substantial success in this respect; in consumption terms, the majority had certainly enjoyed, and were aware of having enjoyed, considerable upward mobility and often in the relatively recent past.[1] Thus, it is not perhaps so remarkable after all that in the way these men envisaged the social order their own subordination should not be the feature of greatest salience, and that their image of the class structure should tend to be one that was most typically formed from the standpoint of the consumer and 'family man' rather than from that of the producer and employee. In other words, before resorting to claims of 'false' consciousness, it is important to recall that the social experience of many of our respondents was of a kind that could reasonably lead them to be less impressed by the weakness and vulnerability of their class position than by the extent to which they had been able to achieve economic advance within the existing social framework.[2]

Finally, it may also be suggested that such experience, interpreted in the way in question, is one major source of our affluent workers' optimism about their economic future. As we have previously shown, the majority in our sample who were conscious of having raised their living standards appreciably within the recent past were much more likely than the remainder to believe that similar gains would be made in the years immediately ahead: that is to say, a marked tendency prevailed to extrapolate experience into expectations—at least in the case of experience of a positive kind.[3]

In conclusion of this chapter, therefore, we would argue that our respondents' hopes and aims for the future are to be seen as shaped for the most part within a consciousness of society that cannot be adequately apprehended in terms of existing formulae. The workers comprised by our critical case could not be said to show a high degree of status consciousness nor yet of class consciousness in the traditional sense. Indeed, some

---

[1] See *IAB*, table 64, p. 139.

[2] It is important to note again in this connection that only 4% of the workers we studied had ever been unemployed for longer than three months (and 88% never at all); and that when interviewed only 7% regarded their present job as being 'fairly insecure' and 1% as 'very insecure'. See pp. 37–8 above. For further general discussion of the difficulties inherent in the notion of 'false' consciousness, see David Lockwood, *The Blackcoated Worker: a Study in Class Consciousness* (London, 1958), pp. 201–13.

[3] See *IAB*, pp. 138–41.

proportion of them could perhaps be best understood as exemplifying Durkheim's claim that in modern industrial society *représentations collectives* become increasingly indeterminate. At the same time, though, a good deal of evidence has also been produced to suggest that among the men we studied some new mode of social consciousness was emerging: one in which differences in prestige and power, as expressed through actual social relationships, take on less significance than differences in wealth, income and standards of consumption seen as the quantitative attributes of individuals or aggregates. At all events, such 'commodity' consciousness, as we may perhaps call it, and the largely destructured image of the social hierarchy that it implies, would certainly mediate most appropriately between the nature of our affluent workers' aspirations and what we have already established about the characteristic patterns that the interaction of choice and constraint has imposed upon their social lives.

6. Conclusion: the affluent worker in the class structure

In the preceding chapters we have focused on three major aspects of our affluent workers' everyday lives which must be regarded as having a crucial bearing on the thesis of *embourgeoisement*: their work, their patterns of sociability, and their aspirations and social perspectives. Broadly speaking, our findings show that in the case of the workers we studied there remain important areas of common social experience which are still fairly distinctively working-class; that specifically middle-class social norms are not widely followed nor middle-class life-styles consciously emulated; and that assimilation into middle-class society is neither in process nor, in the main, a desired objective. In short, the results of our enquiry are not at all what might have been expected had the thesis of *embourgeoisement* been a generally valid one. On the contrary, our evidence is sufficient to show how the thesis can in fact break down fairly decisively at any one of several points. The following paragraphs summarise our major arguments in this connection.

(i) The findings discussed in chapter 3 underline the argument that increases in earnings, improvements in working conditions, more enlightened and liberal employment policies and so on do not in themselves basically alter the class situation of the industrial worker in present-day society. Despite these changes, he remains a man who gains his livelihood through placing his labour at the disposal of an employer in return for wages, usually paid by the piece, hour or day. Advances in industrial technology and management may in some cases result in work-tasks and -roles becoming more inherently rewarding or at any rate less stressful; but it is by no means clear that any overall tendency in this direction is established. Certainly, new forms of industrial organisation also give rise to new forms of strain or deprivation in work—as, for example, those associated with the imperatives of scale, with multiple-shift working or with the blocking of promotion opportunities for men on the shop floor. Moreover for many industrial workers, and especially for those who do not possess scarce skills, obtaining earnings sufficient to support a middle-class standard of living may well mean taking on work of a particularly unrewarding or unpleasant kind—work, that is, which can be experienced only as labour. And indeed for men in most manual grades the achievement of affluence is likely to require some substantial amount of overtime working on top of a regular working week which is already longer than that of white-collar employees. Finally, it is evident that many types of industrial work, and often those that afford high earnings, exert a seriously restrictive effect upon out-of-work life; in this respect again shifts and overtime are major factors, and the impact of the former at least will become more rather than less widely felt. Thus, it may be claimed that ongoing trends of change in modern industry are not in fact ones which operate uniformly in the direction of reducing class differences and divisions. And, to the extent that such a reduction *is* occurring, we would appear to be witnessing as much the emergence of a white-collar labour force as the creation of 'blue-collar organisation men'. None the less, characteristic differences in the work situations of manual and nonmanual employees still widely persist, as do equally characteristic differences in their work experience and in their patterns of work-related behaviour both within the work situation and beyond.

(ii) Just as proponents of the *embourgeoisement* thesis have exaggerated the effects on class structure of higher wages and of changes in the physical and social environment of work, so too have they overstated the effects of rising standards of consumption and of changes in the physical and social environment of domestic life. The styles of life of those relatively affluent manual workers and their families who live in new housing areas undoubtedly tend to differ, in various well-documented ways, from those typical of more traditional working-class communities. But the results of our study reviewed in chapter 4 bring out the point that such changes need not betoken the adoption of specifically middle-class models of sociability; and indeed the life-styles that we recorded would seem better interpreted in terms of the adaptation of old norms to new exigencies and opportunities than in terms of any basic normative reorientation.[1] What is clearer still is that affluence, and even residence in localities of a 'middle-class' character, do not lead on, in any automatic way, to the integration of

[1] As a general theoretical point, it might be suggested that such piecemeal adaptations or modifications of existing norms, under the influence of 'exogenous' changes, are a far more common form of normative change than that involving actual shifts in reference groups and group affiliations on the lines classically set out by Merton (see *Social Theory and Social Structure*, ch. 8). It will be recalled that in 'Affluence and the British Class Structure' we use Merton's model in order to bring out the full extent of what was being—for the most part implicitly— claimed by those who advanced the idea of *embourgeoisement*. On the relationship between exigencies and norms, see also Platt, 'Some Problems in Measuring the Jointness of Conjugal Role-Relationships'.

manual workers and their families into middle-class society. As is shown by the couples we studied, remarkably few 'social' relationships with white-collar persons may in fact be formed; and, so far as we could tell in our case, not primarily because of white-collar exclusiveness but rather because our affluent workers and their wives had no particular desire to develop such relationships and in general tended to follow a family-centred and relatively privatised pattern of social life.

(iii) As is implied by the last mentioned point, a further doubtful link in the argument for *embourgeoisement* is that which connects a high level of aspiration for economic advancement with a similar concern for status ascent. Again as our Luton findings can demonstrate, the connection is, at all events, not a necessary one. Among the couples in our sample, as was seen in chapter 5, powerful motivations to gain higher material standards of living did not in the main appear to be accompanied by status striving. Rather, what was notable was the degree to which, despite their consider-able gains as consumers, our respondents' orientations to the future were still conditioned by their unchanged class situation as producers; and further, the fact that while their social horizons were largely free from traditionalistic limitations, this did not result in the acceptance of dis-tinctively middle-class social perspectives. In this as in other respects, one very obvious but often disregarded observation may be made: namely, that a break with working-class traditionalism need not take the form of a shift in the direction of 'middle-classness', and that evidence of the former change cannot therefore be taken as evidence of the latter.

In these specific instances, our study exposes points at which the *embourgeoisement* thesis, or at least certain specific contentions which it embodies, would seem vulnerable to empirical or even logical objec-tions. On this basis alone, therefore, we could claim that the thesis has often been presented so as to make *embourgeoisement* appear a far more inexorable process than in fact it is. In addition, there are two more general considerations which must at this stage be re-emphasised; these underpin the various arguments advanced above and together enable us to attach some broader significance to the result of our investigation.

First, it is important to recall that, as shown in preceding chapters, those of our respondents who did in one way or another display recog-nisably middle-class attitudes or behaviour almost always included a high proportion of persons with white-collar connections—connections not directly, if at all, attributable to their present affluent condition. If, for example, we were to consider the very small minority in our sample who could perhaps be regarded as 'middle-class' workers, we would, on any reasonable definition of the group, find prominent within it couples with conjugal white-collar affiliations through both their families of origin and their occupational experience. Taking, say, the 17 couples in the sample (7% of the total) who reported regular leisure companions of entirely white-collar status, it turns out that 10 (or 59%) of these are couples with white-collar connections of a familial and an occupational kind.[1] What this means, then, is that in so far as our study does provide findings which are *prima facie* consistent with the idea of *embourgeoisement*, closer examination quite often indicates that the social processes that are involved are *not* those proposed in the *embourgeoisement* thesis. In other words, the phenomenon of manual wage workers with middle-class life-styles and middle-class friends is not only of little quantitative significance in the case we studied: it is also, as we have earlier suggested, as much open to explanation in terms of downward as of upward social mobility, and such factors as occupational histories and patterns of marriage would appear to be at least as relevant as increased incomes, new homes and higher standards of consumption.[2] If we leave out of account those couples in our sample whose 'middle-classness' might be attributable to downward mobility in some form or other, the evidence for *embourgeoisement* resulting from other processes—including affluence, changes in residence and so on—becomes slight indeed. And if, on the other hand, we concentrate our attention on those couples who were entirely without white-collar affiliations of the kind we considered, then such evidence disappears almost altogether. It is clear from our findings that no more than one or two of the 70 couples in question here could be realistically represented as being even 'on the road' to a middle-class pattern of social life; and for the large majority, middle-class influences and middle-class 'social' contacts would seem to be of quite negligible importance.[3]

[1] See also the statistics given on p. 113 above.

[2] It should be said that on all the various indicators of 'middle-classness' employed in previous chapters, differences in relation to incomes, housing, ownership of consumer durables etc. do not occur in the regular manner of differences according to white-collar affiliations—and further, that such 'material' factors for the most part produce no significant differentiation at all when white-collar affiliations are held constant. The one important exception—the association between area of residence and white-collar social contacts—is discussed in the text. In other words, the analysis here works out on much the same lines as when the dependent variable was voting allegiance; see *PAB*, ch. 4. It is, of course, possible that in so far as couples' white-collar affiliations are through their own previous occupations rather than through kinship, *both* these affiliations *and* their middle-class social characteristics might need to be explained in terms of some underlying set of attitudes and aspirations. If this were so, the value of white-collar affiliations as an independent variable would be diminished. However, from what we know about the nature and timing of our respondents' white-collar jobs, the possibility does not strike us as a very likely one.

[3] Bringing together items recorded at earlier points, we may recall that only a third of these couples reported entertaining at home once a month or more *and* ever entertained non-kin; that, including kin, only 12% of the persons so entertained were of white-collar status; that,

The second point which it is essential to keep in mind is, of course, the critical nature of the case we studied—critical in the sense of being so selected that if in this case the *embourgeoisement* thesis could not be substantially confirmed then serious doubt would have to fall on the idea of this process being at all a widespread one within present-day British society. As we described at some length in chapter 2, the sample of workers on which our enquiry centred was one drawn from a population whose social characteristics and social setting were such as to favour, in almost every respect, the validation of the *embourgeoisement* thesis, following the logic of arguments advanced by its various proponents. An absolutely 'ideal' case from this point of view did not appear to be an empirical possibility; but, on the basis of a detailed assessment, the case we eventually decided upon was shown to come near enough to the ideal specification to allow the strategy of the critical case still to be used. Given then the overall nature of the results that this case produced, we believe that we have grounds for generalising from it in a significant, if negative, manner. Specifically, we would claim that it is unlikely that our findings contrary to the *embourgeoisement* thesis would be seriously or extensively contradicted by the results of similar studies of other samples of manual workers in British society with different social characteristics and located in different kinds of work and community *milieux*. That is to say, it appears to us that the idea of appreciable numbers of manual workers and their wives 'turning middle class', in the way that has been frequently suggested, is shown by our research to be a highly questionable one.

Our position here is one which could be satisfactorily put to the test only through further empirical investigation. But one other means, whereby it might be sought at least to throw some doubt on the generalisation we have made would be by querying whether the case we studied was in fact as critical as we have taken it to be. This is clearly a basic issue, but it is one on which at the outset we stated our arguments in full; and these may stand. The only point which it is perhaps desirable to reiterate at this stage is the following: that in deciding upon the place and population for our research we were guided as closely as possible by the way in which the *embourgeoisement* thesis *was actually formulated and argued for in the existing literature*. It is therefore possible that our Luton study may not have critical status in relation to any revisions of the thesis

again including kin, only 8% of their regular leisure companions were white-collar persons; that between them—i.e. 140 respondents—they had only eight memberships in formal associations of a kind likely to encourage white-collar 'social' contacts; and that *none* of their children of secondary school age—42 in all—had got to a grammar school.

which bring in new causal factors or which drastically change the relative weights given to ones previously adduced: but this can scarcely detract from the significance of our results for the original formulation.[1] Moreover it seems unlikely that a version of the thesis could be produced which was so radically altered that the conditions of our enquiry would not be biassed in its favour at least to some considerable extent. Thus the absence of evidence in support of the thesis can be reasonably construed as having implications that go beyond the particular case in question.

These, then, are the conclusions which we would draw from our study relating specifically to the matter of *embourgeoisement*. However, the fact that they are so predominantly negative must lead us also to regard with some scepticism the broad evolutionary perspectives on western industrialism in which, as was described in chapter 1, the emergence of a 'middle-class' society is seen as a central process, resulting more or less automatically from continuing economic growth. In particular, we must be sceptical of the reliance that is placed on rising affluence, advances in technical organisation in industry and changing patterns of urban residence as forces likely in themselves to bring about a radical restructuring of the stratification hierarchy. Such developments may certainly be expected to have a powerful effect on the material conditions of life and on the material attributes of members of the working class, as indeed of all strata; for example, on their incomes and possessions, on the kinds of job they do, on the kinds of houses and localities they live in, and so on. But, as we understand it, social stratification is ultimately a matter of sanctioned social relationships; and while major changes in the respects above mentioned will obviously exert an influence on such relationships, this is not *necessarily* one which transforms class and status structures or the positions of individuals and groups within these structures. A factory worker can double his living standards and still remain a man who sells his labour to an employer in return for wages; he can work at a control panel rather than on an assembly line without changing his subordinate position in the organisation of production: he can live in his own house in a 'middle-

[1] It is also important to remember that while *embourgeoisement* has often been presented as an incipient process, as yet involving only a 'vanguard' section of the working class, it has at the same time been always regarded as one which will progressively develop on a society-wide scale. Thus, it is scarcely relevant to suggest as cases which would be 'more critical' than our own ones which incorporate features of a highly localised kind or of a kind unlikely to have an increasing impact on working-class life. In the light of our own findings it might be argued that the most truly critical case would be one that maximised the probability of white-collar affiliations. But whether respondents could be found in appropriate *milieux* (e.g. small employment units, predominantly white-collar neighbourhoods, etc.) without going contrary to the conditions just mentioned is highly doubtful.

class' estate or suburb and still remain little involved in white-collar social worlds. In short, class and status relationships do not change entirely *pari passu* with changes in the economic, technological and ecological infrastructure of social life: they have rather an important degree of autonomy, and can thus accommodate considerable change in this infrastructure without themselves changing in any fundamental way.

However, while our main point remains that the *embourgeoisement* thesis, and the general view of industrialism of which it forms part, seriously exaggerate the changes in stratification that have accompanied the development of industrial economies, this point should perhaps be accompanied by two disclaimers. First, we do not, of course, seek to rule out the possibility of more basic changes occurring in the pattern of social stratification, and conceivably ones in the direction of a more 'middle-class' society, at some future stage. In this regard we would only observe that such changes would appear to depend on certain fairly radical institutional alterations—in industrial organisation, in educational systems and so on—of a kind which have not yet occurred to any marked extent, and which are unlikely to do so unless purposive action of a political character is undertaken to that end. Secondly, and more importantly, in rejecting the idea of *embourgeoisement* as part of a logic of industrialism we in no way wish to imply that the effect of economic development on working-class social life has been a negligible one. On the contrary, our own research indicates clearly enough how increasing affluence and its correlates can have many far-reaching consequences—both in undermining the viability or desirability of established life-styles and in encouraging or requiring the development of new patterns of attitudes, behaviour and relationships.

In this connection we may usefully return to the notion of 'normative convergence' between certain manual and nonmanual groups which we initially suggested as a more plausible interpretation than that of *embourgeoisement* of ongoing changes on the boundaries of the working and middle classes. It will be recalled that this process was seen as chiefly involving in the case of white-collar workers a shift away from their traditional individualism towards greater reliance on collective means of pursuing their economic objectives; and in the case of manual workers, a shift away from a community-oriented form of social life towards recognition of the conjugal family and its fortunes as concerns of overriding importance. So far as the latter aspect is concerned, our findings clearly show how a family-centred and privatised style of life was indeed the norm among the manual workers we studied, and how the economic advancement of their families was a matter of paramount importance to them. It was also seen in chapter 4 that while there were significant differences in modes of sociability between couples in our manual and white-collar samples, a marked emphasis on home and family life was a feature common to both.

More unexpectedly, an absence of solidaristic orientations was revealed among our Luton workers not only in their pattern of out-of-work sociability but in their working lives as well, and in fact in the general way in which they interpreted the social order. As we have earlier described, the meaning that they gave to the activities and relationships of work was a predominantly instrumental one; work was defined and experienced essentially as a means to the pursuit of ends outside of work and usually ones relating to standards of domestic living. At the same time, class consciousness was even less in evidence than status consciousness; and in so far as coherent images of the class structure were to be found, these most often approximated 'money' models in which extrinsic differences in consumption standards, rather than relationships expressing differences in power or prestige, were represented as the main basis of stratification.

Thus, while the results produced by our critical case can lend little support to the idea of the 'middle-class' worker, they do on the other hand provide ample material to characterise at least one manifestation of that hitherto somewhat shadowy figure, the 'new' worker. How far other studies would replicate our Luton data in their specific detail (as opposed to their generally negative indications in regard to *embourgeoisement*) is a question to which we cannot suggest a definite answer. However, it is certainly not difficult to find evidence of privatised life-styles among other samples of the new working class that have thus far been investigated;[1] and in a previous publication we have set out our reasons for believing that in their industrial attitudes and behaviour the men in our Luton sample may prove to be 'prototypical' even if they are not perhaps highly typical of the present time.[2]

If we assume, then, that the workers we studied are not entirely *sui generis*, it becomes of relevance to consider in the remaining part of this chapter some of the possible wider implications of the more positive findings of our research as presented in this and in earlier reports. In

[1] See, for example, the review of findings in Klein, *Samples from English Cultures*, vol. 1, ch. 5.
[2] See *IAB*, pp. 174–8. This is not to imply that existing evidence of instrumentally oriented industrial workers is particularly scarce. See, e.g., the references given in n. 2, p. 67 above; also Zweig, *The Worker in an Affluent Society, passim*.

particular, it will be of interest to return to the perspectives of some of the arguments reviewed in chapter 1 in which the working class figures not simply as one stratum within a class hierarchy, statically conceived, but rather as a social force or historic agency, charged with the potential for radical industrial and political action and thus for transforming the society within which it exists. To the extent that among the present-day working class both workplace and communal solidarism appear to be in decline, and work is seen merely as a means of sustaining a mode of social life dominated by home and family, two broad but directly opposing possibilities can be argued for. Briefly, they may be set out thus.

(i) Even if *embourgeoisement* is not occurring on any significant scale, it is still likely that within the working class the commitment to collective means of achieving economic goals—most notably, the commitment to trade unionism—is weakening, and likewise support for 'labour' object-ives and for the Labour Party in national politics. In other words, it may be envisaged that the new worker, as a man who has been able to gain a good deal for himself within the existing system, will move towards a conservative and individualistic, rather than a radical and collectivist, out-look on economic and political issues.

(ii) Alternatively, the experience of work as devoid of intrinsic reward, the privatisation of out-of-work life and the prevalence of 'commodity' consciousness may all be taken as indicative of a condition of profound alienation and unfreedom within the 'consumer society', but of a con-dition from which some mass movement of protest and rebellion must (or at any rate could) eventually stem. In other words, the new worker, as a man systematically denied his true needs in the midst of affluence in order to keep the existing system in being, is still to be seen as objectively, even if not as yet subjectively, in fundamental opposition to this system.

Our limited enquiry does not of course enable us to evaluate these rival speculations in any conclusive manner: it can, however, provide a basis for examining some of the variety of assumptions and propositions which they involve. In the two sections which follow, we consider each view in turn.

The idea that under the economic and social conditions of advanced industrialism trade unions begin to lose their functions and thus their appeal for the industrial labour force is one which has by now gained some prominence in the American literature. It is argued, for example, that especially in the presence of the modern large-scale enterprise, the collec-tive protection of workers' interests becomes less and less necessary; that affluent workers develop a preference for individual independence; and that employees at all levels tend increasingly to identify with their firms and their managements.[1] In the British case, by comparison, the implications of 'affluence' for the unions and the union movement have been surprisingly little discussed. As we earlier noted, attention tended to focus rather on the likely consequences for party politics and voting behaviour; most notably, during the late 1950s and early 1960s, on the possibility of a secular decline in electoral support for Labour.[2] However, more recently there has undoubtedly been growing comment on working-class disenchantment with unionism, chiefly as the result—it is suggested —of unions often appearing, even to their own memberships, to be back-ward-looking in their policies and obstructive and unco-operative in their industrial practices. For instance, on the basis of studies of workers in English urban constituencies, two recent authors have claimed that while among these workers unions were still widely regarded as necessary agencies of defence, they were 'rather infrequently praised with basic enthusiasm, and often criticised for a variety of alleged faults and failings'. The writers conclude that 'Agreement with the unions' goal of improving the lot of ordinary people very often does not involve a thoroughgoing approval of unions as institutions or political organisations.'[3]

To what extent, then, are interpretations of this kind supported by the results of our Luton enquiry? Given that the population we studied can be considered as in some way a 'vanguard' one, do our findings point to a decline in workers' involvement in unions and in their sympathy for union principles and goals? A detailed discussion of our respondents' attitudes and behaviour in regard to trade unionism is available in an

---

[1] These arguments are most forcefully expressed in Galbraith, *The New Industrial State*, chs. 22 and 24. See also Blauner, *Alienation and Freedom*, pp. 154, 162–5, 181; and, for a somewhat different perspective, S. Barkin, 'The Decline of the Labor Movement', in Andrew Hacker (ed.), *The Corporation Takeover* (New York, 1964). Clark Kerr *et al.*, *Industrialism and Industrial Man*, pp. 292–3, offer a more sophisticated view of unions being transformed into specialised interest groups operating in a context of 'bureaucratic gamesmanship'. Galbraith, as an arch-exponent of the view that industrial societies are following convergent paths of development, clearly anticipates that his analysis will come to have relevance for more than the American case alone.

[2] See above, pp. 21–3. While the actual course of political events clearly encouraged speculation on these lines, there were no comparable grounds for representing affluence as a threat to unionism. During the period in question, union membership continued to grow (although density was slightly down) and the most striking development was the increase in the numbers of white-collar workers in unions—a process suggesting 'proletarianisation' rather than *embourgeoisement*. In the United States, on the other hand, total union membership has been in decline since 1957, despite rising numbers in non-agricultural employment.

[3] Robert McKenzie and Allan Silver, *Angels in Marble: Working Class Conservatives in Urban England* (London, 1968), p. 133. (The findings and assessments referred to relate to samples of workers of all political persuasions and not to Conservative workers alone.)

earlier publication;[1] the aspects which appear particularly relevant in the present context may be restated as follows.

(i) Taking our sample of workers as a whole, 87% were union members. Skefko is in fact '100% union', while in Vauxhall and Laporte the proportions of our respondents unionised were 79% and 68% respectively. However, it was not the case that unionism in these two latter plants was on the wane. On the contrary, membership was growing and indeed, so far at least as semi-skilled workers were concerned, Vauxhall and Laporte could be regarded as quite valuable recruiting grounds for the unions represented. As many as 46% of the assemblers and process workers in our sample who belonged to unions had not been members before entering their present employment.[2] Thus, in the case we studied, the growth of large-scale enterprises, in an area outside the older industrial regions of the country, was associated with a marked *strengthening* in union organisation. It would appear that workers attracted to these plants by the prospect of affluence still in a majority of cases joined unions even when this was not compulsory and when they had no previous commitment to unionism.[3]

(ii) When our respondents were asked why they had first joined a union, around a third of the Skefko employees referred simply to the compulsory nature of membership, and it became evident that among workers in all three firms a further quarter to a third had become unionists with little volition on their own part.[4] Taken together, these presumably reluctant or unenthusiastic recruits clearly outnumbered the minority—20% overall—who stated that they had become union members as a matter of principle or duty. It certainly could not be claimed, then, that for the majority of workers in our sample as a whole the appeals of trade unionism were immediately obvious. At the same time, though, some note must also be taken of the kinds of reasons that were most often given for becoming union members by men in Vauxhall and Laporte. Just on half stated that they had joined in order to gain the advantages of union representation *vis-à-vis* management (for example, over grievances) or of union legal assistance and friendly society benefits. That is to say, these men were

[1] *IAB*, ch. 5.
[2] All these men had had other employers.
[3] On the lack of trade union tradition in the Luton area, see above, pp. 45–6. It may be noted that in both Vauxhall and Laporte the percentage of unionists among the more affluent workers included in our sample was *higher* than the estimated percentage for all manual workers in these plants.
[4] E.g. men who had joined as a result of informal workmate pressure or simply because they did not like to refuse when asked to join.

attracted by what would often be the *individual*, or at any rate highly sectional, advantages of belonging to a labour organisation.[1] And advantages of this kind, it should be remembered, are likely to remain of some considerable importance even where workers have strong guarantees of high wages and continuity of employment.[2]

Moreover, as a matter of more general significance, our interview findings also indicate that in all firms alike the majority of union members did in fact have recourse to union officials when problems concerning their work or work conditions arose.[3] It would seem, thus, that regardless largely of the manner in which they became members, once in a union our affluent workers usually found it of some value to them. In only one occupational group—the setters—was there any association between being initially an unwilling unionist and subsequently having little or no contact with union officials.

(iii) Those of our findings most readily consistent with the idea of a lack of *rapport* between the worker and his union were undoubtedly those concerning members' participation in the union branch and their views on union power. As regards the branch, interest was by any standards at a particularly low level in all groups other than the craftsmen; leaving aside the latter, only 2% reported attending branch meetings regularly and only 8% attended such meetings as enabled them to vote regularly in branch elections. Even counting in the craftsmen, 60% of union members had never been to their branch at all. From the explanations that were offered for this failure to participate, it was clear that, particularly by comparison with the demands and attractions of home and family life, branch activities were of quite negligible concern to the bulk of our respondents and could hold little claim on their time and energy. Moreover, even in the context of their industrial lives, the unionists in our sample typically regarded the branch as something of an irrelevancy. Its affairs appeared remote from what was of major

---

[1] I.e. those advantages which Olson has referred to as 'selective incentives' for union membership—as opposed to the 'public goods' provided via collective bargaining—and which, he implies, constitute the only strictly rational grounds for joining a union. See Mancur Olson, *The Logic of Collective Action: Public Goods and the Theory of Groups* (Cambridge, Mass., 1965).

[2] Indeed in this connection Galbraith is seemingly aware of a serious difficulty for his argument of the declining functionality of trade unions. He recognises that in regard to the framing and administering of systems of work rules and in processing grievances unions must continue to play a centrally important role in industrial relations. It is, however, difficult to understand why he believes that in this way unions will help to increase worker identification with the firm to the detriment of their own strength. See *The New Industrial State*, pp. 276–7.

[3] *IAB*, pp. 104–5.

importance to them in their work: that is, pay and conditions in their own shops and plants. The branch seemed in fact to be often thought of as dealing with matters which, in the words of one man, 'really only concern the union—not the men on the shop floor'.

Given, then, such a tendency among our respondents to dissociate themselves from their union, at least above the level of the workplace, their views on union power are somewhat less surprising than they might otherwise be, although they remain quite striking. In response to a direct question, as many as two-fifths—41%—of the union members in our sample were found to agree rather than disagree with the statement that the trade unions had too much power in the country; a proportion not enormously different from that of 57% found among the non-unionists. Further, it may be noted that when asked about their attitude to the alliance existing between the trade unions and the Labour Party, 54% of those unionists giving a clear-cut answer expressed their *dis*approval as against 46% approving.

Here, therefore, it would seem that in the case of the workers we studied there is fairly unambiguous evidence not merely of apathy but further of some appreciable degree of disaffection in regard to unions and the union movement. On this basis, it might plausibly be suggested that, given high-paying and stable employment, the existence of instrumental attitudes to work and a family-centred mode of life does constitute a threat to 'union-mindedness' and thus to union influence. But, once again, there are other aspects of our findings which do not fall so readily into line with such an interpretation. Most significantly, our interviews with unionists, as well as producing the results reviewed above, *also* revealed that *at workplace level* participation and interest in union matters were in fact quite widespread. For example, at shop steward elections no fewer than 83% of all unionists reported voting regularly; and in the one instance where shop meetings were held these attracted majority attendances. Moreover, as already mentioned, most unionists from time to time consulted with their steward on work-related problems, and when asked how often they discussed union affairs with their workmates, a third of our respondents (32%) answered 'very often' or 'a good deal' and almost half (47%) 'now and then'—thus leaving only a fifth (21%) who could be regarded as more or less uninvolved. Thus, while many of our respondents might be out of sympathy with the unions at a national level, and most showed complete indifference towards the activities of the branch, this did not stand in the way of their quite extensive engagement in unionism in the context in which, one would suggest, its functions and its value were most evident to them.[1]

In this, as in other respects that have been noted, the results of our Luton enquiry do not therefore fit easily with the view that within the new working class of the affluent society trade unionism is destined to lose its hold. There can be little doubt that for the great majority of the workers we studied unionism was far from being a central interest in their lives; and it is equally clear that only very rarely was unionism understood in the sense of a socio-political movement. Most typically, our respondents appeared to see their union as a 'service' organisation, of advantage to them in defending and furthering their personal economic interests in the immediate circumstances of their daily work. But while this may point—as we believe it does—to significant changes that are in train in the character of unionism and in the meaning of union membership,[2] there is no necessary implication that workers' attachment to unionism, or to the underlying belief in the importance of collective means, will thereby be weakened. In other words, there appears to be no reason why trade unionism should not become increasingly 'self-interested' and 'particularistic' in its emphasis without losing its appeal and its strength. Indeed, shifts in these directions may perhaps best be interpreted as highly functional adaptations both to the changing work situations and to the changing wants and expectations of industrial employees.[3]

Just as affluence and its alleged social and psychological consequences have been regarded as solvents of working-class collectivism in industrial

[1] It may be observed that in the enquiry by McKenzie and Silver, referred to above (p. 166), the questions asked on trade unionism appear to have related chiefly to 'the unions' and their activities in quite general terms. In the light of our own findings, we would suggest that a more positive—and balanced—pattern of response would have been achieved, at least in the case of union members, if attention had also been directed towards unionism as it operated at their places of work.

[2] The increasing importance of workplace unionism is amply documented in the research papers of the Royal Commission on Trade Unions and Employers' Associations (The 'Donovan' Commission). There seems little doubt (i) that the number of shop stewards relative to union members is growing, and also the extent to which stewards are involved in bargaining procedures; (ii) that systems of workplace industrial relations are developing spontaneously on a wide scale and are operating in a largely self-contained and self-regulating manner; (iii) that for a large majority of union members, their steward *is* the union; and (iv) that most members feel relatively satisfied with the way in which workshop unionism and bargaining actually function. See in particular Research Paper 10, W. E. J. McCarthy and S. R. Parker, *Shop Stewards and Workshop Relations* (London, H.M.S.O., 1968).

[3] They may also be regarded, as we have earlier pointed out, as a further aspect of normative convergence between manual and nonmanual groups focused on unionism of a politically uncommitted and highly instrumental type. See Goldthorpe and Lockwood, 'Affluence and the British Class Structure', p. 152.

life, so in the political field they have been represented as the source of a shift away from a Labour orientation towards a new working-class Conservatism. In this respect, the British literature can readily provide examples of the arguments that have been advanced, although these have taken on at least three major forms. First, as we observed in chapter 1, the idea of *embourgeoisement* was itself often regarded as the link between affluence and the electoral defeats of the Labour Party in the course of the 1950s. The claim made was in effect that workers who had adopted a middle-class style of life and who identified with the middle class were giving expression to their new sense of status by changing their party allegiance.[1] Secondly, one may note the much more straightforward thesis of the 'prosperity voter'. In this case, the usual argument during the 1950s was that a shift to the Right was taking place among the more affluent sections of the working class because of the experience of rapidly rising living standards under Conservative rule.[2] However, a more general version of the thesis may be found which proposes simply that the higher a manual worker's income, the greater the probability that he will be Conservative—or, at any rate, not Labour—in his political outlook and affiliations.[3] Thirdly, there is the relatively sophisticated idea that affluence and its correlates create an increasing number of manual workers who are 'socially marginal'—still rank-and-file members of the industrial labour force but with middle-class incomes and levels of consumption. Thus, it is held, the uncertain social identification of these individuals and the cross-pressuring to which they are exposed is likely to result in a decline in support for Labour if only through an increase in abstentions or, possibly, in Liberal voting.[4]

In so far as the results from the case we studied imply that among the new working class assimilation into middle-class society is neither occurring nor desired to any significant extent, these results must also of course go against the idea that a process of this nature underlies a secular movement of working-class votes from the Labour to the Conservative Party. However, even while controverting the *embourgeoisement* thesis, our find-

---

[1] See, for example, Lipset, 'The British Voter', part 1, p. 11.

[2] Cf. Abrams, 'New Roots of Working Class Conservatism'.

[3] See, for example, Richard Rose, 'Class and Party Divisions: Britain as a Test Case', *Sociology*, vol. 2, no. 2 (May 1968); and more generally the references to the literature on the 'more money—more contentment—more conservatism' thesis given in Richard F. Hamilton, *Affluence and the French Worker in the Fourth Republic* (Princeton, 1967), pp. 4, 135–6 *et passim*. The names of Galbraith and Kerr again occur, along with those of Daniel Bell, Lipset and David Riesman.

[4] See, for example, Butler and Rose, *The British General Election of 1959*, pp. 15–16; and Crosland, 'Can Labour Win?'

ings could still conceivably back up either or both of the latter two of the arguments set out above. In examining whether or not this is so, we shall again be largely—though not entirely—concerned with data which we have earlier published in detail; consequently, we again adopt a summary form of presentation.

(i) The most important single fact to emerge relating to the politics of the affluent workers we studied was that the large majority were, and generally had been, Labour supporters. Considering the votes cast by our respondents for the three main parties at the General Election of 1959, no less than 80% went to Labour; and at the time our interviews were carried out (May 1963 to February 1964) 79% of intended votes at the forthcoming election were also in Labour's favour. Even allowing for the fact that our sample was composed of males in the younger age-groups, the level of Labour voting was certainly not less—and, if anything, was somewhat higher—than that indicated for manual workers generally by the results of national surveys.[1] Some slight tendency did exist for men who believed they had experienced marked increases in living standards to be less likely than others to back Labour. But at the same time no overall shift to the Right was discernible within our sample during the period in which the political effects of affluence were supposed to have been most felt. On the contrary, a notable feature was the *stability* of Labour support.[2] Thus, our findings are certainly not what would have been expected following the argument which links the achievement of affluence with increased working-class Conservatism. Rather, they are in line with the results of studies made in other advanced societies which also indicate that manual workers can attain relatively high standards of living and still remain strong adherents of left-wing or labour-oriented parties.[3]

(ii) That no straightforward connection exists between affluence and voting was also revealed by more detailed analyses of our data. Among the highest paid of the workers we studied and among those who were house owners (or buyers) a slightly lower level of Labour voting than among the rest of the sample was indeed to be found. However, at the same time a

[1] *PAB*, pp. 14-15.
[2] E.g. of men who voted Labour in 1955, 95% did so again in 1959; and of the Labour voters in this election, 91% were intending Labour voters in 1964. By comparison, the Conservative voters in the sample showed far less consistency in their political allegiance. See *PAB*, pp. 15-16.
[3] See, for example, for the United States, Arthur Kornhauser, Albert J. Mayer and Harold L. Sheppard, *When Labor Votes: a Study of Auto Workers* (New York, 1965) and Bennett M. Berger, *Working-Class Suburb* (Berkeley, 1960), ch. 3 esp.; for France, Hamilton, *Affluence and the French Worker in the Fourth Republic*; and for Germany, Hamilton, 'Affluence and the Worker: the West German Case'.

far stronger association existed between voting and the extent of workers' white-collar affiliations; and when this latter factor was held constant, indicators of affluence ceased to be related to vote in any systematic manner. Those men with the most extensive white-collar connections were the least likely to be Labour supporters, regardless of income level or house ownership.[1] In other words, our data in this respect conform closely to the rule that has emerged in preceding chapters: that those of our affluent workers whose attitudes and behaviour most closely approximate a middle-class pattern are those distinguished by the likelihood of their past or present exposure to white-collar styles of life and personal influence.[2]

In this way our findings in fact do more than indicate—along with those of several other sociological enquiries—that there is no important relationship between affluence and Conservative (or non-Labour) voting within the British working class:[3] they also suggest why an association of this kind, as revealed in certain opinion polls, may well be misleading. That is, because in these polls such other relevant factors as the social origins of respondents and their work histories have not been taken into account and could therefore have created a largely spurious association between measures of affluence and political allegiance.[4] At all events, in

---

[1] *PAB*, pp. 49–59. The data in question relate to white-collar family and occupational connections analysed in the same way as in the present volume. Following a hypothesis suggested by P. M. Blau ('Social Mobility and Interpersonal Relations', *American Sociological Review*, vol. 19, (1954)) we have subsequently examined the further effect on vote of white-collar affiliations through *friends*. Blau's hypothesis is that 'those mobile persons who have established extensive interpersonal relations with others in their new social class should not differ in their conduct from the rest of its members'. While not perhaps entirely adequate, the best measure of social integration we could employ was based on the answers to the question concerning the two or three people with whom spare time was most often spent. By controlling for the occupational status of the spare-time companions of the mobile and immobile men in our sample, we obtained patterns of voting which tended to confirm Blau's hypothesis. However, the size and nature of our sample makes it impossible to draw reliable statistical conclusions from this analysis, and the matter must be left open for further investigation.

[2] It may be noted that the level of Labour voting among those workers with both family and occupational white-collar ties was in fact closer to that of men in our white-collar sample who were of working-class social origins than it was to that of other manual workers with no white-collar affiliations of the kind we considered.

[3] See also Runciman, '*Embourgeoisement*, Self-Rated Class and Party Preference', and *Relative Deprivation and Social Justice*, ch. 9; Eric A. Nordlinger, *The Working Class Tories* (London, 1967), ch. 7; Cannon, 'Ideology and Occupational Community', and McKenzie and Silver, *Angels in Marble*, ch. 3.

[4] Within our sample, those workers with the more extensive white-collar affiliations tended to be the higher paid and to be more often house owners or buyers. See *PAB*, p. 56, table 27. Moreover, it may be noted that in considering Gallup Poll data in relation to the proposition that 'Workers who are more prosperous are less likely to vote Labour than those who are less prosperous', Rose observes that these surveys provide no direct information on income and

the absence of substantiating evidence which is not open to doubts of this kind the 'prosperity voter' must surely remain a very hypothetical figure indeed.

(iii) Turning next to the argument which connects a decline in the working-class Labour vote to the increased social marginality of certain groups of manual workers, we may note that its main empirical basis has been found in one repeated result of survey research: namely, that persons of manual status who none the less claim to be 'middle-class' are less likely to vote Labour than such persons who describe themselves as 'working-class'. This same relationship is indeed clearly evident in our own data, as can be seen from table 21. However, while being confirmatory in this respect, our interview findings also enable us to point to a number of difficulties in the position in question.

First, it may be observed that in our sample of affluent workers as many as 67% regarded themselves as 'working' (or 'lower') class, as against only 14% claiming a definite 'middle-class' status and a further 8% taking the view that they could be described equally well as 'working' or 'middle' class.[1] In view, therefore, of the nature of our sample, it would appear that there was surprisingly little feeling of social marginality among our respondents—certainly less than would be expected on the basis of the arguments under consideration, even supposing for the moment that a 'middle-class' self-rating invariably indicates marginality.[2]

Secondly, it is important to recognise that although workers who claim 'middle-class' status may be less likely than others to vote Labour, this tells one nothing at all about the causal processes that are involved. No-

that 'earnings can only be inferred from questions concerning motor car and telephone ownership'. Such a procedure must thus considerably increase the probability that factors other than income are entering into the analysis. Rose in fact wisely concludes that 'It would be safest to infer that the fact of high wages is less immediately important in regard to vote than goods purchased with wages and their relation to life styles.' He does not, however, appear to recognise how little evidence he has in the end adduced in favour of his proposition—nor the full extent of that which is negative. See 'Class and Party Divisions', pp. 146–7.

[1] Class self-ratings were asked for in the course of the unstructured section of our interviews which was concerned with respondents' images of the social order. See above, p. 145 and appendix C.

[2] The figure of 22% being prepared to regard themselves as 'middle-class' is indeed somewhat lower than that recorded in most surveys based on national working-class samples. E.g. in studies already referred to, Martin ('Some Subjective Aspects of Social Stratification') found 26% of middle-class 'identifiers'; Abrams (in Abrams and Rose, *Must Labour Lose?*), 40%; Runciman, 33%; Nordlinger, 23%; and McKenzie and Silver, 12%. Differences in the nature of the samples and in the methods used in establishing self-ratings mean that such figures must not be taken too seriously. But, at all events, it is clear that despite their affluence and the characteristics of their social *milieux*, the workers we interviewed showed no *marked* propensity to upgrade themselves in the manner in question.

TABLE 21. *Voting intention* (General Election, 1964) by self-rated class*

	Voting intention					
Self-rated class	Lab.	Cons.	Lib.	Uncertain or abstain		N†
	Percentage					
'Middle'	55	21	9	15	100	33
'Middle or working'	63	11	11	16	101	19
'Working', 'lower'	75	8	6	12	101	153

* An essentially similar result is shown if actual vote, 1959, is substituted for voting intention.
† Excludes 24 cases where some other or no class self-rating was given.

TABLE 22. *Voting intention by self-rated class and by conjugal white-collar affiliations*

White-collar affiliations	Self-rated class	Voting intention					
		Lab.	Cons.	Lib.	Uncertain or abstain		N*
		Percentage					
Via family *and* job	'Middle' and 'middle or working'	60	20	10	10	100	20
	'Working', 'lower'	69	19	6	6	100	32
Via family *or* job	'Middle' and 'middle or working'	44	17	11	28	100	18
	'Working', 'lower'	75	4	7	14	100	73
Neither	'Middle' and 'middle or working'	72	14	7	7	100	14
	'Working', 'lower'	77	6	4	13	100	47

* Excludes 24 cases where some other or no class self-rating was given and 1 case where there is no information on white-collar affiliations.

one has shown that a worker first becomes conscious of approximating a middle-class position and *then* changes his voting behaviour; and it would be at least as plausible to suggest that those workers who, for some other reason, do not vote Labour will for this same or a related reason tend to think of themselves as socially superior to their Labour-voting fellow workers. In this connection the data presented in table 22 are of some interest. They reveal that among the workers we studied middle-class

identification was associated with having extensive white-collar affiliations[1] and, furthermore, that when the latter variable is controlled the
relationship between self-rated class and vote becomes much less apparent.
Among men with both family and occupational white-collar connections
and among those having no such connections, there is no very great difference in the level of Labour support as between middle- and working-class
identifiers. It is only in the intermediate group that a wide gap persists. In
addition, further analysis shows that the middle-class identifiers in the
sample who were intending Conservative or Liberal voters in 1964 were in
fact, with only one exception, men who had *never* been attached to the
Labour Party.[2] Thus, while the numbers at our disposal are unfortunately
too small to allow any firm conclusions to be drawn, the data in point
would seem sufficient, at any rate, to cast doubt on the idea that middle-
class identification is a major *cause* of manual workers deserting a Labour
allegiance.

Finally, it must be remarked that when a manual worker claims to be
'middle-class', it *cannot* be assumed that such a claim does always reflect
a position, and an awareness, of social marginality. On the contrary, we
may note that 58% of our middle-class identifiers are men who adhere to
what we have termed 'money' models of the class structure; that is,
models in which they in fact tend to see themselves as belonging to a large
central class comprising the bulk of wage and salary earners. And in the
case of respondents holding such a model, we find that the relationship
between class self-ratings and party choice is once again notably weakened:
as many as 67% of the middle-class identifiers were intending Labour
voters as against 77% of those describing themselves as 'working' or
'lower' class.[3]

---

[1] Counting in cases where respondents described their class in terms other than 'middle',
'working' or 'lower', we find that among men with both family and job white-collar affiliations
35% believe they could be regarded as 'middle-class' as compared with 19% in the rest of the
sample. Moreover, in the latter group there is a concentration of those saying that 'working'
or 'middle' would be equally appropriate designations. Considering only unambiguous
middle-class identifiers, we find still 32% among respondents with both types of affiliations as
against only 9% among the remainder.

[2] Of the remaining 13 men, 8 were regular Conservative supporters, two had shifted between
voting Conservative or Liberal or abstaining, one had shifted between Liberal and Labour
support, and two had never yet voted.

[3] In contrast, we may observe, on the one hand, that the 10 respondents adhering to 'power'
models were all working-class identifiers and all Labour supporters; and, on the other, that
7 of the 19 men holding 'prestige' models were middle-class identifiers and that 5 of the 7
were Conservative or Liberal supporters. One is thus led to suggest that the regularly found
association between self-rated class and vote—which, though significant, is not *strong*—is
largely the result of a particularly marked propensity to vote Labour among manual workers

In sum, we may say that among the 'new' workers we studied it seems improbable that there was more than the merest handful of men who manifested social marginality through a claim to middle-class status and who, on account of a middle-class identification arising in this way, were led to *withdraw* their support from the Labour Party.

(iv) By way of complementing the foregoing arguments, one other feature of our findings on the politics of our sample may be alluded to. That is, that among the sizable majority of Labour adherents, by far the most common kind of reason given for attachment to the Labour Party was one couched in 'class' terms: Labour was typically seen as the party *of* the working class, as the party for which a manual worker would natur-ally vote.[1] In other words, among our affluent workers politics still often carried a class meaning, and the main subjective basis of their Labour support would thus appear to be generally the same as that which has been shown to exist among the British working class at large.[2]

At the same time, though, it is through a closer examination of the nature of our respondents' attachment to Labour that we arrive, para-doxically, at those of our findings which are most consistent with the view that affluence and its correlates tend to undermine a genuinely 'labour' orientation—or, at least, do not readily co-exist with a radical and highly partisan working-class political outlook. For instance, al-though within our sample Labour voting was frequently explained in terms of class, this did not mean that politics were widely represented as a manifestation of the class struggle. Much more commonly, 'class' support for Labour was given simply on the grounds of the party being somewhat more likely than the Conservatives to favour the working-class interest: 'inclined to do that bit more for the working man', as one re-spondent put it. In addition, it is significant that next in importance to 'class' reasons for voting Labour were ones of a quite overtly instrumental and calculative kind[3]—reasons, that is, which in their nature implied no abiding commitment. Thus, while it is perhaps easy to exaggerate the extent to which the working-class interpretation of Labour politics has ever been of a radically class-conscious character, it would certainly

---

describing themselves as 'working class' *within the context of an image of the social order that approximates a 'power' model;* and of a propensity not to vote Labour among such workers who regard themselves as 'middle class' *within the context of an image approximating a 'prestige' model.*

[1] *PAB*, pp. 16–19.
[2] See, for example, Abrams, in Abrams and Rose, *Must Labour Lose?*, pp. 12–14; McKenzie and Silver, *Angels in Marble*, pp. 106–13.
[3] *PAB*, p. 19.

appear that among the workers we studied Labour support with this meaning was, at any rate, rarely present in an overt form—a conclusion which is, of course, very much in line with our previous discussion of their social imagery.[1]

Lastly, in this connection, our respondents' attitudes on the place of trade unions in politics are also of some relevance. As earlier noted, a majority of the unionists in our sample disapproved of the alliance with the Labour Party: conversely, we find that this was also the view of 44% of Labour voters and indeed of 43% of those men who were both union members and Labour supporters.[2] Such comments as were made suggested a quite widespread feeling that the unions should 'keep out of politics'. And consistent with this was the further finding that among the Labour-voting unionists only half were knowingly paying their union's political levy, while nearly a quarter reported that they had contracted out.[3] It is thus evident enough that for most of the men in our sample the traditional conception of the relationship between the Labour Party and the unions had little immediate appeal; no underlying ineluctable unity in their philosophies and goals was apparently perceived.

How, then, can we best draw together the diverse observations that we have been led to make on the whole question of the probable future modes of action of the new working class in both the industrial and political spheres? While the complexity of the matter is obviously such as to make any simple statement perilous, the results of our study would appear to offer grounds for at least the two following conclusions as regards the British case. First: that it is mistaken to suppose that the economic and social attributes characteristic of 'vanguard' groups within the industrial labour force are incompatible with their continued adherence to the traditional *forms* of working-class collectivism; that is, trade unionism and electoral support for the Labour Party. Secondly, however, that although these groups may still regard the unions and the Labour Party as organisations which have some special claim on their allegiance, their attachment

---

[1] On the basis of data from a national sample, Butler and Stokes classify as many as 39% of working-class Labour voters as persons for whom politics is a representation of *opposing* class interests, as compared with 47% who see politics in terms of *simple* class interests. Among middle-class Conservatives the corresponding figures were 13% and 12%. As Butler and Stokes note, these results can be associated with the idea of contrasting dichotomous and hierarchical images of society. See D. Butler and D. Stokes, *Political Change in Britain* (forthcoming).

[2] See *IAB*, pp. 111–12. For the craftsmen, the figure in question fell to 32% as against 49% for the setters and semi-skilled men.

[3] *PAB*, pp. 28–9. For evidence that the level of contracting-out among our respondents is higher than average, see *IAB*, pp. 110–11.

to them *could* certainly become of an increasingly instrumental—and thus conditional—kind, and one devoid of all sense of participation in a class *movement* seeking structural changes in society or even pursuing more limited ends through concerted class action.[1] In short, the idea of any necessary decline in working-class collectivism within the affluent society may be rejected as theoretically and empirically unsound: but the meaning of this collectivism and the nature of its objectives are clearly not impervious to those changes in working-class life with which our study has been centrally concerned.

In turning now to the second possible interpretation of the new working class—that based on the idea of alienation—it may be remarked at the outset that in this case problems of empirical assessment are particularly great. To begin with, 'alienation', as used in this connection, is not a specifically sociological concept: it is rather a notion expressive of a certain human and social philosophy which often figures crucially in a rhetoric of revolution. It is not intended to be tested against fact. Furthermore, as we have earlier implied,[2] some ambiguity exists as to whether alienation in this usage is to be understood as a *latent* or a *manifest* condition. According to writers such as, say, Marcuse or Gorz, alienation is displayed on a wide scale among the working classes of neo-capitalist societies in the form primarily of compulsive and escapist consumption; numbed by the abundant satisfaction of their 'false' needs and in other ways systematically manipulated, the masses exist in a state of generally acquiescent, if occasionally uneasy or fractious, servitude. On the other hand, though, a writer such as Mallet is concerned to argue that within advanced capitalism long-term changes are occurring which give rise to an actual *awareness* of alienation, at least on the part of certain groups of workers; and in this case the emergence of some new form of radical class consciousness and associated socio-political action is foreseen. Thus, while these two versions of 'alienation' are not necessarily incompatible,[3] it is important to try to distinguish which emphasis is predominant in any argument that is being examined, since, as will be seen, rather different sets of issues tend to be raised.

As regards, firstly, the idea of latent alienation, it may be said that this

---

[1] This is one undoubted possibility: another, and quite different, one is suggested in the last section of this chapter.

[2] See above, pp. 18–20.

[3] Gorz, for example, shows some sympathy for Mallet's views: *Stratégie Ouvrière et Néocapitalisme*, pp. 105–6. Marcuse, on the other hand, appears more doubtful; see *One-Dimensional Man*, pp. 28–31.

offers an undoubtedly persuasive means of summing up many of the salient findings that we have reported on the attitudes and behaviour of the workers we studied. For example, the overriding concern they display with increasing their standards of domestic consumption, the extent to which their future objectives are defined in terms of such standards, their home-centred and typically privatised style of life—all these are features which could be regarded as aptly exemplifying, to use Gorz's words, 'une civilisation de la consommation individuelle': a form of society, that is, in which 'l'individu est sollicité de s'évader de sa condition de producteur social, de se reconstituer un microcosme *privé* dont il jouirait et sur lequel il règnerait en souverain solitaire'.[1] Moreover, the fact that our respondents' own images of the social order were rarely structured in terms of class oppositions or status hierarchies, and the prevalence rather of largely destructured 'money' models, would appear to show quite strikingly the extent to which the 'civilisation of individual consumers' was indeed represented in their social consciousness—inhibiting their awareness of the inequalities of power and forms of exploitation upon which the existing order rests. Finally, and most crucially, the idea of alienation appears closely applicable to our respondents' experience of their work and to the meaning and place that work typically held in their social lives. In this respect, indeed, Marx's original characterisation of 'alienated labour' can stand as a not greatly exaggerated account of our major conclusions:

... work is *external* to the worker ... it is not part of his nature ...; consequently, he does not fulfil himself in his work but denies himself, has a feeling of misery rather than well-being, does not develop freely his mental and physical energies but is physically exhausted and mentally debased. The worker, therefore, feels himself at home only during his leisure time, whereas at work he feels homeless. His work is not voluntary but imposed, *forced labour*. It is not the satisfaction of a need, but only a *means* for satisfying other needs.[2]

It could, then, certainly be claimed that the alienated worker (in the above sense) is, at all events, far more readily recognisable in our research data than the worker 'on the move towards new middle-class values and middle-class existence'. However, while this is so, it is also the case that there are a number of respects in which the findings of our study do not fall so neatly into line with the 'latent alienation' thesis, and that we thus remain sceptical concerning certain of its underlying assumptions.

---

[1] *Stratégie Ouvrière et Néocapitalisme*, p. 66.

[2] Karl Marx, 'Alienated Labour' in 'Economic and Philosophical Manuscripts of 1844', trans. T. B. Bottomore, *Karl Marx: Early Writings* (London, 1963).

One such assumption, for instance, is that alienation, as seen in a pre-occupation with 'false' consumer needs, derives fundamentally from the work situation; from the nature, that is, of work-tasks and relationships. As Gorz puts it, in a passage we earlier quoted in full:

It is precisely because the worker is not 'at home' in 'his' work; because, denied him as creative active function, this work is a calamity, a *means* solely of satisfying needs, that the individual is stripped of his creative, active needs and can find his own power only in the sphere of non-work—the satisfaction of the passive needs of personal consumption and domestic life . . .[1]

Or, in the words of an Italian socialist writer, Bruno Trentin: 'the "alienated consumer" is the person who, in his consumer needs, reflects his alienation as an agent of production'.[2]

In this way, therefore, the neo-Marxist position comes close to that of largely non-Marxist industrial sociologists who have taken employees' immediate experience of work within a given form of technical organisation as critically determining their industrial attitudes and behaviour at all levels and, in some cases, as also shaping their more general socio-political orientations. But, as we have argued at length elsewhere, such a position is not one which accords well with the findings of our own—or of a now increasing number of other—investigations. Specifically, it may be objected that there is in fact no direct and uniform association between immediate, shop-floor work experience and employee attitudes and behaviour that are of wider reference. This is so because the effects of technologically determined conditions of work are always *mediated* through the meanings that men give to their work and through their own definitions of their work situation, and because these meanings and definitions in turn *vary* with the particular sets of wants and expectations that men bring to their employment. Thus, among the workers we studied, no systematic relationship was to be found between the degree to which their work might be considered as objectively 'alienating' and, say, the strength of their attachment to their jobs, the nature of their relationships with workmates, or their stance in regard to their employing organisation.[3]

Consequently, it becomes difficult to see the instrumental attitudes and behaviour that our respondents in the main displayed as being primarily and basically the effect of their—often significantly differing—tasks and roles within the organisation of production. Rather, their propensity to accept work as essentially a means to extrinsic ends would seem better

[1] See above, pp. 16–17.
[2] From *Tendenze del Capitalismo italiano* (Rome, 1962). Quoted in Gorz, 'Work and Consumption', p. 348. Cf. Marcuse, *One-Dimensional Man*, p. 8.
[3] See *IAB*, chs. 2, 3 and 4.

understood as something that to an important degree existed independently of, and prior to, their involvement in their present work situations. This latter interpretation, moreover, is strongly confirmed by a fact that we earlier emphasised: namely, that many of our respondents, and especially of those in routine, semi-skilled jobs, had previously performed work of an intrinsically more rewarding or at least less 'alienating' character, although no doubt in return for appreciably lower earnings than they currently enjoyed.[1] Thus, if we consider the assemblers in our sample—as representing the popular archetype of 'alienated labour'—we find that 10% had previously been employed *chiefly* in nonmanual jobs, 13% as skilled craftsmen, and another 16% in various forms of relatively skilled manual work; further, only 19% had *never* held a job more skilled than their present one, and as many as 58% had at some stage been in either nonmanual or craft employment. At the same time, 76% of these men referred to the level of pay as a reason for staying in their present jobs, and in the case of 31% this was the only reason offered.[2]

For some proportion of the workers we studied, therefore, exactly the reverse of the argument advanced by the theorists of alienation would appear to apply. Rather than an overriding concern with consumption standards reflecting alienation in work, it could be claimed that precisely such a concern constituted the motivation for these men to take, and to retain, work of a particularly unrewarding and stressful kind which offered high pay in compensation for its inherent deprivations.[3] It might indeed still be held that to devalue work rewards in this way for the sake of increasing consumer power is itself symptomatic of alienation—perhaps even of alienation in an extreme form. But in this case, of course, the idea

[1] See above, pp. 55–7, also *IAB*, pp. 32–6.

[2] See *IAB*, pp. 27–36 and also John H. Goldthorpe, 'Attitudes and Behaviour of Car Assembly Workers: a deviant case and a theoretical critique', *British Journal of Sociology*, vol. 17, no. 3 (September 1966).

[3] Such a pattern of behaviour should not, moreover, be thought of as particularly unusual. See, for example, the research reports cited in *IAB*, p. 33, n. 2; p. 39, n. 2; p. 61, n. 1; also Ingham, 'Organisational Size, Orientation to Work and Industrial Behaviour'. It should be added here that the main way in which alienation theorists differ from industrial sociologists who have emphasised the implications of technology is that the former also see as a crucial factor in the work situation the nature of property relationships. Thus, they might reply to our argument above that within capitalist society all wage labour is basically alienating and that therefore choice between different types of work, in the way we are concerned with, is largely illusory. Such a claim means denying the validity or importance of the mass of empirical research which shows that certain types of work-task and -role are regularly experienced as less depriving and as more inherently rewarding than others. A real difficulty in trying to explore the neo-Marxian theory of alienation, by means of empirical research, is in fact that of knowing exactly what connection is being presumed between the nature of work-tasks and -roles on the one hand and the bases of industrial authority on the other.

of work as being invariably the prime source of alienation has to be abandoned and its origins must be sought elsewhere; specifically, in whatever social-structural or cultural conditions generate 'consumption-mindedness' of the degree in question.

In this regard, furthermore, we may take up one other doubt about the bases of the alienation thesis. As a secondary factor to the nature of work in maintaining the working class in a state of latent alienation, the influence of advertising and of the media of mass communication generally has regularly been cited.[1] This claim, we may note, would seem to endow media effects with a much greater potency than has thus far been demonstrated by empirical research;[2] but, quite apart from this, it is obviously inadequate in itself to explain why *some* workers should be far more motivated to force up their consumption standards than others—even to the point of sacrificing their working lives. Since the mass media are in their very nature a potential source of influence on all members of the 'mass' society, what is required is some account of how individuals and groups are *differentially* exposed and responsive to the models of consumption that the media present. We have ourselves already advanced a number of relevant hypotheses, together with some supporting evidence, which attach importance to such factors as life-cycle phase, local community structure, and geographical, residential and social mobility; factors, that is, which seem likely to determine the extent to which media influences will be countered or unopposed or even reinforced by *interpersonal* influences. However, there is obviously still a serious lack of investigation in this field. *If* giving priority to 'the passive needs of personal and domestic life' is to be taken as constitutive of alienation, then, one would suggest, serious analysis calls for the development of a new empirical sociology of consumption rather than for the refurbishing of an old philosophical anthropology of production.

Finally, though, the point may be underlined that to label attitudes to work and consumption, such as those which our respondents displayed, as 'alienation' (leaving aside all questions of their source) is in effect to make a form of social diagnosis which in the end cannot be rejected by force of logic or evidence and which, by the same token, others are in no way constrained to accept. For our own part, we would simply observe that it is not to us self-evident why one should regard our respondents'

[1] See, for example, Gorz, *Stratégie Ouvrière et Néocapitalisme*, pp. 58–69, 111–18; Marcuse, *One-Dimensional Man*, pp. 4–9, and 'Liberation from the Affluent Society', in David Cooper (ed.), *The Dialectics of Liberation* (London, 1968).

[2] See the reviews provided in Joseph T. Klapper, *The Effects of Mass Communication* (Glencoe, 1957), and Denis McQuail, *Towards a Sociology of Mass Communications* (London, 1969).

concern for decent, comfortable houses, for labour-saving devices, and even for such leisure goods as television sets and cars, as manifesting the force of 'false' needs; of needs, that is, which are 'superimposed upon the individual by particular social interests in his repression'.[1] It would be equally possible to consider the amenities and possessions for which the couples in our sample were striving as representing something like the minimum material basis on which they and their children might be able to develop a more individuated style of life, with a wider range of choices, than has hitherto been possible for the mass of the manual labour force. And in particular, given the harsh dilemma that our respondents frequently faced between more inherently rewarding work and greater economic resources with which to carry through their family projects—a dilemma largely avoided by those in more advantageous class positions— we would not be inclined to speak *de haut en bas* of 'stunted mass-produced humanity', 'made-to-measure consumers' or 'sublimated slaves'.[2]

The second version of the alienation thesis that we have alluded to envisages that under certain conditions, currently being created by the development of capitalist society, working-class alienation will in fact become manifest and will express itself in forms of class action of a radical kind. As we have earlier remarked, an argument on these lines has perhaps been worked out most fully by Serge Mallet.[3] For Mallet, it will be recalled, the crucial development is the increasing importance within western economies of technologically advanced, capital-intensive plants in which production operations are of a highly integrated character. In such plants, Mallet contends, the close interdependence of managements and employees and the solidarity which tends to grow up between different groups of employee favour the emergence of a new trade unionism of a syndicalist type, capable, in the long term, of revitalising the working-class movement.

An initial observation which may be made on this analysis is that it again reveals a preoccupation with the nature of work-tasks and -roles and of work environment as the determinants of socio-political perspec-

---

[1] Marcuse, *One-Dimensional Man*, p. 5. Perhaps Marcuse and like thinkers, as well as prophets of *embourgeoisement*, need to be reminded that 'a washing machine is a washing machine is a washing machine'.

[2] In further investigating the undoubtedly negative aspects of an instrumental orientation to work and a privatised out-of-work life, a more heuristically valuable notion than 'alienation' might be that of 'identity'. See, for example, the insightful comments in Thomas Luckmann and Peter Berger, 'Social Mobility and Personal Identity', *European Journal of Sociology*, vol. 5, no. 2 (1964), and also in Luckmann, *Das Problem der Religion in der modernen Gesellschaft* (Freiburg, 1963).

[3] See above, pp. 18–19.

tives. Mallet, in fact, almost entirely neglects the out-plant lives of the members of the new working class with which he is concerned. His grounds for doing so, which he makes no attempt to substantiate, consist essentially of a version of the 'dual social identity' thesis which we have earlier referred to: 'La classe ouvrière a effectivement cessé de vivre à part... L'ouvrier cesse de se sentir tel lorsqu'il sort de l'usine.'[1] Thus, he claims, it is only by studying the workers in question 'en tant que producteurs' that the distinctive characteristics of their class situation can be understood.

The ways in which this argument might be called into doubt, both logically and empirically, should by now be evident enough.[2] However, even if we leave these aside, there remains our basic objection to the general approach which Mallet adopts: namely, that the wider social and social-psychological implications of a given type of work environment are to a significant degree *indeterminate* so long as the orientations to work of the employees involved are not also specified. In our own investigation, we were not able to study workers under extremely advanced technological conditions. But we were able to show that across several contrasting work environments, ranging from small-batch machine production to process production, a broad *similarity* in many aspects of workers' attitudes and behaviour was the notable feature: a similarity which could be seen as deriving from a shared orientation to work of a markedly instrumental kind. Moreover, it may be added that the process workers in our sample— the group, that is, working within the most integrated production system— were, if anything, less concerned than men in other groups with possibilities for 'participation' in plant or in work affairs generally. For example, the process workers contained the lowest proportion of trade unionists who believed that the unions should try to get workers a share in management (22%); the lowest proportion of 'regular' or 'occasional' attenders at union branch meetings (0%); and the lowest proportion of men reporting that they consulted their shop stewards 'very often' or 'a good deal' (17%). Further, they also revealed the lowest level of participation in work-based clubs and societies—only 4% being classed as regular attenders—and the lowest proportion (34%) attracted by the idea of promotion.[3]

[1] *La Nouvelle Classe Ouvrière*, p. 9.
[2] It is particularly remarkable that Mallet should have been led to an acceptance of the 'dual social identity' view on the basis of French data and experience. For a more detailed and considered discussion of the matter, including some critical comment on Mallet, see Jean-Marie Rainville, *Condition Ouvrière et Intégration Sociale* (Paris, 1967).
[3] See *IAB*, pp. 90–2, 98–109, 119–20. While the number of process workers we interviewed was decidedly small (N = 23) it is important to remember that these men were the élite of the Laporte production employees; i.e. the highest paid, chiefly on account of their seniority and of the responsibility entailed in their jobs. Thus they would appear to be a specially appropriate sample to consider in the present connection.

7+

Thus, what one is led to conclude, and other more extensive research than our own now bears this out, is that a production system which is highly integrated in a technical or functional sense does not in any automatic way tend to produce a high degree of social integration of employees in the plant—either in the manner envisaged by Mallet or in that suggested by Blauner and other writers previously considered.[1] For one thing, it would seem probable that automated or process production systems may, in fact, in certain respects inhibit social integration;[2] but, more importantly, the possibilities for, and constraints upon, the organisation of social relationships which such systems entail must be seen simply as setting limits to patterns that are actually determined by wider social-structural and cultural influences. On this basis, it could well be argued that the emergent forms of worker action and labour relations described by Mallet in the enterprises he studied are far more a 'French' phenomenon—a product, say, of French trade union structure and ideology, of French styles of management, of the pattern of French economic development and so on—than they are a phenomenon of technologically advanced plants *per se*.

Lastly, in regard to Mallet, we may note that the findings of our own enquiry do appear consistent with a possibility which he considered, but then discounted, as an alternative to the idea that syndicalism at plant level will lead on to a new stage in the 'global' class struggle. That is, the possibility that workers in modern, high-productivity enterprises will adopt an increasingly particularistic approach to industrial relations, thus giving rise to a new 'corporatism' and the consolidation of a new labour aristocracy. Certainly among the workers we studied there was a general appreciation of the extent to which their individual prosperity depended upon the economic fortunes of the firms in which they were presently employed. The majority revealed a preparedness for 'teamwork' and 'accommodation' in their attitudes towards their firms, even while being eager to press for as large a share in the proceeds of such co-operation as they could possibly get.[3] Moreover, if it is accepted, as Mallet apparently does accept, that the typical goals and aspirations of the new working class are for secure and rising incomes and higher living standards, then it is

---

[1] See in particular the detailed report by Friedrich Fürstenberg, 'Structural Changes in the Working Class: a situational study of workers in the Western German chemical industry' in J. A. Jackson (ed.), *Sociological Studies I: Social Stratification* (Cambridge, 1968). In a variety of ways, Fürstenberg's findings reveal interesting similarities with our own as reported in this and previous publications.

[2] See above, pp. 40–1.

[3] See *IAB*, pp. 72–89.

difficult to see why such a stance *vis-à-vis* employers is not a largely rational one. At all events, the point can scarcely be evaded that even in enterprises where a concern with increasing worker participation and control develops, this need not be oriented towards class, as opposed to sectional, objectives nor need it entail any commitment to radical change in the wider economic or social order. Rather than representing alienation made manifest, *syndicalisme gestionnaire* could be simply an advanced form of instrumental collectivism.[1]

It will, then, by now be evident that, in our view, interpretations of the new working class in terms of alienation, whether this is seen as a latent or a manifest state, give rise to a variety of doubts and objections. In so far as such interpretations are open to critical examination from a sociological standpoint, they reveal weaknesses of both an analytical and empirical kind. Basically, we would argue, these weaknesses stem from the insistence of alienation theorists on the crucial significance of the nature of work activity and relationships to any understanding of working-class social being and consciousness. This insistence stands in direct contrast with (and has sometimes served as a useful corrective to) the tendency of adherents of the *embourgeoisement* thesis to concentrate their attention on consumption and domestic life, and to leave almost entirely out of account the worker as producer. However, as against both these emphases, we would maintain that the relative importance of these two different areas of social life and experience to the understanding of working-class perspectives and modes of action is not an issue to be decided *a priori*: it is, rather, a central one for sociological enquiry.

In the two preceding sections of this chapter, we have reviewed critically two very divergent perspectives on the new working class and its probable future as a socio-political force: what we might perhaps refer to as the

---

[1] Mallet's argument to the effect that: 'C'est le caractère global de l'économie de notre époque qui est la meilleure protection du syndicalisme d'entreprise contre les tendances particularistes ou le repliement corporatiste étroit' is probably the weakest part of his entire analysis. Here, in relying on the effects of necessary contradictions in capitalist economies, he appears to lapse into the dogmatic Marxism which he elsewhere deplores. See *La Nouvelle Classe Ouvrière*, pp. 70–4. It is interesting to note that a case of a strike at a French electronics plant during the events of May–June 1968, which is presented as supporting Mallet's general position, in fact shows that the aim of demands for *cogestion* was essentially to increase operating efficiency and profitability so as to make possible higher wage and salary levels for all employees. See Jacques Leenhardt, 'La Nouvelle Classe Ouvrière en Grève', *Sociologie du Travail*, no. 4 (1968). This paper is intended to qualify the findings of an earlier study which went directly contrary to Mallet's views in showing a lack of solidarity between technicians and manual workers: Christiane Barrier, 'Techniciens et Grèves à l'Electricité de France', *Sociologie du Travail*, no. 1 (1968).

liberal and the neo-Marxist points of view. To end with, it is not our intention to try to develop a third such perspective, or at least not one that is of at all a comparable kind. As will be seen, our ambitions are, advisedly, far more limited.

Despite the many ways in which they are obviously in direct conflict, the two interpretations that we have considered have at least one major underlying similarity: that is, they are alike in deriving from some kind of evolutionist position. Their proponents typically claim on the one hand to have some grasp of the inherent 'logic' of industrialism; or, on the other, to possess an understanding of the long-term dynamics of capitalism. Consequently, they are equally inclined to see the future problems and possibilities of the working class as being, as it were, already immanent at least in its most 'advanced' sections. However, our arguments against both liberal and neo-Marxist analyses have been largely intended to raise questions as to the reliability of certain relationships which appear basic to the developmental schemes that these analyses imply. These are such questions as: *Must* the achievement of 'middle-class' incomes by manual workers and their families presage a decline in their commitment to labour-oriented political parties? *Is* a preoccupation with personal and domestic consumption the specific consequence of alienating conditions of work? *Do* the most advanced industrial technologies have a built-in propensity to create enterprises that are highly integrated socially as well as functionally?

To the extent, then, that in these and similar respects we entertain serious doubts, our own position must be a less crudely deterministic one.[1] Different sections of the working class find themselves in differing situations, and this is likely to remain the case for the foreseeable future. The situation of the 'new' working class we would see as being a relatively *open* one; that is to say, one in which a quite wide range of possibilities is inherent, although the chances of their realisation may vary. What actually occurs will depend to a significant extent on factors which the two interpretations discussed do not take adequately into account.

For instance, rather than seeing in instrumental attitudes to work and in

---

[1] It should be said that neo-Marxist writers of the present do differ notably from Marxists of an earlier period in revealing some uncertainty as to whether capitalism will in fact prove to be unstable and thus permit the 'final' stage of historical development—from capitalism, to socialism—to be accomplished. In *One-Dimensional Man*, for example, Marcuse evinces some considerable pessimism in this respect. At the same time, though, it is evident that Marcuse, no less than say, Galbraith, accepts the idea that modern societies are being forced on to convergent paths of development, even if the ultimate model on which this process is focused is that now emergent in America rather than a socialist one.

privatisation the clear signs of a secular decline in working-class collectivism or the superimposition of 'false' needs, we would claim that what is undoubtedly in evidence here is that in the pursuit of higher living standards certain other wants and expectations are being devalued or suppressed, but not to the extent that deprivation ceases to be felt. There exists, in other words, a situation of some tension. Moreover, it is in our view likely that a sense of deprivation will tend to increase as improvements in material standards reach the point at which old wants are satisfied and aspirations of a new type arise—aspirations that are less closely related to consumption of a private character and less easily fulfilled. To illustrate but one possibility, it may be recalled that among our Luton couples parents' aspirations for their children appeared already to be running well beyond the latter's actual chances of success within the existing system of educational provision. Thus, in circumstances of this kind, the *potential* support for politics of social change is evident enough: but whether this potentiality is realised and, if so, how, will depend upon the degree and the manner in which the awareness of deprivation becomes articulated and directed.

Similarly, the absence, as in the case of the workers we studied, of well-defined images of the social order, other than 'money' models of a rather peculiar abstractness, does not have to be interpreted either as betokening a basic incompatibility between class consciousness and mass society or as 'false' consciousness. It too, in our opinion, most obviously suggests 'openness': a situation in which social consciousness is not delimited by the fixed horizons of either deferential or proletarian traditionalism and in which there are indeed few established cultural prescriptions serving to define the nature of the social order. As a result, individual conceptions tend to be variable, inchoate or at any rate incomplete, and therefore to be relatively malleable.

Thus, in our perspective on the new working class and on the question of what its political significance will be, the 'degrees of freedom' that exist become a consideration of central importance. To introduce such an emphasis would seem desirable if only to counterbalance the necessitarian tendencies inherent in other interpretations. But, furthermore, we would underline the heuristic value in bringing out in this way the role that must be assigned to political *leadership*: that is, to purposive action on the part of élites and organisations, aimed at giving a specific and politically relevant meaning to grievances, demands and aspirations, which have hitherto been of a sub-political kind, and at thus mobilising mass support for a programme or movement.

So far as the British case is concerned, it is the future performance in this respect of the Labour Party and its affiliates which may be presumed to be of major consequence. In the past, the parochial character of traditional working-class collectivism was given wider and more explicit formulation by a Labour movement whose goals and ideologies were capable of transcending the particularism of communal solidarity. At the present time, however, the instrumental collectivism of the new working class is confined to local and narrowly economic issues and lacks any comparable articulation at the level of national politics. As is evident from our own and other enquiries, the new worker often regards politics as being of only marginal relevance to the concerns of his private life;[1] still less than the traditional worker, one would suggest, does he recognise connections between his personal hopes and fears and public issues. Thus, both the opportunity and the task for creative political leadership that now face the Labour Party are considerable, no matter how at any particular moment its electoral fortunes may stand. While at one level of analysis the new working class must obviously be seen as a product of economic and social structural changes of a long-term kind, what it becomes as a socio-political force could well be critically influenced by what the Labour Party seeks to make of it.

For example, one obvious possibility is that the basis of Labour strategy will continue to be essentially the same as it has been since at least the mid-1950s. That is to say, the position may be maintained that increasing affluence and concomitant changes in working-class social life imply the progressive erosion of the traditional Labour vote, and that consequently these threats have to be countered by modifying the image and indeed the policies of the party in an appropriate direction: specifically, by ridding them of their distinctively 'class' character and making them more attractive to those groups, including the new working class, which now constitute the all-important 'middle ground' of electoral politics.

The first comment that must be made on this position is that convincing support for the basic claim—that affluence tends to weaken working-class attachment to Labour—has never been adduced, and that, as we have seen, empirical investigation has tended largely to disconfirm this connection. It is, therefore, difficult to accept entirely at face value the argument typically advanced by those advocating a 'centrist' strategy that this is one made *necessary* by the changing nature of economic and social con-

[1] See, for example, *PAB*, pp. 22–4, 29–32; also Willmott, *The Evolution of a Community*, pp. 106–7.

190

ditions—that it represents the only realistic and responsible line of development of Labour politics within the affluent society. Rather, we would
suggest, such advocacy must be understood as being itself a political
initiative—an attempt at political leadership—intended to take the party
away from radical politics of a class-oriented kind because a move in this
direction is regarded as inherently desirable. Far from reflecting, as is often
claimed, a hardheaded recognition of 'the end of ideology', the strategy of
winning the middle ground must be seen as being in fact inspired by
ideology more than by sociology. Ideas of *embourgeoisement*, of the socially
marginal worker, and so on have not so much prompted the concern to
weaken Labour's working-class identification as served as convenient and,
for a time, plausible legitimations for this shift.

However, the fact that the strategy in question is *not* empirically well-
grounded has significant consequences. It means, for example, that
Labour has in one sense underestimated the potential firmness of its
support among the working class and thus the possibilities offered by re-
taining—and developing—its class base. On the other hand, though, it
means that the effect that affluence and its concomitants most probably
have had on the working-class Labour vote has been neglected. That is,
the tendency for a purely affective or customary attachment to Labour to
give way to one of a somewhat more calculative kind: an attachment likely
to be more dependent on Labour clearly and consistently demonstrating
that it *is* the party of the working man. This neglect would appear to have
become particularly far-reaching in its implications in the course of the
second Wilson administration. Government economic policies—notably
in regard to prices and incomes and industrial relations—have not been
manifestly favourable to working-class interests, and there have been few
compensating measures of a radically redistributional or otherwise egalitarian kind. Under such circumstances, it is not hard to envisage the frustration of the affluent worker's private economic ambitions leading to still
further attenuation of the links between localised, trade union collectivism and electoral support for the Labour Party. Indeed, opinion poll data
over the period 1967–9 point clearly enough to a considerable shift of
working-class sentiment away from Labour; and the one enquiry that has
been made into underlying attitudes points to the conclusion that the
likely defectors are individuals who 'had looked to the advantages which a
Labour Government could bring in terms of prices, full employment,
social benefits' and now feel cheated mainly because it is these direct
personal advantages that have been withheld.[1]

[1] See 'The Lost Labour Voter', *Socialist Commentary* (February 1969).

Thus, at the time of writing (1969) it seems probable that working-class abstentions, apart from any actual voting swing to the Conservatives, will result in electoral defeat for Labour in 1971 or earlier; and this could perhaps mark the beginning of another lengthy period of Conservative rule. But even if this were to occur, it is important to recognise that it would not necessarily result in the Labour Party leadership abandoning its centrist strategy. On the contrary, it might well be that the proponents of this strategy would successfully argue that the loss of working-class support brings out more clearly than before the need for Labour to become a 'national' party capable of appealing to all social strata. In this way, therefore, it is evident that the radical potential of the working class, old and new, could remain unrealised indefinitely, and conceivably to the point of extinction. Richard Hamilton has neatly summed up the whole matter as follows:

Ironically, the 'end of radical politics' in many countries may well be the result of a self-fulfilling prophecy. The intellectuals supporting this view succeed in convincing political leaders. These leaders, in turn, believing that people will no longer respond to traditional liberal and leftist issues, now stress other concerns. The newly moderate leaders lose elections (because many voters no longer see them as standing for the issues that interest them). The election results are then taken as additional proof of the rejection of radical politics on the part of the newly affluent masses. The response of the leadership is to call for still more moderation.[1]

It may indeed be that the inner logic of this sequence is so compelling that, on any sober assessment, it is this more than anything else that we must expect in Britain in the 1970s and after. Nevertheless, even if this is so, it does not remove the relevance or importance of stressing that other, very different, possibilities still *do* exist and still *could* be realistically pursued. Most notably, as the direct opposite of the attempt to lose its class identification and win the middle ground, it is still open to the Labour Party to take as its major objective that of strengthening its hold on the working class as conventionally understood (bearing in mind the fact that less than two-thirds of manual workers and their wives regularly vote Labour) while establishing itself also among the growing white-collar labour force of men and women occupying subordinate technical and administrative posts. At the same time, it could seek to distinguish itself from the Conservative Party with increasing sharpness in a number of respects.

[1] *Affluence and the French Worker in the Fourth Republic*, p. 292. Cf. Westergaard, 'The Withering Away of Class', pp. 110–13.

Such a strategy would entail a reversion by Labour to a clear commitment to the interests of the mass of wage-earning, rank-and-file employees, and an endeavour to advance these interests not merely by promoting general economic expansion but also by thorough-going egalitarian measures over a wide front. This would no doubt lead to strenuous political conflict and also probably to a heightening of social antagonisms. But it must be remembered that when working-class voters explain that they back the Labour Party because it is likely to be 'just that little bit more for the working man', there is no suggestion that they approve of the nicety with which Labour seeks to retain their support, or that they would be opposed to policies more manifestly in their favour. Rather, as we have seen, such policies are likely to become increasingly necessary if their allegiance is to be kept firm.

Moreover, an intensification of socio-political debate and a widening awareness of the extent of inequality in British society would be of definite advantage to Labour as regards a second important possibility: namely, that of politicising the new aspirations that may be expected to emerge among the working class in the wake of affluence. Rising ambitions for children's careers have already been mentioned; and one might further suggest, for example, a growing concern for an improved urban environment and demands for more extensive public provision for recreation and leisure generally. New aspirations in these directions are not a long step away from wanting high material standards of living in a domestic context; but they are ones much more likely to be blocked in a society whose institutions are far more efficiently geared to producing private affluence than to organising equal opportunities for individual growth and self-fulfilment. Thus, support for policies designed to realise such aspirations would in fact virtually imply support for policies of a radical cast in relation to education, social welfare, town and regional planning, and so on.

Finally, Labour could go yet one stage further in refusing to accept the—essentially Conservative—doctrine that the efficient management of the economy is the key to electoral success. For the Labour Party to attempt to compete with the Conservatives on these terms alone is in effect for it to agree on the enemy's ground; and there is implied, moreover, the damaging admission—for any party with radical pretensions—that political debate centres on means rather than on ends. The contrary possibility that exists is therefore for Labour to seek actively to stimulate and shape political demands which may as yet be relatively weak and unformed but which are of a kind that the Conservative Party would find it

7*

difficult to accommodate. The most obvious examples here are demands
for some substantial measure of employee participation in the control
of industrial enterprises and, more generally, for the democratisation
of economic decision-making and for greater accountability in the use of
economic power from plant and community level upwards.[1] In other
words, the party could choose to construe its political task as being not
merely that of responding to wants and expectations already manifest
among its potential supporters, but further as that of endeavouring to
expand and diversify such wants and expectations in ways that would
carry radical implications.

At a time when a Labour government is giving overriding priority to
'getting the economy right' and when the preservation of consensus is
claimed to be vital to this end, ideas for the revival of class-based politics
are not likely to have any immediate attraction for the party leadership.
They are in fact depicted as irresponsible and beyond the bounds of the
practical: in consequence, of course, the chances of their being actualised
are automatically diminished. On the other hand, it may be added, these
same ideas, relating as they do to a strategy that accepts the existence of
parliamentary institutions, would face rejection by most of the neo-
Marxist Left as evidence merely of a 'necrophiliac' attachment to social
democracy: from this standpoint too, radical politics are regarded as being
at an end—unless, that is, a revolutionary upheaval can in some way be
triggered off.

In our own estimation, however, both of these negative positions must
be interpreted as to some very large degree reflecting the political preferences—and hopes—of their adherents. The possibility of the Labour
Party adopting and efficiently pursuing radical objectives is not in fact
denied by any lessons of history nor by any results of sociological investigation or analysis. What these sources do reveal is the variety of the
factors that tend to inhibit Labour leaders from embarking on such a
course—not least, awareness of the extent of the problems to be overcome
and of the force of the opposition to be met. But the possibility itself is not

[1] As regards employee participation, our own findings offer some illustration of the scope that
exists for building up and formulating demands that may currently be expressed only at a low,
and largely sub-political, level. As previously noted (*IAB*, pp. 108–9) there was no very extensive support among our affluent workers (the craftsmen apart) for the idea that their
unions should seek to increase their involvement in management. However, the fact that among
men with such generally restricted wants and expectations in work there should be a sizable
minority (about a third overall) who *did* wish for a greater voice in the running of their firms,
suggests that such a concern could at all events be more readily developed than, say, a greater
interest in participation in the 'plant community'—or the union branch.

thereby excluded.[1] It is there to be taken up by a leadership with sufficient political nerve and skill; and the chances of success of such an attempt, as regards both the survival of the Labour Party and the achievement of basic structural reforms, cannot at all events be reckoned as appreciably less than those of either consensus politics or revolution.

Thus, our conclusion must be that if the working class does in the long term become no more than one stratum within a system of 'classless inegalitarianism', offering no basis for or response to radical initiatives, then this situation will not be adequately explained either as an inevitable outcome of the evolution of industrialism or as reflecting the ability of neo-capitalism to contain the consequences of its changing infrastructure by means of mass social–psychological manipulation. It will to some degree be also attributable to the fact that the political leaders of the working class *chose* this future for it.

[1] This is not for a moment to deny that the need exists for far more study of the inhibiting factors in question. The sociology of the leadership of left-wing democratic parties has scarcely been advanced since Michels; yet this must be regarded as an essential complement to studies of the social composition and character of their mass support.

Appendix A. The occupational classification used in the study

The occupational classification set out in the first column of table A1 below was constructed on the basis of previous efforts by British sociologists, notably that of Hall and Caradog Jones.[1] The particular occupational classifications used in this and other reports on the research have been derived from this more comprehensive eightfold classification through collapsing categories in whatever ways appeared most useful from case to case. The threefold classification into 'white-collar', 'intermediate', and 'manual' occupations that is used in the present monograph is given in the last column of table A1.

In allocating particular occupations to classes of occupations we followed the general rule of choosing the 'lower' alternative in all borderline cases or cases where our information was incomplete or ambiguous. The examples given below are selected in order to give some idea of the range of occupations included in given categories as well as of 'typical' occupations.

[1] J. Hall and D. Caradog Jones, 'The Social Grading of Occupations', *British Journal of Sociology*, vol. 1 (January 1950).

TABLE A1. *Occupational classification*

Occupational status level	Examples	Summary classification used as basis for 'white-collar affiliation' groupings
1 (a) Higher professional, managerial and other white-collar employees	Chartered accountant, business executive, senior civil servant, graduate teacher	
(b) Large industrial or commercial employers, landed proprietors	—	
2 (a) Intermediate professional, managerial and other white-collar employees	Pharmacist, non-graduate teacher, departmental manager, bank cashier	
(b) Medium industrial or commercial employers, substantial farmers	—	'White-collar'
3 (a) Lower professional, managerial and other white-collar employees	Chiropodist, bar manager, commercial traveller, draughtsman, accounts or wages clerk	
(b) Small industrial or commercial employers, small proprietors, small farmers	Jobbing builder, taxi owner–driver, tobacconist	
4 (a) Supervisory, inspectional, minor officials and service employees	Foreman, meter-reader, shop assistant, door-to-door salesman	
(b) Self-employed men (no employees or expensive capital equipment)	Window cleaner, jobbing gardener	'Intermediate'
5 Skilled manual workers (with apprenticeship or equivalent)	—	
6 Other relatively skilled manual workers	Unapprenticed mechanics and fitters, skilled miners, painters and decorators, p.s.v. drivers	'Manual'
7 Semi-skilled manual workers	Machine operator, assember, storeman	
8 Unskilled manual workers	Farm labourer, builder's labourer, dustman	

Appendix B. Membership in formal associations

We show first below the schema which was used in classifying the associational memberships of our respondents.[1] The examples given are intended to indicate the kind of association which figured (or in the case of type 1, which might have figured) most frequently in the cell in question.

Nature of functions	Probable composition of membership in terms of occupational status*		
	Predominantly white–collar	Mixed	Predominantly manual
Diffuse	1 Freemasons Conservative clubs	2 Buffaloes Free Foresters Royal Air Force Association Townswomen's Guild	3 Working men's clubs British Legion Clubs 'Sports and social' clubs
Intermediate	4 Golf clubs Flying club Works sailing club	5 Cricket clubs (some) Rifle club Luton Girls' Choir Works photo club	6 Pigeon clubs Angling clubs Football clubs (some) Weightlifting and body-building clubs
Specific	7 Grammar school P.T.A.'s Residents' associations (some)	8 Modern school P.T.A.'s S.J.A.B. W.V.S. Charitable bodies Gardening clubs	9 Tenants' associations Allotment societies

* The information used in classifying associations in this respect was obtained during preliminary fieldwork in Luton and in the firms on which our sample is based; or, where necessary, by enquiring into specific cases.

Table B1 then shows how the memberships of our affluent workers and their wives were distributed between the types of association that the schema distinguishes.

[1] This was influenced to some extent by C. Wayne Gordon and Nicholas Babchuk, 'A Typology of Voluntary Associations', *American Sociological Review*, vol. 24, no. 2 (February 1959).

TABLE B1. *Associational memberships by type of association*

Type of association*	Number of memberships claimed		
	Husbands	Wives	All
1	0	0	0
2	10	31	41
3	41	19	60
4	4	1	5
5	59	7	66
6	23	0	23
7	6	4	10
8	49	41	90
9	14	12	26
TOTAL MEMBERSHIPS	206	115	321

	Percentage of total memberships claimed		
	Husbands	Wives	All
Associations with predominantly white–collar memberships and diffuse or 'intermediate' functions; or with predominantly white–collar or 'mixed' memberships and diffuse functions (types 1, 2 and 4)	7	28	14
Associations with 'mixed' memberships and 'intermediate' functions (type 5)	29	6	20
Associations with predominantly manual memberships or with specific functions (types 3, 6, 7, 8 and 9)	65	66	65
TOTALS	101	100	99

Appendix C. The collection and analysis of data on respondents' images of class

In the course of the 'home' interview schedule (see below, pp. 212–25) we put the following question, which was deliberately worded in a rather vague way, to each of the men in our sample: 'People often talk about there being different classes—what do you think?' Except in those cases where the existence of classes was firmly denied the answer given to this question was then taken as the starting point for a general discussion of class of a relatively unstructured kind. The schedules had printed on them a check-list of issues on which interviewers were to seek to establish each respondent's views, but the order in which issues were raised could be varied, following the natural flow of the discussion, and interviewers were instructed to try so far as possible to formulate their questions *in ways consistent with what they had already learnt about respondents' ideas and conceptions*. The following is an extract from the brief which was prepared for the guidance of interviewers on this section of schedule.

This series of questions as a whole is designed to elicit the respondent's picture of the class structure and of his own position in it (and to find out how far he is sensitive to status divisions). However, it is important that he should not be pressed to think in terms of unfamiliar concepts; this means that the probing must be done very carefully, and related directly to the answers given. But despite this, one must attempt to get answers that are moderately clear and self-explanatory on paper.

It may not be possible to get the material divided up as has been done in our headings, but this doesn't matter; encourage the respondent to stick to them as much as can be done without constraining his spontaneity, and have no inhibitions about referring back to a point that has already been partly covered when you come to it later.

As throughout the interview, you should write down as nearly as possible exactly what the respondent says; where there isn't time to catch the exact words, get the gist of it and the exact wording only for especially significant phrases. It's better to get down disjointed phrases that convey the feel of the situation than to have some parts verbatim and others omitted, although it should never be allowed to become so disjointed that the trend of the argument is lost.

The content of the general instructions should be thoroughly learnt; particular examples are however not meant to suggest that these are the answers we want to get, but simply to give some idea of the possibilities before we've had time to learn this from experience. Where opening questions (on particular issues) are suggested, they should be used unless there is some good reason (in the nature of the respondent's previous answers) against it. We want to establish as much uniformity of interviewing practice as we can without making it impossible to talk to each respondent roughly in his own terms.

The brief then went on to explain in detail the nature of the issues in which we were interested. These in effect called for coverage of respondents' views on almost every major aspect of social stratification: the main lines of class division; the composition of classes; the determinants of the class position of individuals and groups; subjective class identification; the extent and channels of social mobility; the causes of the phenomenon of classes in general; and the nature of ongoing or probable changes in the class structure.

Through this method of interviewing, as may be imagined, a considerable quantity of material was accumulated: in a large majority of cases, this section of the interview schedule produced a document of upwards of 2,000 words. Following a careful initial reading of these documents, it proved possible for the most part to devise manageable systems of coding which at the same time appeared reasonably adequate to the degree of heterogeneity which was displayed. However, in view of the relatively unsystematic and often *nuancé* character of the material, it was also clearly desirable to demonstrate the *reliability* of our codes in the sense that their use by different individuals on the same cases would produce similar results. Consequently, a test was undertaken in which 50 cases were coded by five persons, each case being coded by two of the five selected at random. Each person coded 20 cases in all and had five cases in common with each of the other four. Through this test it was revealed that some appreciable variation occurred in the reliability of codes for particular items, and it was eventually decided that a number of these—where the average disagreement between coders was calculated at > 15%—should be abandoned. With the codes then remaining, the average disagreement between coders was calculated at < 10%.[1] The 'approved' codes, in terms of which data were subsequently processed and tabulated, pertained to the following items:

(i) The number of major social classes distinguished by respondents.

(ii) The kind of terminology respondents used in specifying these classes.

(iii) Respondents' views on the major factor determining the class position of individuals and groups.

(iv) The position respondents saw themselves as holding within the class structure.

(v) Respondents' explanations of why individuals and groups held the class positions which they did.

(vi) Respondents' assessment of the extent of upward social mobility.

(vii) Respondents' views on the necessity and desirability of the class system.

Those items in regard to which codes were not approved were, fortunately, not crucially important ones so far at least as the investigation of our respondents, basic conceptions of the class structure were concerned.[2] However, in the case of one item of undoubted interest in this connection—respondents' views on the positioning of class 'boundaries'—no detailed method of coding of a generally satisfactory kind could be worked out by the time that the reliability test was made. Thus, information on this matter which is included in the discussion of

---

[1] We wish to acknowledge the assistance we received from Mr P. C. Carroll in devising this test and in carrying out both the test and final coding. Assistance with the test coding was also kindly given by Messrs M. Anderson, A. F. Heath and G. Salaman.

[2] They were in fact largely items on which we had allowed multiple codes—e.g. perceived channels of mobility—and in such cases the possibilities for disagreement between coders are obviously increased.

Appendixes

our respondents' images of class is derived from the direct inspection of schedules. It will be observed that in this respect no detailed analysis is attempted.

As was earlier noted, a forthcoming paper will present and discuss more of our material on class imagery than is incorporated in the present work.

Appendix D. The interview schedules

Wherever data from our interviewing programme has been presented in the text, we have followed the practice of giving in the text, or in a footnote to it, the wording of the questions from which the data were derived. The present appendix supplements this information by setting out our two main interviewing schedules in almost complete form. What has been omitted, for reasons of space, are the various charts or 'grids' on which the responses to a number of questions were recorded and, in some cases, simultaneously coded. At various points we have added explanatory notes, which are contained in square brackets. The notes in italics are instructions to the interviewer which appeared on the original schedules. Questions marked with an asterisk are those which were brought together to form the interview schedule for our white-collar sample. In some few instances their wording was modified slightly so as to make them appropriate for white-collar respondents.

It may be observed that no results have been presented in this or other reports on our research from several items included in our schedules. The reasons for such omissions vary. For example, in some cases either the questions put or the problems on which they were intended to throw light were not well-conceived and the information produced was thus of little use. In other cases, the results are of interest but we have simply not found it possible to incorporate them into the structure of the reports we have produced. Available tabulations of results from all the items in question may be had on application to the authors.

WORK SCHEDULE

Date: *Number:*

Section 1: Work history
In this section distinguish carefully 'job' in the sense of working for a specific firm and in the sense of the actual work-task carried out.

1. When did you *first* come to work here at Vauxhall/Skefko/Laporte?

2. Since then, have you ever left, either of your own accord or because of redundancy?
   If 'Yes': When was that?
   Why?
   When did you come back?

3. Have you ever worked anywhere except Vauxhall/Skefko/Laporte?
   If 'No': move to question 5.
   If 'Yes': ask question 4.

4. (a) What was the last job you did before coming here in [date last joined present firm].
   - (i) Name of firm
   - (ii) Location of firm
   - (iii) Actual type of job
   - (iv) Skill level
   - (v) Industry

(b) What were the main jobs you had before that; say those you had for a year or more? *Specify by actual type of job.*
   - (i) *earliest*
   - (ii)
   - (iii)
   - (iv)
   - (v)
   - (vi)

Prompt if necessary re military service and job done in forces.

(c) And how many different jobs have you had altogether since starting work including your present one? *If man is in doubt—say 'well roughly then'.*

(d) Did you like any of your other jobs more than the one you have now? *If 'Yes'* : Which ones?
Why?

* 5. Have you ever thought of leaving your present job at Vauxhall/Skefko/Laporte?
If 'Yes' : Why?
Have you done anything about it? *Prompt if necessary* : '*such as looking for a job in the paper*'.
If 'Yes' : What was that?
Ask all : What is it then that keeps you here?

6. *For those who have worked elsewhere than at present firm.* Had you ever worked on [present type of job] before coming to Vauxhall/Skefko/Laporte?

* 7. (a) What sort of work does your father do or what was his last job, if he is no longer alive or retired?
* (b) Has/had he been in that kind of work for most of his life?
If 'No' : *Probe for other main jobs done ; be sure to get skill level.*

Section 2: The worker and his job

* 1. What exactly is your present job? Could you tell me briefly in your own words just what it is that you do?

2. Have you done any other jobs in Vauxhall/Skefko/Laporte?
If 'No' : *move to question 4.*
If 'Yes' : What were they?

3. Do you prefer the job you're doing now to others you have done in Vauxhall/Skefko/Laporte?

If 'Yes' : Why is that?

If 'No' : Which of your other jobs did you prefer?

Why?

4. *Ask all.* Are there any other shop-floor jobs in Vauxhall/Skefko/Laporte which you would rather do than your own?

If 'Yes' : What are they?

Why would you prefer those?

Have you ever thought of asking to be transferred to one of these jobs?

If 'Yes' : Have you done anything about it? *Specify*

If 'No' or uncertain : Do you think your job is one of the best going then?

* 5. *Hand card.* Here are some of the things often thought important about a job: which one would you look for first in a job? And which next?

Interest and variety

Good pay and the chance of plenty of overtime

Good workmates

A supervisor who doesn't breathe down your neck

Pleasant working conditions

A strong and active union

6. So far as these two things are concerned would you say that your present job is

First rate?

Pretty good?

Not too good?

Very bad?

7. Do you find your present job physically tiring?

8. Would you say it puts a great strain on your nerves? *Prompt if necessary* : *'Does it make you feel jittery at the end of the day?'*

9. Do you find it monotonous?

10. [Vauxhall] Can you 'work up the line' or 'build a bank' in your job?

If 'No' : Why is that?

[Skefko] Do you set yourself an output target—say, so many pieces of work per day?

If 'Yes' : Do you ever work faster to get within reach of the target early on and then take it easy for a bit?

[This question was not asked of Laporte workers.]

11. Do you ever find the pace of the job too fast?

12. Do you find you can think about other things while doing your job?

If 'Yes' : What do you think about?

13. Which would you prefer: a job where someone tells you exactly how to do the work or one where you are left to decide for yourself how to go about it?

14. If there was one thing about your job here you could change what would it be? *At some point ask all:* 'How do you feel about shiftwork?'

Section 3: Worker and work group

1. (*a*) In your job, how much do you talk to your workmates? Would you say

    A good deal?
    Just now and then?
    Hardly at all?

    (*b*) When do you talk to them? Mainly during work or during breaks?

    (*c*) *If* 'good deal' *or* 'now and then' : What sort of things do you talk about, is it mainly about work or mainly about things outside the factory?

* 2. How would you feel if you were moved to another job in the factory more or less like the one you do now but away from the men who work near to you? Would you feel

    Very upset?
    Fairly upset?
    Not much bothered?
    Not bothered at all?

3. How many of the men who work near to you would you call close friends? *If none move to question 7.*

4. When do you see him/them outside of the factory?

5. How well do you know his wife and family/their wives and families? Would you say you know them

    Very well?
    Quite well?
    Just to say hello to?
    Not at all?

6. Do any of them/does he live near you, say, within ten minutes' walk?

* 7. (*a*) How do you get on with your foreman? Would you say you got on
    Very well?
    Pretty well?
    Not so well?
    Very badly?
    (*b*) Why is this?

8. If '*pretty well*', '*not so well*' *or* '*very badly*' : Do you think it possible for a worker to get on really well with his foreman?
    If '*No*' : Why not?
    If '*Yes*' : What would have to be changed to make this possible in your case?

* 9. (*a*) How about the idea of becoming a foreman? Would you like this

206

Very much?
Quite a lot?
Not much?
Not at all?

*   (b) Why do you say this?

10. Have you ever thought seriously of becoming a foreman?
If 'Yes': What have you done about it?

11. Just supposing you did become a foreman, what do you think your mates would feel about it? *Probe for admiration; envy; sense of betrayal; amusement, etc.*

Section 4: Worker and firm

* 1. *Check back to section 1, question 5 and ask if appropriate.* You said you stayed at Vauxhall/Skefko/Laporte because ... Do you think there are many firms which would give you these advantages?

* 2. How would you say Vauxhall/Skefko/Laporte compares with other firms you know of as a firm to work for. Would you say it was
Better than most?
About average?
Worse than most?

* 3. (a) Which workers get a better deal for themselves; those in nationalised industries or those in private enterprise concerns like Vauxhall/Skefko/Laporte?

*   (b) Why?

4. Do you think this firm is run as efficiently as it might be?
If 'No': Have you ever made any suggestions for improving efficiency?

5. Do you think work study men are more concerned to make things go smoothly for everyone or chiefly to make the worker keep up a fast pace all the time?

* 6. *Hand card.* Here are two opposing views about industry generally. I'd like you to tell me which you agree with more. Some people say that a firm is like a football side—because good teamwork means success and is to everyone's advantage. Others say that teamwork in industry is impossible —because employers and men are really on opposite sides. Which view do you agree with more?

* 7. This firm has an exceptionally good industrial relations record. Why do you think this is?

8. How do you feel about the number of office workers in Vauxhall/Skefko/Laporte? Would you say there are
Too many?

Not enough?

About right?

9. What do you think about the pay of men in clerical jobs in Vauxhall/Skefko/Laporte as compared with your own? Would you say they earned

Too little?

Too much?

About right?

If asked about amount earned by clerical workers say 'Anything from £12–20 per week.'

*10. (a) Do you think the firm could pay you more than it does without damaging its prospects for the future? *Prompt if necessary about markets.*

* (b) Why?

11. (a) You are paid by [method of payment in operation]: some workers in other firms are on piece-rates/time-rates and many office workers get paid a fixed salary with nothing extra for overtime. Which method of payment would you prefer?

A salary

Hourly rates

Piece-rates

(b) Why?

12. It is possible that at some time in the future workers may get their wages by cheque. How would you feel about this? Would you be

Generally against?

Not much bothered?

Generally in favour?

*13. In this firm there are different canteens for shop-floor workers, office workers and managers. Do you think this is on the whole a good thing or should all canteens be open to everybody?

14. Are you a special section member of the [works club], that is, more than an 'ordinary member'?

If 'Yes': What activities do you take part in? Probe for rough degree of regularity.

Have you ever held an official position in the [works club] or one of its sections?

If 'Yes': What was that?

When did you hold it?

15. (a) [Vauxhall] How do you think Vauxhall cars compare with other makes, price for price. Would you say they are

Better?

About the same?

Worse?

(b) Do you have a car?

If 'Yes': Is it a Vauxhall?

If 'No': What make is it then? (Specify)

15. [Skefko/Laporte] How do you think Skefko/Laporte products compare with those of other engineering/chemical firms. Would you say they are:

> Better?
>
> About the same?
>
> Worse?

Section 5: Worker and union

* 1. (a) Are you a member of a trade union?
>> *If 'No': move to question 13.*
>> *If 'Yes': Which?*
>> When did you join?
>> Why did you join then?
> (b) Were you ever a member of another union before you joined the ...
>> *If 'Yes': specify.*
> (c) Do you pay Labour Party dues?
>> *If 'No': Have you contracted out then?*

2. (a) How often do you go to union shop meetings? Would you say you went
>> Regularly?
>> Occasionally?
>> Rarely?
>> Never?
> (b) When did you last go to one?

3. (a) How often do you go to union branch meetings? Would you say you went
>> Regularly?
>> Occasionally?
>> Rarely?
>> Never?
> (b) And when did you last go to one?

4. *If 'rarely' or 'never' to 2 and 3 above*: Why is it then you don't bother with union meetings?
> *If 'rarely' or 'never' to 3 only*: Why is it you go to shop meetings but don't bother with branch meetings?

5. How about voting in the elections for shop stewards. Would you say you voted
>> Regularly?
>> Occasionally?
>> Rarely?
>> Never?

6. And how about voting in union branch elections? Would you say you voted
>> Regularly?
>> Occasionally?
>> Rarely?
>> Never?

7. *If 'rarely' or 'never' to 5 and 6 above :* Why is it then you don't bother about voting in union elections?

If 'rarely' or 'never' to 6 only : Why is it you vote in shop steward elections but not in branch elections?

8. Some people say unions should just be concerned with getting higher pay and better conditions for their members. Others think they should also try to get workers a say in management. What are your views?

* 9. Do you think a union should consider the economic position of a firm when pressing for a wage increase or is its job to concentrate solely on the benefit of its own members?

10. Have you ever thought of standing as a union official?
   If 'Yes' : Have you done anything about it?
   If 'Yes' : What?

*11. How often do you talk to your workmates about union affairs
   Very often?
   A good deal?
   Now and then?
   Hardly ever?

*12. And what about your shop steward; how often do you talk with him about your work and conditions
   Very often?
   A good deal?
   Now and then?
   Hardly ever?

*13. *For non-union men.* Were you ever a union member?
   If 'Yes' : Which union was that?
   Why did you leave?
   If 'No' : Have you ever seriously thought of joining a union?
   If 'Yes' : Why didn't you then?
   If 'No' : Do you have any serious objections to joining a union?
      If 'Yes': Why is this? *Probe e.g. if he would join if no affiliation to Labour Party.*
      If 'No' : Is it just that you have never bothered to join then?

14. (*a*) If the union called a strike, would you come out?
   (*b*) Why?

*15. *Ask all.* Do you think union officials are more interested in gaining power for themselves or in fostering the welfare of the union?

Section 6: Security and prospects

* 1. Have you ever been out of a job for any length of time, say for more than a month?

If 'Yes': When was that? *Probe for experience in depression years, if old enough.*

For how long?

* 2. (*a*) How secure do you think your job is in Vauxhall/Skefko/Laporte? Would you say it is
        Dead safe?
        Fairly safe?
        Rather insecure?
        Very insecure?

*   (*b*) What makes you say that? *Probe for security via seniority etc. as opposed to economic prospects.*

* 3. If '*dead safe*' or '*fairly safe*' or D.K: If you were offered a job where you could earn £5 a week more than you do now but which was rather insecure, would you take it?

    If '*rather insecure*' or '*very insecure*': If you were offered a job where you earned £5 a week less than you do now but which was fairly safe, would you take it?

* 4. *Hand card.* Here is a list of things that might help a man to move up in the world. Which do you think would help most?

    And the next?

Ambition	Hard Work
Education	Intelligence
Character	Luck
Knowing the right people	

5. How much would you say your standard of living had risen over the last ten years? *Ensure no confusion with 'cost of living'.* Would you say it had risen.
        A great deal?
        Quite a lot?
        Not very much?
        Not at all?

6. (*a*) How about the next five years? Would you expect things to be
        Better?
        About the same?
        Worse?
  (*b*) What makes you say that?

* 7. One way a worker might improve his position (even if you aren't too keen on the idea) is by getting promotion, say, to a foreman's job. If you decided to have a go at this how would you rate your chances of getting to be a foreman? Would you say they were
        Very good?
        Fairly good?
        Not too good?
        Hopeless?

If 'not too good' or 'hopeless' : What do you think would stop you becoming a foreman?

If 'very good' or 'fairly good' : Quite a lot of men don't manage to become foremen. What makes you think you can do it?

* 8. (*a*) If a worker of ability really put his mind to it, how far up this firm do you think he could get in the end?

    (*b*) Can you recall anyone who has got to [level mentioned in 8*a*]?

* 9. Another way a man might improve his position is by starting up in business on his own. Have you ever thought of doing this?

    If 'Yes' : Did you take the matter any further?

        If 'Yes' : What did you do?

        If 'No' : Why not?

HOME SCHEDULE

Date :

'*Work*' *interview number* . . . .   '*Home* ' *interview number* . . . .

We've seen you at work already, Mr X, so now we'd like to ask you about your life outside work, and in particular what you do in your spare time. We're not after private details, but just the general pattern of the things you do.

Section 1 : Residence

Husband and/or wife

1. Before we start talking about your spare time, may I ask how long have you and your wife been here in Luton?

    If moved into Luton as a couple : Where did you live before? *State nearest town and county.*

    Why did you move to Luton?

    What sort of changes did this involve? *Probe for advantages and disadvantages, especially social ones.*

2. How long have you been living in this particular house?

    If different from 1 : Where in Luton did you live before? *Get name of street.*

Husband

* 3. (*a*) Which of these descriptions would you say fits this area best? *Hand card.*

    A very mixed area

    A rather select area

    An ordinary working-class area

    A pretty rough area

    A nice quiet and respectable area.

* (*b*) Do you like this part of Luton, or would you like to live somewhere else?

> *If likes area :* Why is that?
> *If would like to move :* Where is it that you would like to live? *Specify as precisely as possible.*
> Which of the descriptions we were using before do you think would fit [above area] best? *Show card.*
> Have you tried to do anything about moving? *Prompt : such as saving for deposit.*

Section 2 : Leisure

Now we come to your spare time. We'll often ask about the other people you did things with, because on the face of it it seems that people tend to go around with other people very much like themselves, and we're interested to see how far this is true in Luton.

Husband and wife

* 1. (*a*) Now I know it's difficult, but could you try to think back and tell me what were the main things you did last weekend?

* (*b*) And what were the main things you did in your spare time on [last two week-days]? *Show chart for recording activities and explain. Get other people's names for convenient reference ; and ask for each :* 'Is he a workmate, a friend or a relative?' *'Main things' means activities which took about an hour or more.*

Husband

* 2. (*a*) Would you say that is typical of the way you spend your spare time? Is there anything else that you usually do? *Prompt where appropriate :* 'How about when you're on another shift?'

> *If not typical :* What else do you do?

   (*b*) How about overtime—how much are you doing at present?

Wife

* 3. (*a*) And how about you, Mrs X, was that typical of the way you spend your spare time? Is there anything else that you usually do? *Prompt where appropriate :* 'Does it make any difference when Mr X is on the other shift?'

> *If not typical :* What else do you do?

* 4. During the last week, did you happen to visit anyone in the daytime?

> *If 'Yes' :* Who was that?
> Was there any special reason, or was it just a social visit?

* 5. Did anyone come to see you?

> *If 'Yes' :* Who was that?
> Was there any special reason, or was it just a social visit?

Husband and/or wife

* 6. (*a*) How about your neighbours—how much do you see of them? *Ask about either side of house.*

(*b*) Do you know what they do? *i.e. their occupation.*

Husband and wife

* 7. Who would you say are the two or three people that you most often spend your spare time with? *Make clear, apart from spouse and children. Ask for each and record on chart*

(*a*) Name and relationship

(*b*) How did you get to know him/her?

(*c*) How long have you known him/her?

(*d*) Where does he/she live?

(*e*) What kind of work does he/do she and her husband do?

Husband

* 8. Do you have any good friends you see less often, for some reason or other?

Prompt: 'How about schoolfriends, or men you knew in the services?'

If 'Yes': When do you see them?

Where do they live?

What sort of work do they do?

How did you get to know them?

Wife

* 9. Do you have any good friends you see less often for some reason or other?

If 'Yes': When do you see them?

Where do they live?

What sort of work do they do?

How did you get to know them?

Husband

Now we come to talking about friends generally . . .

10. (*a*) We all know that there are some kinds of people we feel completely at ease with, while with others we feel a bit awkward. Could you say what sort of people you feel completely at ease with?

(*b*) And what sort of people would you feel a bit awkward with?

*11. (*a*) Given a free choice, which of these kinds of people would you most like to have as your friends? *Hand card.*

People with a good education

People who have a bit of class about them

People with a similar background and outlook

People who're good company even if they can be a bit common at times

People who do interesting and responsible work

214

*   (b) Why is that?

*   (c) What kind of people do you have in mind?

*12. (a) And which of these kinds of people would you be most likely to be put off making friends with? *Hand card.*

> People whose work puts them in a different class
> People who're a bit common
> People from a very different background and outlook
> People who live in a way that I'd find it hard to keep up with
> People who talk about things I don't understand

*   (b) Why is that?

*   (c) What kind of people do you have in mind?

*13. People have different ideas of what a close friend is—what would you call a close friend?

Husband and/or wife

*14. We've been talking about your friends and your spare-time activities— how about having other couples round, say for a meal, or just for the evening: how often would you say you do this, on average?

> *If ever:* When did you last do this?
> Who is it you have round—are they friends, or relatives, or who? (*List by name, and get occupation if not given previously.*)
> What is it you do when they come round?
> > *If not relatives and not previously mentioned:* How did you get to know these friends?
> *If never:* Does that include relatives?

*15. Now here's one about just you and your husband/wife: how often would you say you have an evening out together, on average? *Can be with friends but* without *children.*

> *If ever:* What sort of things do you usually do?
> When did you last have an evening out together like this?

*16. How about family outings including the children: about how often would you say you have one, on average?

Husband and wife

*17. Do you belong to any clubs or organisations or anything like that? Here's a list (*show card*) with some examples of the kind of thing we mean—these are only examples.

Workingmen's or social club	Church or church group
Political party	Sports club
Parent-Teacher Association	W.E.A. class
Tenants' Association	British Legion

> *If any, ask for each:* Are you just an ordinary member, or have you held any particular position in it?

Where relevant : About how often do you go to it?

Would you describe any of the people you meet there as friends rather than just acquaintances?

> *If 'Yes'* : Did you meet them through [name of association], or were you friends before?

Husband and wife

*18. Do you hold an official position in any other body, such as your trade union, or being on the local council, or running a Scout troop?

> *If 'Yes'* : What is it/are they?

19. Are there any clubs or societies that you have ever wanted to join, but didn't?

> *If 'Yes'* : Was there any special reason why you didn't join?

Husband and wife

20. Are there any clubs or societies that you have belonged to in the past, but don't now?

> *If 'Yes'* : Was there any special reason why you left?

Husband and/or wife

*21. What newspapers or magazines do you read in the family? *Prompt*: 'Are there any just for the children?'

*22. What did you do for your last holiday?

> *If not abroad* : Do you ever go abroad for your holidays?

Section 3 : Kinship

Husband and wife

Take out family tree and explain.

* 1. You mentioned seeing some of your relatives / You haven't mentioned seeing any of your relatives, so could I ask a bit about what relatives you have, and where they live and so forth? *Fill in family tree.*

If any relatives in Luton area :

* 2. Apart from what you've already told me about, do you see much of any of your relatives in this area? *Specify which relative and nature of joint activity in each case. Only include those on family tree.*

If any relatives outside Luton :

* 3. What about your relatives outside Luton—how far do you keep in touch with them? *Only those on family tree.*

216

Husband and wife

4. Is there any one of your relatives who you think has done particularly well for himself?

   If 'Yes': Who is that?

   Why do you regard him as having done well for himself?

Section 4: Wife's work

Wife

1. (a) Now I'd like to ask about your work; could you tell me about the jobs you've done, please? What was the first job you had ...? *etc. Draw line across chart for time of marriage.*

   For earlier jobs after marriage:
   (b) Why did you give that job up? *Take each separately, numbering as on chart.*

   If has job at present:
* (c) What are the hours you work now?

   If has child under 15:
* (d) What do you do about the child(ren)?

Section 5: Conjugal roles

Husband and/or wife

1. Now I'd like to ask who it is who decides when certain things are to be done—it might be one or other of you, or both of you together, or sometimes one and sometimes the other. Who decides

* (a) What you'll do for your holidays?
* (b) That you'll buy something new and expensive for the house? *Prompt:* 'For instance, a new suite, or a refrigerator.'
* (c) What colour to have the wallpaper and paint when you're decorating?

* 2. Do you and your wife/husband discuss together how you should spend the money?

   If 'Yes': What sort of thing do you discuss? *Probe for plans and time perspective implied.*

Husband and/or wife

* 3. What sort of arrangements do you have about the housekeeping money?

   If wife works

* 4. What happens to Mrs X's pay packet?

* 5. (a) Would you say that over the last 10 years your living standard has gone up, or down, or stayed about the same?
* (b) Well, comparing yourself with other people, would you say that you have done better than they have, worse, or about the same?

8+   217

*   (*c*) Who is it that you're thinking of, when you say that you've done better/worse?

6. Have you ever talked about the possibility of you/your husband going after promotion, or setting up in business on your/his own?

7. Now I'd like to ask which of you does various things—again, it might be generally one of you, both of you together, or sometimes one and sometimes the other.

*   (*a*) Who is it who washes up?

*   (*b*) Who is it who does the main shopping of the week?

*   (*c*) Who is it who takes the children out (or did when they were younger)— I mean when you're both at home?

*   (*d*) Who is it who puts the children to bed (or did when they were younger) —again I mean when you're both at home?

Section 6: Children and education

Husband and/or wife

1. Do you discuss the children's education together?
   If 'Yes' : What sort of things is it you talk about?

Husband

2. (*a*) Coming to your own education now, could you tell me what schools you went to?
   (*b*) How old were you when you left school?
   (*c*) Did you have any more education or training after that? (*Probe : any part-time?*)

Wife

3. (*a*) Coming to your own education now, could you tell me what schools you went to?
   (*b*) How old were you when you left school?
   (*c*) Did you have any more education or training after that? (*Probe : any part-time?*)

Husband or wife

For each child, where relevant

* 4. (*a*) What primary school does/did X go to? *Record name of school.*

    If 11 + :
   (*b*) What secondary school does/did X go to? *Record name of school.*
   (*c*) Has/did X take(n) any exams or certificates at school?
       If 'Yes' : list subjects taken, passed and failed.

    If 15 + :
   (*d*) Has X left school yet?

218

If 'Yes' : How old was he/she when he/she left?

If left school:
(e) Has he/she had any further education or training since he/she left school?
If 'Yes' : What was that?

If not under full time education:
(f) What kind of job does he/she have now?
Has he/she ever had any other jobs? *Record whole job history.*

Enter all above information on chart for all children in order of birth.

For oldest boy (girl if no boys) still at secondary school.

Husband and wife
* 5. (a) If you had to pick the three of these subjects which you think would be most important for X to learn, which would you choose? *Show list, and check those chosen.*

Art	Mathematics
Domestic Science	Needlework
English Literature	Science
French	Technical Drawing
Geography	Typing
History	Woodwork

* (b) Why do you think that? *Take subjects one by one if relevant.*

Husband and/or wife
* 6. (a) Do you know what X wants to be? What is it?

If knows:
Is that the kind of job you hope that X will eventually settle down in?
If 'No':
What do you hope for, then?

If doesn't know:
What kind of job *do* you hope that X will eventually settle down in, then?
Why is that?

Where appropriate:
* (b) Would you be prepared for X to spend 3 years at university if this was necessary for him to become a [preferred occupation]?
* (c) What sort of chance do you think there is that he will get that sort of job: would you say it was more or less certain, about fifty-fifty, or not much chance?
* (d) Why do you think that?
* (e) Have you discussed this with any of his teachers?
* 7. Supposing you knew of a better job than he could get in Luton going in

another part of the country, would you want X to go and take it, or would you rather he stayed in Luton?

For oldest boy (girl if no boys) not yet at secondary school

* 8. (a) What schools are there that X might go on to when he leaves primary school? *Prompt: independently of ability.*
*   (b) Are there any others?
* 9. (a) What kind of school would you like him/her to go to if you had the choice?
*   (b) Why's that?
*   (c) What sort of chance do you think there is that he will get to a [preferred type school]: would you say it was more or less certain, about fifty-fifty, or not much chance?
*   (d) Why do you think that?

If not covered elsewhere:
*   (e) Have you discussed this with any of his/her teachers?

If not already asked for another child

*10. (a) If you had to pick the three of these subjects which you think it would be most important for X to learn, which would you choose? *Show list, and check those chosen.*

Art	Mathematics
Domestic Science	Needlework
English Literature	Science
French	Technical Drawing
Geography	Typing
History	Woodwork

*   (b) Why do you think that? *Take subjects one by one if relevant.*

Ask where any children

Husband and/or wife

*11. (a) Do you think there is anything parents can do to help children do well in school?
     If 'Yes': What sort of things?
   (b) Is there anything else besides what you do now that you would like to be able to do?
     If 'Yes': What sort of thing?

Ask everyone (even without children)

*12. There's been a lot of talk recently about schoolteachers' pay: taking into account the kind of work they do, do you think they get too much, too little, or about right? *If asked: the average teacher in a secondary modern would get about £20 a week when he was in his thirties.*

I've asked a lot of questions about your children's education; now I'd like to ask some more general things about bringing up children. First of all . . .

Wife

*13. Have you ever read any books or magazines telling you how to look after the children?

> *If 'Yes'* : Can you remember what they were? *List names.*
>
> What did you think of what they said—have you tried to act on their advice?
>
> If the book told you to do one thing and your mother had said another thing, which would you trust more?

Husband and/or wife

*14. Do you/did you read to the children or tell them stories before they go/went to bed (when they were younger)?

> *If 'Yes'* : Which of you does/used to do it?

Ask everyone, even without children

Wife

*15. Here is a list of a lot of things you might think are desirable in a child; which three of the things listed on this card would you say are the *most* important in a boy of about 10? *Show card.*

> That he is honest
> That he is happy
> That he is considerate of others
> That he obeys his parents well
> That he is dependable
> That he has good manners
> That he has self-control
> That he is popular with other children
> That he is neat and clean
> That he is curious about things
> That he is ambitious
> That he is able to defend himself

Husband and wife

16. Now here are two imaginary situations, and I'd like you to say for each one what you would do if this happened in your family. The first one is that . . .

* (a) Your son of about 10 is playing ludo with some of his friends. He is losing, and gets angry and starts to quarrel with the others. They make fun

221

of him, and he loses his temper completely, knocks over the board, and rushes out of the room. What would you do?

* (b) Your son is playing soldiers in the garden. He gets very excited with the game and runs about wildly. He pulls up garden canes to use as swords, knocks off flower heads with them, and marches up and down over flower beds. What would you do?

* (c) Which of these two episodes would upset you more?

Section 7 : Politics

Well, now we come to a slightly different kind of question: so far we've been concentrating on your own family affairs; at this stage could we turn to your ideas on some topics outside the family, so as to get a rounded picture of the way you look at things?

Husband

* 1. (a) It seems likely that there will be a General Election soon—do you think it will make a great deal of difference whether the Conservatives or Labour win, or won't it make much difference which side wins?

    If difference :
    In what ways would it make a difference?

    If no difference :
    Why do you feel that it won't make much difference?

* 2. (a) When the election comes, how do you think you will vote?
* (b) Well, could you tell me how you've voted for the last few elections? Let's begin with the last one, 1959—how did you vote then? . . . What about the one before that? *If in difficulty, ask : 'Can you remember how you voted in 1945 ?'*

    If no change from 1945 (or earliest vote) until future intention :
* (c) Now you seem pretty attached to the Conservative/Labour Party—can you tell me why this is?

    For each change, significant abstention, or uncertainty for next election ask :
* (d) Why is that . . . ? *Phrase appropriately.*

  3. Within the past few weeks, have you discussed political issues with anyone?
    If 'Yes' : Who was this?
    What did you talk about?

  4. Coming back to your friends, would you say that their political leanings are generally like yours, generally different, or mixed?

  5. Is there anyone you know whose views on politics would carry a lot of weight with you?
    If 'Yes' : Who is that?

* 6. Some people say there's one law for the rich and another law for the poor— would you agree or disagree, on the whole?

222

* 7. As you know, most trade unions support the Labour Party; do you approve of this, or do you think they ought to keep themselves separate?

* 8. Some people say that the trade unions have too much power in the country: would you agree or disagree, on the whole?

* 9. Some people say that big businessmen have too much power in the country: would you agree or disagree, on the whole?

10. Here's a question on how you feel about strikes; which of these statements would come nearest to *your* attitude? *Show card*.

> I don't believe that going on strike could ever benefit me, and I would not do so under any conditions.

> I would not be prepared to go on strike unless this was the only way to defend my rights, and the strike had the full support of the union.

> I would be prepared to strike if necessary to secure fair treatment at my place of work, whether or not top union officials approved of this.

> I would be prepared to strike at any time that it was necessary to support the interests of workers and to help the working-class movement anywhere in the country.

Section 8: Class

* 1. People often talk about there being different classes—what do you think? [For details of the conduct of this part of interview see appendix C.]

* 2. Many things affect a person's standing in the community—among the most important are a man's job, and the money he earns. Could you put these six people in the order of what *you* think is their standing in the community? You can bracket some of them together at the same level if you want. *Show card*.

> Grocer with his own shop, making £20 a week
> Accountant, making £25 a week
> Building site labourer, making £15 a week
> Factory worker, making £20 a week
> Scrap iron dealer, making £25 a week
> Bank clerk, making £15 a week

Section 9: Expenditure and savings

For our final section of all I have a few questions about saving and spending: first of all . . .

Husband and/or wife

1. I'd like to ask you if you use a number of different ways of putting aside your money:
* (a) Do you have a Post Office savings account?
* (b) Do you have a bank account?

If 'Yes' : Is it a joint account?
Do you have a cheque book?

*   (c) Do you have anything in a building society or savings bank or National Savings?

*   (d) Do you have anything in stocks and shares, or a unit trust?

*   (e) Do you have any kind of insurance policy?
If 'Yes' : What kind?
If life : For how much?

* 2. Do you contribute to a pension scheme at work?
If 'Yes' : How much are the contributions?

* 3. Do you put anything away as savings?
If 'Yes' : What is it that you save for? Is it for retirement, or to buy particular things, to pay regular bills, or what?
Do you save regularly, or just now and then?
If regularly : Do you put away a fixed amount, or does it vary?
If fixed : How much is it you put away?
If wife works : Who is it who does the saving?

* 4. Do you have a car?
If 'Yes' : Does your wife drive too?
If 'Yes' : Do you have any difficulty about who should use the car?

* 5. Do you have a refrigerator?
If 'Yes' : Did you buy it cash down, or was it on H.P.?

* 6. Do you have a telephone?

* 7. Is this your own house, or a council house, or what? *Phrase in relation to circumstances.*
If own : How did you find this house and choose it?
How did you make the arrangements for buying it?

Husband

Now we come to talk about the family income

* 8. (a) Could you tell me what your *highest* week's earnings in the last year was, roughly?

*   (b) And what was the *lowest* week's?

*   (c) Could you tell me your average weekly earnings—I mean including ordinary amounts of overtime, and after deductions—from your main job? Which of these categories would it come into?

     A. under £15   B. £15–17   C. £18–20
     D. £21–23   E. £24–26   F. £27–29
     G. £30 +

*   (d) Well, taking into account what the other people in the family earn and anything you get from other sources, such as family allowances, lodgers, and any other jobs you do, would you tell me which of these categories the average weekly income of the whole family comes into? [categories as in previous question]

Well, that's all about money. Now that you've answered all these questions, here's one final general one.

* 9. Looking 10 years ahead, what improvement in your way of life would you most hope for?

References

Abrams, Mark, 'New Roots of Working Class Conservatism', *Encounter* (May 1960).

Abrams, Mark and Rose, Richard, *Must Labour Lose?* (London, 1960).

Acton Society Trust, *Management Succession* (London, 1956).

Anderson, Perry, 'Origins of the Present Crisis', and 'Problems of Socialist Strategy', in Anderson and Robin Blackburn (eds.), *Towards Socialism* (London, 1965).

Argyris, Chris, 'The Organisation—What makes it Healthy?', *Harvard Business Review*, vol. 37, no. 5 (1958).

Aron, Raymond, *La Lutte de Classes* (Paris, 1964).

Bahrdt, H. P., 'Die Angestellten' and 'Die Industriearbeiter', in Marianne Feuersenger (ed.), *Gibt Es noch ein Proletariat?* (Frankfurt, 1962).

Bakke, E. W., *The Unemployed Man* (London, 1933).

Banks, J. A., *Prosperity and Parenthood* (London, 1954).

Baran, Paul A. and Sweezy, Paul M., *Monopoly Capital* (New York and London, 1966).

Barkin, S., 'The Decline of the Labor Movement', in Andrew Hacker (ed.), *The Corporation Takeover* (New York, 1964).

Barrier, Christiane, 'Techniciens et Grèves à l'Electricité de France', *Sociologie du Travail*, no. 1 (1968).

Bell, Colin, *Middle Class Families* (London, 1968).
  'Mobility and the Middle Class Family', *Sociology*, vol. 2, no. 2 (May 1968).

Belleville, Pierre, *Une Nouvelle Classe Ouvrière* (Paris, 1963).

Bendix, Reinhard, *Work and Authority in Industry* (New York, 1956).
  Nation Building and Citizenship (New York, 1964).

Berger, Bennett M., *Working-Class Suburb* (Berkeley, 1960).

Bernard, Jessie, 'Class Organisation in an Era of Abundance', *Transactions of the Third World Congress of Sociology*, vol. 3 (London, 1956).

Black, E. I. and Simey, T. S. (eds.), *Neighbourhood and Community* (Liverpool, 1954).

Blackburn, Robin, 'The Unequal Society', in Blackburn and Alexander Cockburn (eds.), *The Incompatibles: Trade Union Militancy and the Consensus* (London, 1967).

Blau, Peter M., 'Social Mobility and Interpersonal Relations', *American Sociological Review*, vol. 19 (1954).

Blauner, Robert, *Alienation and Freedom: the Factory Worker and his Industry* (Chicago and London, 1964).

Blumberg, P., *Industrial Democracy: The Sociology of Participation* (London, 1968).

Bott, Elizabeth, *Family and Social Network* (London, 1957).

Bottomore, T. B., 'Social Stratification in Voluntary Associations', in D. V. Glass (ed.), *Social Mobility in Britain* (London, 1954).

Business Week, 'Worker Loses His Class Identity', 11 July 1959.

Butler, D. E. and Rose, Richard, *The British General Election of 1959* (London, 1960).

Butler, D. and Stokes, D., *Political Change in Britain* (forthcoming).

Cannon, I. C., 'The Social Situation of the Skilled Worker', University of London Ph.D. thesis, 1961.

'Ideology and Occupational Community', *Sociology*, vol. 1, no. 2 (May 1967).

Cauter, T., and Downham, J. S., *The Communication of Ideas* (London, 1954).

Centers, Richard, *The Psychology of Social Classes* (Princeton, 1959).

Central Office of Information, *Social Changes in Britain* (December 1962), reprinted in *New Society*, 27 December 1962.

Chombart de Lauwe, P., 'Y-a-t-il encore une Classe Ouvrière?', *Revue de l'Action Populaire*, no. 134 (January 1960).

Clarke, D. G., *The Industrial Manager: His Background and Career Pattern* (London, 1966).

Clements, R. V., *Managers: A Study of their Careers in Industry* (London, 1958).

Crosland, Anthony, *Can Labour Win?*, Fabian Tract 324 (London, 1960).

Crozier, Michel, *The Bureaucratic Phenomenon* (London, 1964).

Le Monde des Employés de Bureau (Paris, 1965).

Cyriax, George and Oakeshott, Robert, *The Bargainers* (London, 1960).

Dahrendorf, Ralf, *Class and Class Conflict in Industrial Society* (London, 1959).

'Bürger und Proletarier: Die Klassen und ihr Schicksal', in *Gesellschaft und Freiheit* (Munich, 1961).

Dale, J. R., *The Clerk in Industry* (Liverpool, 1962).

Dennis, N., Henriques, F. and Slaughter, C., *Coal is Our Life* (London, 1956).

Détraz, Albert, 'L'Ouvrier Consommateur', in Leo Hamon (ed.), *Les Nouveaux Comportements Politiques de la Classe Ouvrière* (Paris, 1962).

Douglas, J. W. B., *The Home and the School* (London, 2nd ed., 1967).

Dubin, R., 'Industrial Workers' Worlds: A Study of the "Central Life Interests" of Industrial Workers', *Social Problems*, vol. 3 (January 1956).

Dufty, N. F., 'White Collar Contrasts', *International Journal of Comparative Sociology*, vol. 4 (1963).

Eldridge, J. E. T., *Industrial Disputes* (London, 1968).

Etzioni, A., 'Organizational Control Structure', in J. G. March (ed.), *Handbook of Organizations* (New York, 1965).

Faunce, W. A., 'Automation and the Automobile Worker', *American Sociological Review*, vol. 28 (August 1958).

Fertility Tables, 1961 Census (England and Wales), (London, H.M.S.O., 1966).

Fineberg, J. (ed.), *Lenin: Selected Works*, vol. 5 (London, n.d.).

227

References

Firth, R., *Two Studies of Kinship in London* (London, 1956).

Flanders, Allan, *The Fawley Productivity Agreements* (London, 1965).

Floud, J. E., Halsey, A. H. and Martin, F. M., *Social Class and Educational Opportunity* (London, 1957).

Fortune, The Editors of, *The Changing American Market* (New York, 1955).

Frankenberg, Ronald, *Communities in Britain* (London, 1966).

Fürstenberg, Friedrich, 'Structural Changes in the Working Class: a situational study of workers in the Western German chemical industry', in J. A. Jackson (ed.), *Sociological Studies I: Social Stratification* (Cambridge, 1968).

Galbraith, J. K., *The New Industrial State* (London, 1967).

Galtung, Johan, *Theory and Methods of Social Research* (London, 1967).

Geiger, Theodor, *Die Klassengesellschaft im Schmelztiegel* (Cologne and Hagen, 1949).

Glass, D. V., 'Fertility Trends in Europe since the Second World War', *Population Studies*, vol. 12, no. 1 (March 1968).

Goldthorpe, John H., 'Social Stratification in Industrial Society', in P. Halmos (ed.), *The Development of Industrial Societies*, Sociological Review Monograph No. 8 (Keele, 1964).

'Attitudes and Behaviour of Car Assembly Workers: a deviant case and a theoretical critique', *British Journal of Sociology*, vol. 17, no. 3 (September 1966).

'Images of Class among Affluent Manual Workers' (forthcoming).

Goldthorpe, John H. and Lockwood, David, 'Not so Bourgeois After All', *New Society*, 18 October 1962.

'Affluence and the British Class Structure', *Sociological Review*, vol. 11, no. 2 (July 1963).

Goldthorpe, John H., Lockwood, David, Bechhofer, Frank and Platt, Jennifer, *The Affluent Worker: Industrial Attitudes and Behaviour* (Cambridge, 1968).

The Affluent Worker: Political Attitudes and Behaviour (Cambridge, 1968).

Gordon, C. Wayne and Babchuk, Nicholas, 'A Typology of Voluntary Associations', *American Sociological Review*, vol. 24, no. 2 (February 1959).

Gorz, André, *Stratégie Ouvrière et Néocapitalisme* (Paris, 1964).

'Work and Consumption', in Perry Anderson and Robin Blackburn (eds.), *Towards Socialism* (London, 1965).

Le Socialisme Difficile (Paris, 1967).

Gross, Ronald, 'The Future of Toil' in Arthur B. Shostak and William Gomberg (eds.), *Blue-Collar World: Studies of the American Worker* (Englewood Cliffs, 1964).

Hall, J. and Caradog Jones, D., 'The Social Grading of Occupations', *British Journal of Sociology*, vol. 1 (January 1950).

Hamilton, Richard F., 'The Income Differential between Skilled and White Collar Workers', *British Journal of Sociology*, vol. 14 (December 1963).

'The Behaviour and Values of Skilled Workers', in Arthur B. Shostak and

William Gomberg (eds.), *Blue-Collar World: Studies of the American Worker* (Englewood Cliffs, 1964).

'Affluence and the Worker: the West German Case', *American Journal of Sociology*, vol. 71 (September 1965).

Affluence and the French Worker in the Fourth Republic (Princeton, 1967).

Hausknecht, M., *The Joiners* (New York, 1962).

Heraud, B. J., 'Social Class and the New Towns', *Urban Studies*, vol. 5, no. 1 (February 1968).

Hinden, Rita, 'The Lessons for Labour', in Mark Abrams and Richard Rose, *Must Labour Lose?* (London, 1960).

Hoggart, Richard, *The Uses of Literacy* (London, 1958).

Hubert, Jane, 'Kinship and Geographical Mobility in a Sample from a London Middle-Class Area', *International Journal of Comparative Sociology*, vol. 5 (March 1965).

Hyman, Herbert, H., *Interviewing in Social Research* (Chicago, 1954).

IAB, see Goldthorpe *et al.*, *The Affluent Worker: Industrial Attitudes and Behaviour*.

Ingham, G. K., 'Organisational Size, Orientation to Work and Industrial Behaviour', University of Cambridge Ph.D. thesis, 1968.

Jackson, Brian and Marsden, Dennis, *Education and the Working Class* (London, revised ed., 1966).

Jennings, Hilda, *Societies in the Making* (London, 1962).

Karsh, B., 'Work and Automation', in Howard Boone Jacobson and Joseph S. Roucek (eds.), *Automation and Society* (New York, 1959).

Kerr, Clark, 'The Prospect for Wages and Hours in 1975', in *Labor and Management in Industrial Society* (New York, 1964).

Kerr, Clark, Dunlop, John T., Harbison, Frederick H. and Myers, Charles A., *Industrialism and Industrial Man* (London, 1962).

Kerr, M., *People of Ship Street* (London, 1958).

Klapper, Joseph T., *The Effects of Mass Communication* (Glencoe, 1957).

Klein, Josephine, *Samples From English Cultures* (London, 1965).

Kornhauser, Arthur, Mayer, Albert J. and Sheppard, Harold L., *When Labor Votes: A Study of Auto Workers* (New York, 1965).

Kuper, L., 'Blueprint for Living Together', in Kuper (ed.), *Living in Towns* (London, 1953).

Lee, D. J., 'Class Differentials in Educational Opportunity and Promotions from the Ranks', *Sociology*, vol. 2, no. 3 (September 1968).

Leenhardt, Jacques, 'La Nouvelle Classe Ouvrière en Grève', *Sociologie du Travail*, no. 4 (1968).

Lintas Research, *The Changing Consumer* (London, 1961).

Lipset, S. M., 'The British Voter', *The New Leader*, 7 and 21 November 1960. 'The Changing Class Structure of Contemporary European Politics', *Daedalus*, vol. 63, no. 1 (1964).

Little, Alan and Westergaard, John, 'The Trend of Class Differentials in Educational Opportunity in England and Wales', *British Journal of Sociology*, vol. 15, no. 4 (December 1964).

References

Lockwood, David, *The Blackcoated Worker: a Study in Class Consciousness* (London, 1958).

'The "New Working Class"', *European Journal of Sociology*, vol. 1, no. 2 (1960).

'Sources of Variation in Working Class Images of Society', *Sociological Review*, vol. 14, no. 3 (November 1966).

Lockwood, David and Goldthorpe, John H., 'Dr Abrams on Class and Politics: a Second Opinion', cyclostyled paper available from the Department of Applied Economics, Cambridge (1962).

Luckmann, Thomas, *Das Problem der Religion in der modernen Gesellschaft* (Freiburg, 1963).

Luckmann, Thomas and Berger, Peter, 'Social Mobility and Personal Identity', *European Journal of Sociology*, vol. 5, no. 2 (1964).

Mackenzie, Gavin, 'The Economic Dimension of *Embourgeoisement*', *British Journal of Sociology*, vol. 18 (March 1967).

Mallet, Serge, *La Nouvelle Classe Ouvrière* (Paris, 1963).

Mann, J. M., 'Sociological Aspects of Factory Relocation', University of Oxford D.Phil. thesis, 1968.

Marcuse, Herbert, *One-Dimensional Man* (London, 1964).

'Liberation from the Affluent Society' in David Cooper (ed.), *The Dialectics of Liberation* (London, 1968).

Marenco, Claudine, 'Gradualism, Apathy and Suspicion in a French Bank', in W. H. Scott (ed.), *Office Automation: Administrative and Human Problems*, (Paris, O.E.C.D., 1965).

Marshall, T. H., *Citizenship and Social Class* (Cambridge, 1950).

Martin, F. M., 'An Inquiry into Parents' Preferences in Secondary Education' and 'Some Subjective Aspects of Social Stratification', in D. V. Glass (ed.), *Social Mobility in Britain* (London, 1954).

Marx, Karl, 'Alienated Labour', in 'Economic and Philosophical Manuscripts of 1844', trans. T. B. Bottomore, *Karl Marx: Early Writings* (London, 1963).

Marx, Karl and Engels, Frederick, *On Britain* (Moscow, 1953).

Mathieu, Gilbert, 'La Réponse des Chiffres', *Les Temps Modernes*, nos. 196-7 (September-October 1962).

Mayer, Kurt, 'Recent Changes in the Class Structure of the United States', *Transactions of the Third World Congress of Sociology*, vol. 3 (London, 1956).

'Diminishing Class Differentials in the United States', *Kyklos*, vol. 12 (October 1959).

'The Changing Shape of the American Class Structure', *Social Research*, vol. 30 (Winter 1963).

McCarthy, W. E. J. and Parker, S. R., *Shop Stewards and Workshop Relations*, Research Paper 10, Royal Commission on Trade Unions and Employers' Associations (London, H.M.S.O., 1968).

McKenzie, Robert and Silver, Allan, *Angels in Marble: Working Class Conservatives in Urban England* (London, 1968).

McQuail, Denis, *Towards a Sociology of Mass Communications* (London, 1969).

Merton, R. K., *Social Theory and Social Structure* (Glencoe, 1957).

Millar, Robert, *The Affluent Sheep* (London, 1963).

The New Classes (London, 1966).

Miller, S. M. and Reissman, Frank, 'Are Workers Middle Class?', *Dissent*, vol. 8 (Autumn 1961).

Mills, C. Wright, *The Marxists* (New York, 1962).

Mogey, J. M., *Family and Neighbourhood* (Oxford, 1956).

Morin, Edgar, 'La Mue d'Occident', in *Introduction à une Politique de l'Homme* (Paris, 1965).

Moser, C. A. and Scott, Wolf, *British Towns* (Edinburgh and London, 1961).

Mosson, R. M. and Clarke, D. G., 'Some Inter-Industry Comparisons of the Background and Careers of Managers', *British Journal of Industrial Relations*, vol. 6, no. 2 (July 1968).

Mott, Paul E., Mann, Floyd C., McLoughlin, Quin and Warwick, Donald P., *Shift Work: the Social, Psychological and Physical Consequences* (New York, 1965).

Mumford, Enid and Banks, Olive, *The Computer and the Clerk* (London, 1967).

Naville, P., 'The Structure of Employment and Automation', *International Social Science Bulletin*, vol. 10, no. 1 (1958).

L'Automation et le Travail Humain (Paris, 1961).

Newson, J. and E., *Infant Care in an Urban Community* (London, 1963).

Nicholson, J. H., *New Communities in Britain: Achievements and Problems* (London, 1961).

Nordlinger, Eric A., *The Working Class Tories* (London, 1967).

Oeser, O. E. and Hammond, S. E. (eds.), *Social Structure and Personality in a City* (London, 1954).

Olson, Mancur, *The Logic of Collective Action: Public Goods and The Theory of Groups* (Cambridge, Mass., 1965)

Orwell, George, *The Road to Wigan Pier* (London, 1937).

Ossowski, Stanislas, 'La vision dichotomique de la stratification sociale', *Cahiers Internationaux de Sociologie*, vol. 20 (1956).

Class Structure in the Social Consciousness (London, 1963).

PAB, see Goldthorpe *et al.*, *The Affluent Worker: Political Attitudes and Behaviour*.

Platt, Jennifer, 'Some Problems in Measuring the Jointness of Conjugal Role-Relationships', *Sociology*, vol. 3, no. 3 (September 1969).

Popitz, H., Bahrdt, H. P., Jures, E. A. and Kesting, H., *Das Gesellschaftsbild des Arbeiters* (Tübingen, 1957).

Postan, M. M., *An Economic History of Western Europe, 1945–1964* (London, 1967).

Powles, William E., 'The Southern Appalachian Migrant: Country Boy turned Blue-Collarite', in Arthur B. Shostak and William Gomberg (eds.), *Blue-Collar World: Studies of the American Worker* (Englewood Cliffs, 1964).

Rainville, Jean-Marie, *Condition Ouvrière et Intégration Sociale* (Paris, 1967).

Rainwater, Lee, 'Persistence and Change in Working Class Life-Style', in

References

Arthur B. Shostak and William Gomberg (eds.), *Blue-Collar World: Studies of the American Worker* (Englewood Cliffs, 1964).

Rex, John, *Key Problems of Sociological Theory* (London, 1961).

Rhee, H. A., *Office Automation in Social Perspective* (Oxford, 1968).

Rich, D., 'Social Relationships in Leisure Time', University of Birmingham Ph.D. thesis, 1951.

'Spare Time in the Black Country', in Leo Kuper (ed.), *Living in Towns* (London, 1953).

Roberts, Geoffrey, *Demarcation Rules in Shipbuilding and Shiprepairing* (Cambridge, 1967).

Rose, Richard, 'Class and Party Divisions: Britain as a Test Case', *Sociology*, vol. 2, no. 2 (May 1968).

Rosser, Colin and Harris, Christopher, *The Family and Social Change* (London, 1965).

Rostow, W. W., *The Stages of Economic Growth: A Non-Communist Manifesto* (Cambridge, 1960).

Runciman, W. G., '*Embourgeoisement*, Self-Rated Class and Party Preference', *Sociological Review*, vol. 12, no. 2 (July 1964).

Relative Deprivation and Social Justice (London, 1966).

Socialist Commentary, 'The Lost Labour Voter', February 1969.

Stacey, Margaret, *Tradition and Change: a Study of Banbury* (Oxford, 1960).

Steiner, George, 'The Decline of the Labour Party', *The Reporter*, 29 September 1960.

Svalastoga, Kaare, *Prestige, Class and Mobility* (Copenhagen, 1959).

Swift, D. F., 'Social Class, Mobility–Ideology and 11+ Success', *British Journal of Sociology*, vol. 18, no. 2 (June 1967).

Sykes, A. J. M., 'Some Differences in the Attitudes of Clerical and Manual Workers', *Sociological Review*, vol. 13, no. 1 (1965).

Timms, D. W. G., 'Distribution of Social Defectiveness in Two British Cities: a Study in Human Ecology', University of Cambridge Ph.D. thesis, 1963.

Touraine, Alain, 'La Vie Ouvrière', in Touraine (ed.), *Histoire Générale du Travail*, vol. 4, *La Civilization Industrielle* (Paris, 1961).

Touraine, Alain and Ragazzi, Orietta, *Ouvriers d'Origine Agricole* (Paris, 1961).

Trentin, Bruno, *Tendenze del Capitalismo italiano* (Rome, 1962).

Turner, Graham, *The Car Makers* (London, 1963).

Turner, H. A., Clack, Garfield and Roberts, Geoffrey, *Labour Relations in the Motor Industry* (London, 1967).

U.S. Department of Labor, *How American Buying Habits Change* (Washington, 1959).

Varga, Eugene, *20th Century Capitalism* (Moscow and London, n.d.).

Veblen, Thorstein, *The Engineers and the Price System* (New York, 1933).

Walker, Nigel, *Morale in the Civil Service: a Study of the Desk Worker* (Edinburgh, 1961).

Weber, Max, *The Protestant Ethic and the Spirit of Capitalism*, trans. T. Parsons (London, 1947).

Wedderburn, Dorothy, 'The Conditions of Employment of Manual and Non-manual Workers', *Proceedings of the Social Science Research Council Conference on Social Stratification and Industrial Relations* (January 1969).

Weir, D. T. H. and Mercer, D., 'Orientations to Work among White-Collar Workers', *Proceedings of the Social Science Research Council Conference on Social Stratification and Industrial Relations* (January 1969).

Weller, Ken, *Truth About Vauxhall*, Solidarity Pamphlet No. 12 (Dunstable, n.d.).

Westergaard, John, 'The Withering Away of Class', in Perry Anderson and Robin Blackburn (eds.), *Towards Socialism* (London, 1965).

Westoff, Charles F., 'The Changing Focus of Differential Fertility Research: the Social Mobility Hypothesis', in J. J. Spengler and O. D. Duncan (eds.), *Population Theory and Policy* (Glencoe, 1956).

Whyte, Jnr. W. H., 'The Outgoing Life', *Fortune*, vol. 49 (July 1953).

Wilensky, Harold, 'Work, Careers and Social Integration', *International Social Science Journal*, vol. 12, no. 4 (1960).

'Orderly Careers and Social Participation: the Impact of Work History on Social Integration in the Middle Mass', *American Sociological Review*, vol. 26, no. 4 (August, 1961).

'Mass Society and Mass Culture', *American Sociological Review*, vol. 29, no. 2 (April 1964).

Willener, A., *Images de la société et classes sociales* (Berne, 1957).

Willmott, Peter, *The Evolution of a Community* (London, 1963).

Woodward, Joan, *Management and Technology* (London, H.M.S.O., 1958).

'Industrial Behaviour—Is there a Science?', *New Society*, 8 October 1964.

Industrial Organisation: Theory and Practice (Oxford, 1965).

Worsley, Peter, 'The Distribution of Power in Industrial Society', in P. Halmos (ed.), *The Development of Industrial Societies*, Sociological Review Monograph No. 8 (Keele, 1964).

Wrong, Dennis, H., 'Class Fertility Differentials in England and Wales', *The Millbank Memorial Fund Quarterly*, vol. 38 (January 1960).

Young, Michael, 'Distribution of Income Within the Family', *British Journal of Sociology*, vol. 3, no. 4 (December 1952).

Young, Michael and Willmott, Peter, *Family and Kinship in East London* (London, 1957).

Family and Class in a London Suburb (London, 1960).

Zweig, F., *The British Worker* (London, 1952).

'The New Factory Worker', *The Twentieth Century* (May 1960).

The Worker in an Affluent Society (London, 1961).

Index

235

Index

Dubin, R., 67 n.
Dufty, N. F., 57 n., 67 n., 73 n., 75 n.
Duncan, O. D., 126 n.
Dunlop, John T., 7 n.
Durkheim, Émile, 156

Earnings
of manual workers studied, 36–7, 61
of white-collar workers studied, 36, 61
Ecological factors
in evolution of working class, 12–14, 19
in patterns of sociability, 111–13
Education
of children, 134–6
parents' involvement in, 137–40
Eldridge, J. E. T., 34 n.
Embourgeoisement, 3, 9, 14, 17, 21, 22–8, 29, 30, 31–2, 34, 35–6, 40, 46–7, 51–3, 54, 74, 79, 83–4, 85, 87, 91 n., 93, 96, 108–110, 111, 114–15, 116–18, 122, 144–5, 157–65, 171, 187, 191
Employee participation, 194
Engels, Friedrich, 1, 3
Entertaining, 89–91, 91–2, 98, 110, 111–13
Etzioni, A., 74 n.

Family limitation, 126–9
Faunce, W. A., 40 n.
Feuersenger, Marianne, 9 n.
Financial planning, 124–6
Fineberg, J., 3 n.
Firth, R., 144 n.
Flanders, Allan, 34 n.
Floud, J. E., 130 n.
Frankenberg, Ronald, 51 n.
Friends (*see also* 'Spare-time associates')
kind of people preferred as, 140–1
relations with, 87–92, 103, 105–6
status of, 109–10, 111–14
Fürstenberg, Friedrich, 186 n.

Galbraith, J. K., 10 n., 11 n., 166 n., 168 n.
171 n., 188 n.
Galtung, Johan, 50 n.
Geiger, Theodor, 5 n.
Glass, D. V., 93 n., 119 n., 126 n.
Goldthorpe, John H., 7 n., 24 n., 31 n., 80 n.,
97 n., 118 n., 145 n., 170 n., 182 n.
Gomberg, William, 13 n., 26 n., 41 n.
Gordon, C. Wayne, 198 n.
Gorz, André, 17 n., 18 n., 19 n., 179–81,
183 n.
Gramsci, A., 17 n.
Gross, Ronald, 41 n.

Hacker, Andrew, 166 n.
Hall, J., 196 n.

Halmos, P., 7 n., 17 n.
Halsey, A. H., 130 n.
Hamilton, Richard F., 21 n., 26 n., 171 n.,
172 n., 192
Hammond, S. E., 118 n., 147 n., 150 n.
Hamon, Leo, 9 n.
Handel, Gerald, 26 n.
Harbison, Frederick H., 7 n.
Hare, John (Lord Blakenham), 47 n.
Harris, Christopher, 93 n., 96 n.
Hausknecht, M., 94 n.
Heath, A. F., 201 n.
'Hegemony', 17–18
Henriques, F., 92 n.
Heraud, B. J., 35 n.
Hinden, Rita, 22 n.
Hoggart, R., 92 n., 118 n., 119, 144 n.
Home- (and family-) centredness (*see also*
'Privatisation'), 25, 27, 101–3, 163–4,
169
Hubert, Jane, 89 n.
Hyman, Herbert H., 50 n.

'Images' of society, social class, 115, 118,
120, 145–56, 176, 178, 180, 189
Incomes
'homogenisation' of, 7–8, 14, 23, 24
manual–nonmanual differences, 21 n.
Ingham, G. K., 67 n., 182 n.
Instrumental collectivism, 26, 170, 187
Instrumental orientation to work, 56, 58, 64,
65, 66–8, 69–70, 74, 80–2, 103, 164–5,
169, 180, 181–3, 185, 189–90
'Integration' of workers into firm, 10–11, 12,
18–19, 59–60, 68–74, 80–2
Interviewing, 49–51

Jackson, Brian, 96 n.
Jackson, J. A., 186 n.
Jacobson, Howard Boone, 41 n.
Jennings, Hilda, 116 n., 144 n.
Job satisfaction, 54–60, 63–4, 65
Jures, E. A., 118 n.

Karsh, B., 41 n.
Kautsky, Karl, 3 n.
Kelly-Wischnewetzky, F., 3 n.
Kerr, Clark, 7 n., 64 n., 166 n., 171 n.
Kerr, M., 93 n., 144 n.
Kesting, H., 118 n.
Kin
relations with, 89–91, 92, 101, 104
separation from, 38, 89, 97
Klapper, Joseph T., 183 n.
Klein, Josephine, 23, 85 n., 86 n., 114, 115 n.,
119 n., 164 n.
Kornhauser, Arthur, 172 n.
Kuper, Leo, 106 n., 116 n., 144 n.

236